Super Foods & Power Juices

OVER **200** EVERYDAY RECIPES

THE AUSTRALIAN
Women's Weekly

Super Foods & Power Juices

Contents

Super
CHARGE
YOUR
Diet

In the modern world where diets seem to be all about weight loss, it's easy to forget that all we need to do is eat well to optimally nourish our bodies, boost vitality and give us the best chance of great health. This is where superfoods come in.

Superfoods are those foods packed with nutrients, minerals, and substances such as antioxidants that benefit us enormously. While it does seem as if there is a new superfood touted every week, they need not be expensive or hard to obtain.

While there is a place for exotic superfoods such as acai or goji berries, or supplements such as maca powder or spirulina, superfoods can be found all around you. Locally grown berries, broccoli, cabbage, watercress, Asian greens, mushrooms, seeds, oats, salmon, mussels, green tea and natural yoghurt are just a few of the foods that easily fall into the category of 'superfood'.

This book is designed to help all of us get more superfoods on our plates to nutrient-boost our diets.

It is almost always better to strive to obtain all the nutrients we need for our health through consuming the great variety of healthy produce that nature provides. The more variety of fresh healthy foods you have in your diet, the more you diversify your intake of nutrients and beneficial compounds. There are many different healthy diets, but what they all have in common is that they are based on wholesome, natural, minimally processed foods.

This book is intended to inspire you to use the most nutritious of those foods to create a mouth-watering menu for you and your family. With handy buttons, pointing out the specific nutritional benefits of each recipe, this collection of superfood recipes makes it easy to plan your meals.

From power-starts, portable and filling lunches, snack ideas, and flavour-packed dinners, to healthy sweets, smoothies and juices, let The Australian Women's Weekly help fill your diet with the type of foods that are the best for you. Healthy eating has never tasted so good!

HEALTHY CHECKLIST

BE SURE TO MAKE TIME TO EAT A WHOLESOME BREAKFAST, TO PREPARE YOUR BODY FOR THE DAY

AIM TO BE ACTIVE FOR AT LEAST 30 MINUTES EVERYDAY. REMEMBER THAT DOING A LITTLE PHYSICAL ACTIVITY IS BETTER THAN DOING NONE.

AVOID OVEREATING SIMPLE CARBOHYDRATES & PROCESSED SUGARS

TRY TO GET 7 TO 8 HOURS OF SLEEP A NIGHT

PLAN TO MAKE ANY MEAL YOU EAT CONSIST MAINLY OF FRESH FRUIT AND VEGETABLES - WHICH CONTAIN PHYTOCHEMICALS, BIOLOGICALLY ACTIVE SUBSTANCES THAT HELP TO PROTECT YOU FROM DISEASE. REGULARLY EATING A VARIETY OF FRUIT AND VEGETABLES LOWERS YOUR RISK OF:

- TYPE 2 DIABETES
- STROKE
- HEART DISEASE
- CANCER
- HIGH BLOOD PRESSURE (HYPERTENSION)

SUPER FOODS

mixed mushrooms

WITH SMOKED SALMON, EGG & SEED TOPPING

PREP + COOK TIME **20 MINUTES** SERVES **4**

20g (¾ ounce) sunflower seeds, chopped coarsely

20g (¾ ounce) pepitas (pumpkin seeds), chopped coarsely

2½ tablespoons olive oil

600g (1¼ pounds) swiss brown mushrooms, sliced thickly

600g (1¼ pounds) oyster mushrooms

1 large clove garlic, crushed

1 fresh long red chilli, seeded, chopped finely

1 tablespoon water

2 teaspoons lemon juice

4 free-range eggs

1 tablespoon vinegar

200g (6½ ounces) smoked salmon

2 tablespoons fresh chervil leaves

1 Heat a large frying pan over medium heat. Add the sunflower seeds and pepitas; cook, stirring, for 2 minutes or until seeds are toasted. Remove from pan.

2 Heat 1 tablespoon of the oil in same pan over high heat, add half the mushrooms; cook, stirring occasionally, for 4 minutes or until browned lightly. Transfer to a large bowl; cover with foil to keep warm. Repeat with another tablespoon of the oil and the remaining mushrooms.

3 Return all mushrooms to pan, stir in garlic, chilli and water; cook for 1 minute or until fragrant. Remove from heat; stir in juice; season to taste. Transfer to a bowl; cover with foil to keep warm.

4 Meanwhile, to poach eggs, half-fill a large, deep frying pan with water, add vinegar; bring to a gentle simmer. Break 1 egg into a cup. Using a wooden spoon, make a whirlpool in the water; slide egg into whirlpool. Repeat with a second egg. Cook eggs for 3 minutes or until whites are set and the yolks remain runny. Remove eggs with a slotted spoon; drain on a paper-towel-lined plate. Keep warm. Repeat poaching with remaining eggs.

5 Divide mushroom mixture among plates, top with eggs, smoked salmon, seed mixture and chervil; season.

I AM
PALEO
GLUTEN-FREE
DAIRY-FREE

QUINOA

porridge

PREP + COOK TIME **20 MINUTES** SERVES **2**

½ cup (100g) white quinoa,
    rinsed, drained
1½ cups (375ml) water
½ cup (125ml) skim milk or
    almond milk
1 medium apple (150g),
    grated coarsely
100g (3 ounces) red seedless grapes,
    halved
2 tablespoons pistachios, toasted,
    chopped coarsely
1 tablespoon honey or pure
    maple syrup

1 Combine quinoa and the water in a small saucepan; bring to the boil. Reduce heat; simmer, covered, for 10 minutes. Add milk; cook, covered, for a further 5 minutes or until quinoa is tender.
2 Stir in apple and half the grapes.
3 Serve porridge warm topped with nuts and remaining grapes; drizzle with honey.

tips We used a pink lady apple in this recipe. Most quinoa comes rinsed, but it's a good habit to rinse it yourself under cold water until the water runs clear, then drain it. This removes any remaining outer coating, which has a bitter taste. Quinoa absorbs a lot of liquid. Depending on how you like your porridge, add a little boiling water at the end of step 1 to thin it out.

I AM
VEGAN
HIGH IN AMINO ACIDS
GLUTEN-FREE

CHIA & ALMOND TOASTED MUESLI

PREP + COOK TIME
20 MINUTES (+ COOLING)
SERVES 4 (MAKES 2 CUPS)

1 cup (90g) rolled oats
2 tablespoons chia seeds
⅓ cup (55g) coarsely chopped almonds
½ teaspoon mixed spice
1 tablespoon pure maple syrup
2 tablespoons sunflower seeds
2 tablespoons LSA (see tips)

1 Preheat oven to 200°C/400°F. Grease and line an oven tray with baking paper.
2 Combine oats, chia, almonds and mixed spice on tray. Drizzle with syrup; toss well.
3 Bake muesli for 10 minutes or until mixture is browned lightly. Cool on tray.
4 Transfer cooled muesli to a medium bowl, add seeds and LSA; stir to combine.

tips *LSA is a ground mixture of linseeds, sunflower seeds and almonds. It is available from supermarkets and health food stores. You can make double or triple the recipe. Store it in an airtight container in the fridge for up to 3 months.*

STRAWBERRY & PASSIONFRUIT BREAKFAST TRIFLE

PREP TIME 5 MINUTES

SERVES 2

2 Weet-Bix (50g), broken into chunks
½ cup (40g) All-Bran cereal
1 cup (280g) low-fat plain yoghurt or soy yoghurt
⅓ cup (80ml) fresh passionfruit pulp
140g (4½ ounces) strawberries, sliced

1 Layer half each of the Weet-Bix and All-Bran in two 1¼-cup (310ml) glasses. Top with half each of the yoghurt, passionfruit and strawberries.
2 Repeat with remaining Weet-Bix, All-Bran and yoghurt. Top with remaining strawberries and passionfruit.

tips Assemble the trifle just before you're ready to eat so the cereals keep their crunch. You will need about 4 passionfruit. You can make the trifle with any seasonal fruit combination or even with canned fruit in natural juices. Canned pears and frozen raspberries work well together.

I AM
HIGH FIBRE
HIGH IN CALCIUM
SUGAR-FREE

chia bircher

WITH GRANOLA & POMEGRANATE

PREP + COOK TIME **25 MINUTES (+ REFRIGERATION)** SERVES **4**

You will need to start this recipe a day ahead. Make a double batch of the granola and store in an airtight container for up to 1 week.

160g (5 ounces) raspberries

2 cups (560g) low fat greek-style yoghurt

¼ cup (40g) white chia seeds

½ teaspoon vanilla extract

1 tablespoon pure maple syrup

¾ cup (60g) traditional rolled oats

½ cup (40g) sliced raw almonds

¼ teaspoon ground cinnamon

1 medium pomegranate (320g), seeds removed (see tip)

1 Reserve 12 of the raspberries. Mash remaining raspberries in a medium bowl with yoghurt until combined. Add chia seeds, extract and 2 teaspoons of the maple syrup. Cover; refrigerate overnight.

2 Preheat oven to 200°C/400°F.

3 To make granola, place oats on an oven tray. Bake for 5 minutes or until lightly browned. Add almonds, cinnamon and remaining maple syrup; mix well. Bake for another 5 minutes or until nuts are golden. Cool on tray.

4 Spoon half the yoghurt mixture into four 1 cup (250ml) jars. Top with half the pomegranate seeds and granola. Repeat layering with remaining yoghurt mixture, pomegranate seeds and granola. Serve topped with reserved raspberries.

tip To remove pomegranate seeds, cut pomegranate in half crossways; hold it, cut-side down, in the palm of your hand over a bowl, then hit the outside firmly with a wooden spoon. The seeds should fall out easily; discard any white pith that falls out with them.

I AM
HIGH FIBRE
HIGH IN CALCIUM
LOW FAT

APPLE PIE

pancakes

PREP + COOK TIME **35 MINUTES (+ COOLING)** SERVES **4**

1 cup (135g) frozen blackberries

⅓ cup (80ml) pure maple syrup

1 cup (150g) wholemeal spelt flour

2 teaspoons baking powder

1 teaspoon ground cinnamon

½ teaspoon mixed spice

1 cup (250ml) buttermilk

1 free-range egg, beaten lightly

2 teaspoons vanilla extract

1 medium pink lady apple (150g),
   unpeeled, grated coarsely

micro mint, to serve

1 Combine blackberries and half the maple syrup in a small saucepan; bring to the boil. Reduce heat; simmer, stirring occasionally, for 10 minutes or until berries soften. Remove from heat; cool.

2 Sift flour, baking powder, cinnamon, mixed spice and a pinch of salt into a medium bowl; gradually whisk in combined buttermilk, egg, extract and remaining maple syrup until batter is smooth. Fold in apple.

3 Heat an oiled, medium non-stick frying pan over medium heat. Pour ¼-cup of batter for each pancake into pan; cook until bubbles appear on the surface. Turn; cook until browned lightly. Remove from pan; cover to keep warm. Repeat with remaining batter to make a total of eight pancakes.

4 Serve pancakes with blackberry compote and mint.

tip You could use frozen mixed berries instead of blackberries.

I AM
HIGH FIBRE
HIGH IN VITAMIN C
LOW FAT

cavolo nero fritters
WITH PICKLED BEETROOT

PREP + COOK TIME **35 MINUTES (+ STANDING & COOLING)** SERVES **4**

3 large zucchini (450g), grated
    coarsely
1 teaspoon salt
3 cavolo nero (tuscan cabbage) leaves
    (30g), trimmed, shredded finely
2 tablespoons finely chopped
    fresh mint
¼ cup (40g) wholemeal plain
    (all-purpose) flour
2 cloves garlic, crushed
2 free-range eggs, beaten lightly
2 tablespoons olive oil
3 small beetroot (beets) (300g),
    peeled, sliced thinly (see tips)
2 tablespoons cider vinegar
100g (3 ounces) fetta, crumbled
¼ cup loosely packed fresh
    mint leaves
2 tablespoons sunflower seeds,
    toasted

HONEY DRESSING
2 tablespoons extra virgin olive oil
1 tablespoon cider vinegar
½ teaspoon honey

1 Combine zucchini and salt in a colander; stand in the sink for 10 minutes to drain. Using your hands, squeeze excess liquid from zucchini. Place zucchini in a medium bowl with cavolo nero, chopped mint, flour, garlic and egg; season. Mix well to combine.
2 Heat oil in a large non-stick frying pan over medium heat. Pour ¼-cups of mixture into pan, flatten slightly; cook for 5 minutes each side or until golden and crisp. Drain on paper towel; cover to keep warm. Repeat with remaining mixture to make a total of eight fritters.
3 Meanwhile, combine beetroot and vinegar in a bowl; season. Stand for 5 minutes. Drain; reserve pickling liquid for honey dressing.
4 Make honey dressing.
5 Arrange fritters, beetroot, fetta and mint leaves on a serving plate. Serve drizzled with dressing and sprinkled with sunflower seeds.

honey dressing Whisk ingredients with reserved pickling liquid in a small bowl until combined.

tips Use a mandoline or V-slicer to slice the beetroot very thinly. Cooked fritters can be frozen; reheat for a quick breakfast.

I AM
VEGETARIAN
RICH IN VITAMINS
LOW CARB

chickpea pancake

WITH FRIED EGGS & CHERRY TOMATOES

PREP + COOK TIME **30 MINUTES (+ COOLING)** SERVES **4**

⅔ cup (100g) chickpea flour (besan)

½ teaspoon ground cumin

¾ cup (180ml) water

1 tablespoon olive oil

1 free-range egg white

1 tablespoon olive oil, extra

170g (5½ ounces) asparagus, trimmed

1 clove garlic, chopped

250g (8 ounces) mixed cherry tomatoes, halved

1 tablespoon red wine vinegar

4 free-range eggs

I AM

VEGETARIAN
HIGH IN PROTEIN
LOW CARB

1 Preheat oven to 180°C/350°F.

2 Place chickpea flour and cumin in a medium bowl; season. Whisk in the water and oil until batter is smooth.

3 Beat egg white in a small bowl with an electric mixer until soft peaks form; gently fold into batter.

4 Heat an oiled 24cm (9½-inch) ovenproof non-stick frying pan over medium heat. Pour batter into pan; cook for 2 minutes or until bubbles form around the edge. Transfer pan to oven; bake for 7 minutes or until pancake is cooked through and light and fluffy.

5 Meanwhile, heat half the extra oil in a large non-stick frying pan over medium heat; cook asparagus for 5 minutes, turning, or until lightly browned and cooked. Remove from pan; keep warm.

6 Add garlic to same pan; cook, stirring for 30 seconds or until fragrant. Add tomatoes and vinegar; cook, breaking tomatoes with the back of a wooden spoon, for 5 minutes or until tomatoes have just broken down. Season. Remove from pan; wipe pan with paper towel.

7 Heat remaining oil in same pan over medium heat. Add eggs; cook for 4 minutes or until whites are set and yolks remain runny.

8 Cut pancake into wedges; serve topped with fried egg, tomato mixture and asparagus.

tip Pancake is best made just before serving.

THE AUSTRALIAN Women's Weekly

Super Foods & Power Juices

THE AUSTRALIAN WOMEN'S WEEKLY TRIPLE TESTED TEST KITCHEN

Contents

Super
CHARGE
YOUR
Diet

COCONUT & MANGO

breakfast bowl

PREP + COOK TIME **40 MINUTES** SERVES **4**

*The quinoa mixture thickens as it cools, so add more
coconut milk or water if you wish to thin it down.
When mangoes are not in season, use pears, apples or
bananas. Use dairy-free chocolate, if you prefer.*

1 cup (200g) white quinoa
1 litre (4 cups) coconut milk
1 cup (250ml) water
⅓ cup (55g) coconut sugar
¼ teaspoon sea salt
¼ cup (25g) finely grated dark chocolate (70% - 85% cocoa solids)
2 tablespoons macadamias, roasted, chopped coarsely
2 tablespoons almonds, roasted, chopped coarsely
2 small mangoes (600g), sliced thinly
¼ cup loosely packed fresh mint leaves, to serve

1 Combine quinoa, coconut milk, the water, half the coconut sugar
and the salt in a medium saucepan over high heat; bring to the
boil. Reduce heat to low; simmer, covered, for 30 minutes or until
quinoa is tender.
2 Serve quinoa mixture topped with remaining coconut sugar,
then chocolate, nuts, mango and mint.

I AM
HIGH IN FOLATE
HIGH IN VITAMIN C
PROTEIN RICH

FIG & RASPBERRY
baked porridge

PREP + COOK TIME **50 MINUTES** SERVES **6**

You can use the same weight of other fruits such as apricots, apples, pears, blueberries, blackberries and plums. Have all your dry ingredients weighed and combined the night before, to make it easier to prepare the next morning.

I AM
HIGH FIBRE
HIGH IN CALCIUM
EGG-FREE

1½ cups (135g) traditional
   rolled oats
1 teaspoon ground ginger
½ teaspoon sea salt
2 tablespoons coconut sugar
⅓ cup (55g) dry-roasted almonds,
   chopped coarsely
3 cups (750ml) milk
2 tablespoons honey
2 tablespoons olive oil
200g (6½ ounces) fresh raspberries
8 fresh figs (480g), torn in half
1 cup (280g) greek-style yoghurt

1 Preheat oven to 180°C/350°F. Grease a 2 litre (8-cup) ovenproof dish.
2 Combine oats, ginger, salt, coconut sugar and half the almonds in a large bowl. Whisk milk, half the honey and the oil in a large jug until combined; add to oat mixture, stirring until just combined. Fold in half the raspberries and 5 of the figs. Spread mixture evenly into dish.
3 Bake porridge for 30 minutes or until oats are tender. Stand for 10 minutes. Top with remaining almonds, raspberries and figs; drizzle with remaining honey. Serve porridge with yoghurt.

one-pan eggs
WITH KIMCHI

PREP + COOK TIME **15 MINUTES** SERVES **4**

Kimchi is a traditional Korean fermented cabbage dish found in Asian supermarkets. Freeze remaining canned tomatoes in a resealable bag for up to 3 months.

¼ cup (60g) virgin coconut oil

1⅓ cups (300g) kimchi

½ x 400g (12½-ounce) can
  diced tomatoes

4 free-range eggs

½ cup (40g) bean sprouts

¼ cup loosely packed fresh
  coriander (cilantro) leaves

¼ cup loosely packed fresh
  mint leaves

1 Heat coconut oil in a medium frying pan with a fitted lid over high heat. Add kimchi and tomatoes; cook, stirring, for 2 minutes or until combined and simmering. Season.

2 Using a wooden spoon, make four indents within the kimchi mixture. Carefully break an egg into each indent. Reduce heat to low; cook, covered, for 5 minutes or until egg whites are just set.

3 Serve immediately topped with sprouts and herbs.

serving suggestion *Serve with char-grilled bread.*

I AM
DAIRY-FREE
GLUTEN-FREE
LOW CARB

THREE-GRAIN MAPLE

syrup porridge

PREP + COOK TIME **50 MINUTES** SERVES **4**

You can make this the night before up to the end of step 1. Reheat with milk or serve cold the next day. Cool any leftover porridge and keep, covered, in the fridge for up to 3 days. Stir in a little extra milk to serve.

I AM
LOW FAT
HIGH FIBRE
EGG-FREE

1 cup (160g) brown rice
½ cup (100g) pearl barley
½ cup (45g) steel cut oats
1.25 litres (5 cups) water
1 cinnamon stick, halved
½ vanilla bean, seeds scraped
½ teaspoon salt
½ cup (125ml) milk
2 tablespoons pure maple syrup
1 ripe persimmon (120g), sliced thinly
125g (4 ounces) blueberries
¼ cup (60g) pomegranate seeds
¼ cup (35g) hazelnuts, toasted, chopped coarsely
¾ cup (200g) vanilla yoghurt
2 tablespoons pure maple syrup, extra
pinch of ground cinnamon

1 Combine rice, barley, oats, the water, cinnamon stick, vanilla bean and seeds and salt in a medium saucepan over high heat; bring to the boil. Reduce heat to low; simmer, covered, for 40 minutes, stirring occasionally to prevent sticking to base of pan, or until grains are tender with a slight bite.
2 Stir in milk and maple syrup; cook, stirring for 5 minutes or until porridge is heated through.
3 Serve porridge topped with persimmon, blueberries, pomegranate seeds, hazelnuts and yoghurt; drizzle with extra maple syrup and sprinkle with ground cinnamon.

RAINBOW CHARD & GARLIC

baked eggs

PREP + COOK TIME **30 MINUTES** SERVES **4**

You can also use silver beet (swiss chard), kale or spinach instead of rainbow swiss chard, if you like. Recipe is best made just before serving.

6 medium rainbow chard leaves
    with stems (330g)
2 tablespoons olive oil
2 cloves garlic, crushed
8 free-range eggs
⅓ cup (80ml) cream
2 tablespoons roasted skinless
    hazelnuts, chopped coarsely
2 tablespoons small fresh flat-leaf
    parsley leaves
bulls blood leaves, to serve

1 Preheat oven to 180°C/350°F. Grease four 1 cup (250ml) shallow ovenproof dishes.
2 Chop chard stems into 5cm (2-inch) lengths; coarsely chop leaves.
3 Heat oil in a large frying pan over medium heat; cook chard stems, stirring for 2 minutes or until just tender. Add garlic and chard leaves; cook, stirring for 2 minutes or until garlic is fragrant and leaves have wilted. Season.
4 Divide chard mixture into dishes. Carefully break two eggs into each dish, then add cream.
5 Bake for 15 minutes or until eggs are just set. Serve topped with hazelnuts, parsley and bulls blood leaves.

serving suggestion *Serve with char-grilled bread.*

I AM
VEGETARIAN
HIGH IN PROTEIN
VITAMIN RICH

FRUIT & NUT

muffins

PREP + COOK TIME **40 MINUTES** MAKES **12**

We used a nut, fruit and seed mix consisting of almonds, cashews, sultanas, chopped dried apricots, pepitas and sunflower seeds. You can use any combination of nuts, dried fruit and seeds you prefer.

I AM
SUGAR-FREE
PROTEIN RICH
LOW FAT

¾ cup (120g) wholemeal self-raising flour
½ cup (75g) white self-raising flour
¾ cup (120g) nut, fruit and seed mix, chopped coarsely
½ cup (140g) vanilla yoghurt
½ cup (125ml) milk
¼ cup (90g) honey
1 free-range egg
¼ cup (60ml) olive oil
1 small pear (180g), chopped finely
⅔ cup (110g) nut, fruit and seed mix, extra, chopped coarsely
2 tablespoons honey, extra

1 Preheat oven to 180°C/350°F. Line a 12-hole (⅓ cup/80ml) muffin pan with paper cases.
2 Combine flours and nut mix in a large bowl. Whisk yoghurt, milk, honey, egg and oil in a jug; pour into flour mixture, stir until just combined. Fold in the pear.
3 Spoon mixture into paper cases; sprinkle with extra nut mix.
4 Bake muffins for 18 minutes or until a skewer inserted in the centre comes out clean. Serve warm muffins drizzled with extra honey

Sunflower seeds are packed with nutrients and are a great source of the antioxidant vitamin E, which plays a role in heart health, as well as protecting the skin from sun damage and aging. They can be eaten raw or lightly toasted, as well as sprinkled into salads, stir-fries or on top of baked goods, such as muffins.

Quinoa, black (top) white (left) and red (see below), is cooked and eaten as a grain, but is, in fact, a seed. It's gluten-free, a good source of protein, contains all the essential amino acids and is high in fibre.

Pepitas, or pumpkin seeds, are rich in healthy unsaturated fats, and are packed with fibre. They are an especially good source of iron, making them a valuable addition to those with vegetarian and vegan diets.

Red quinoa is nutritionally equal to black and white quinoa, however, it has a slightly more fibrous texture, so will hold its shape better after cooking than white quinoa. It is also a little crunchier once cooked.

Linseeds, also known as flaxseeds, are especially rich in fibre; adding just 1 tablespoon to your breakfast cereal delivers three grams of fibre.

White chia seeds are nutritionally equal to black chia seeds (see below); both are fibre-rich and will provide you with a wealth of vitamins, minerals and antioxidants.

seeds

The abundance of seeds and grains on offer at health-food stores and supermarkets these days is truly eye-opening. Many are gluten-free, full of protein and contain all the essential amino acids, making them a perfect food for the ever-growing population of vegetarian and vegan dieters.

Black chia seeds contain protein and all the essential amino acids, making them a great addition to vegetarian and vegan diets.

Activated bukinis, or buckwheat groats, is made with buckwheat. It is gluten-free and has excellent levels of magnesium, B-group vitamins, phosphorus and zinc. It's terrific for vegetarian and vegan diets, as it is relatively rich in protein and contains all the essential amino acids.

Amaranth, like quinoa, is another seed that is used like a grain. It was a staple food of the Aztecs and remains popular in the Americas. It is gluten-free, high in protein, and is an excellent source of iron and manganese.

banana date loaf

WITH HONEY SPICED LABNE

PREP + COOK TIME **1 HOUR 40 MINUTES (+ REFRIGERATION)** SERVES **8**

You will need to start this recipe a day ahead. Muslin is available from fabric or craft stores. You will need 1¼ ripe bananas.

½ cup (55g) chopped walnuts

½ cup (45g) traditional rolled oats

1 tablespoon virgin coconut oil

1 tablespoon pure maple syrup

1 cup (300g) mashed ripe banana (see notes above)

2 teaspoons vanilla extract

¾ cup (180ml) buttermilk

200g (6½ ounces) medjool dates, pitted, chopped coarsely

2 cups (300g) high-fibre self-raising flour

1 teaspoon bicarbonate of soda (baking soda)

1½ teaspoons baking powder

⅓ cup (80g) virgin coconut oil, extra

HONEY SPICED LABNE

500g (1 pound) greek-style yoghurt

2 tablespoons honey

2 teaspoons ground cardamom

1 Make honey spiced labne.

2 Preheat oven to 180°C/350°F. Grease and line a 10cm x 20cm (4-inch x 8-inch) loaf pan with baking paper.

3 Combine walnuts, oats, coconut oil and maple syrup in a bowl. Place half the walnut mixture on a baking-paper-lined oven tray. Bake 10 minutes or until golden; cool.

4 Place banana, extract, reserved labne liquid, buttermilk and half the dates in a blender; blend until mixture is smooth.

5 Sift flour, soda and baking powder into a large bowl. Add banana mixture, remaining dates, extra coconut oil and roasted walnut mixture; stir to combine. Spoon mixture into pan, smooth surface. Sprinkle with remaining walnut mixture.

6 Bake for 1 hour 10 minutes or until a skewer inserted in the centre comes out clean. Leave in pan 15 minutes; turn, top-side up, onto a wire rack to cool completely.

7 Serve bread with labne.

honey spiced labne Line a sieve with muslin; place over a medium bowl. Spoon yoghurt into sieve, gather cloth and tie into a ball with kitchen string. Refrigerate for 24 hours, gently squeezing occasionally to encourage the liquid to drain. Reserve ½ cup of draining liquid to add in step 4. Place labne in a medium bowl with honey and cardamom; mix well. Refrigerate until required.

I AM
HIGH FIBRE
VITAMIN RICH
EGG-FREE

NO-KNEAD FENNEL & BEETROOT
spelt bread

PREP + COOK TIME **50 MINUTES (+ STANDING)** MAKES **8 ROLLS**

You will need to start this recipe a day ahead. We used a cast iron saucepan, but any heavy-based pan can be used. For a sweet variation, add nuts, dried fruit and honey.

1 medium beetroot (beet) (150g), peeled, grated coarsely

3 teaspoons fennel seeds

3 cups (450g) spelt flour

1 teaspoon table salt

1 teaspoon dried yeast

1 tablespoon olive oil

1¼ cups (310ml) warm water

1 teaspoon salt flakes

1 Spread beetroot onto paper towel; stand for 1 hour to dry.

2 Place 2 teaspoons of the fennel seeds in a small frying pan; cook, stirring for 30 seconds or until fragrant.

3 Combine flour, table salt, toasted fennel seeds, yeast, oil, the water and beetroot in a large bowl. Cover with plastic wrap and a tea towel; stand to slowly rise for 14 hours.

4 Place a 24cm (9½-inch) (base measurement) cast iron casserole dish with a firm fitting lid in the oven; preheat to 240°C/475°F. (The dish needs to be as hot as the oven before you put the dough inside.)

5 Turn dough onto a floured surface; shape into a large ball. Divide dough into eight portions; shape each portion into a roll. Arrange rolls, side-by-side, in a circle, on a large sheet of baking paper. Sprinkle with salt flakes and remaining fennel seeds. Cover; stand for 1 hour.

6 Transfer rolls on paper into the hot dish; cover with lid. Bake for 20 minutes; remove lid. Bake rolls for a further 12 minutes or until bread sounds hollow when tapped. Transfer bread to a wire rack. Serve warm or cool.

serving suggestion Serve with ricotta and honey.

I AM
LOW FAT
EGG-FREE
NUT-FREE

WITH ROASTED VEGETABLES

PREP + COOK TIME **30 MINUTES** SERVES **4**

170g (5½ ounces) asparagus,
    trimmed
1 medium red capsicum (bell
    pepper) (200g), cut into 1cm
    (½-inch) strips
2 tablespoons olive oil
750g (1½ pounds) kumara
    (orange sweet potato), peeled,
    grated coarsely
1 medium red onion (170g),
    sliced thinly
2 tablespoons rice flour
1 tablespoon fresh thyme leaves
1 medium avocado (250g), chopped
100g (3 ounces) marinated goat's
    fetta in olive oil, reserve
    1 tablespoon of the oil
kale sprouts, to serve

1 Preheat a flat-based sandwich press on high. Toss asparagus and capsicum in half the olive oil; season. Place in sandwich press, close; cook for 5 minutes or until lightly grilled. Cut asparagus in half lengthways.

2 Meanwhile, squeeze out excess moisture from kumara. Combine kumara, onion, flour, thyme and remaining olive oil in a medium bowl; season.

3 Spoon ⅓ cup measures of kumara mixture, in two batches, on base plate of sandwich press. Close press to flatten; cook for 7 minutes or until crisp and golden.

4 Serve rösti topped with asparagus, capsicum, avocado and crumbled fetta. Drizzle with reserved marinating oil and top with kale sprouts.

tip Rösti and vegetables can also be cooked in a non-stick frying pan.

I AM
NUT-FREE
GLUTEN-FREE
LOW GI

seedaholic bread

WITH ALMOND BUTTER & PEAR

PREP + COOK TIME **2 HOURS 30 MINUTES (+ STANDING & COOLING)** MAKES **10 SLICES**

1½ cups (135g) rolled oats

1½ cups (120g) quinoa flakes

1 cup (150g) sunflower seeds

1 cup (200g) pepitas (pumpkin seeds)

⅔ cup (130g) linseeds (flaxseeds)

½ cup (70g) white chia seeds

½ cup (80g) chopped almonds

½ cup (70g) chopped hazelnuts

½ cup (40g) psyllium husks

2 teaspoons sea salt flakes

3½ cups (875ml) warm water

2 tablespoons raw honey

⅔ cup (140g) virgin coconut oil,
    melted

½ cup (65g) almond butter

2 medium packham pear (250g),
    sliced thinly

2 tablespoons olive oil

1 Grease a 1.5-litre (6-cup), 14cm x 24cm (5½-inch x 9½-inch) loaf pan; line the base and two long sides with baking paper, extending the paper over the edge.

2 Place dry ingredients in a large bowl. Place the water, honey and coconut oil in a large jug; stir until dissolved. Pour over dry ingredients; stir to combine. (The mixture will be firm, if it is too stiff add extra tablespoons of water, one at a time.)

3 Spoon seed mixture into pan; shape with your hands into a loaf shape. Cover surface with plastic wrap; stand at room temperature for 2 hours to allow ingredients to absorb the liquid and set the bread into shape.

4 Preheat oven 200°C/400°F.

5 Bake bread for 30 minutes. Invert bread onto a wire rack on an oven tray; peel away lining paper. Return bread to oven on tray; bake a further 1 hour 20 minutes (see tips) or until a skewer inserted into the centre comes out clean. Leave for 3 hours or until completely cool before slicing.

6 To serve, spread slices of bread with almond butter, top with pear slices; drizzle with olive oil.

tips Psyllium husks are available from vitamin and health food stores. Position the shelf in the oven so the top of the bread sits in the middle of the oven. If the bread starts to overbrown during baking, cover it loosely with foil. Bread will keep in an airtight container in the fridge for up to 2 weeks. Freeze individual slices in zip-top bags for up to 1 month.

I AM
VEGAN
SUGAR-FREE
HIGH FIBRE

Coconut flesh gives you a fibre boost, but is not as rich in vitamins and minerals as tree nuts (almond, brazil, cashew etc).

Coconut flour is a high fibre, low carbohydrate, gluten-free flour made from fresh dried coconut flesh. It has a sweetish taste and is suitable for those on a paleo diet.

Coconut sugar is not made from coconuts, but from the sap of the blossoms of the coconut palm tree. The refined sap looks a little like raw or light brown sugar, and has a similar caramel flavour. It also has the same amount of kilojoules as regular table (white) sugar.

Coconut cream comes from the first pressing of the coconut flesh, without the addition of water; the second pressing (less rich) is sold as coconut milk. Look for coconut cream labelled as 100% coconut, without added emulsifiers.

Coconut oil is extracted from the coconut flesh so you don't get any of the fibre, protein or carbohydrates present in the whole coconut. The best quality is virgin coconut oil, which is the oil pressed from the dried coconut flesh, and doesn't include the use of solvents or other refining processes.

Coconut flakes are a good source of protein, are low in carbohydrates and high in fibre. Sprinkle over muesli, porridge or use on cakes.

Coconut water is the liquid from the centre of a young green coconut. It has fewer kilojoules than fruit juice, with no fat or protein. There are sugars present, but these are slowly absorbed giving coconut water a low GI.

coconut

Coconut and its natural food products are currently all the rage. Once relegated to the 'bad fat' basket, it has been found that coconut contains 'medium chain saturated fats': these are burned more readily for energy than other fats, so are less likely to be stored as fat.

Shredded coconut is thin strips of dried coconut. Add it to muesli, sprinkle over porridge, or use it in cakes and slices.

Young coconuts are coconuts that are not fully mature. As a coconut ages and a sprout develops, the liquid inside the mature husk gradually dehydrates and changes to a light, fluffy, edible texture.

baked turkish eggs

WITH LAMB MINCE

PREP + COOK TIME **25 MINUTES** SERVES **2**

¼ cup (60ml) extra virgin olive oil

1 medium onion (150g), chopped finely

2 cloves garlic, crushed

½ teaspoon ground mixed spice

½ teaspoon ground cinnamon

¼ teaspoon chilli flakes

150g (4½ ounces) minced (ground) lamb

1 large tomato (220g), chopped coarsely

2 tablespoons lemon juice

½ teaspoon stevia granules or norbu (monk fruit sugar)

1 tablespoon finely chopped fresh mint

1 tablespoon finely chopped fresh flat-leaf parsley

4 free-range eggs

¼ cup loosely packed fresh micro mint leaves

¼ cup loosely packed fresh flat-leaf parsley leaves, extra

2 lebanese flatbreads (230g), quartered

CUCUMBER YOGHURT

½ lebanese cucumber (130g)

½ cup (95g) greek-style yoghurt

1 clove garlic, crushed

1 teaspoon finely grated lemon rind

1 Make cucumber yoghurt.

2 Heat 2 tablespoons of the oil in a large frying pan over medium heat; cook onion, garlic, spices and chilli flakes, for 3 minutes or until soft. Add mince; cook, breaking mince up with a wooden spoon, for 5 minutes or until browned. Add tomato, juice and stevia; cook, for 2 minutes. Remove from heat; stir in chopped herbs. Season to taste.

3 Make four indents in mince mixture with the back of a spoon. Carefully crack eggs into indents; season eggs. Cook, covered, over medium heat for a further 6 minutes or until egg whites are set and yolks remain runny.

4 Drizzle with remaining oil; top with cucumber yoghurt, micro mint and extra parsley. Serve with flatbread.

cucumber yoghurt Coarsely grate cucumber; squeeze out excess water. Combine cucumber with remaining ingredients in a small bowl; season to taste.

tips This is a great dish for a group, just multiply the recipe. You can use minced beef, pork or chicken instead of the lamb, if you like.

I AM
PROTEIN RICH
HIGH IN IRON
SUGAR-FREE

super seed bowl

WITH APPLE & YOGHURT

PREP + COOK TIME **10 MINUTES** SERVES **2**

2 medium green apples (300g),
   cut into matchsticks

2 tablespoons lemon juice

½ cup (125ml) coconut water

100g (3 ounces) strawberries,
   sliced thickly

½ cup (140g) greek-style yoghurt

2 tablespoons raw honey

SUPER SEED MIX

2 tablespoons sunflower seeds

2 tablespoons pepitas
   (pumpkin seeds)

1½ tablespoons sesame seeds

1½ tablespoons poppy seeds

1½ tablespoons chia seeds

1½ tablespoons linseeds (flaxseeds)

2 tablespoons dried currants

2 tablespoons goji berries

1 Make super seed mix.

2 Combine apple and juice in a medium bowl.

3 Divide apple mixture and half the seed mix between two bowls, add coconut water. Top with strawberries and yoghurt; drizzle with honey and sprinkle with remaining seed mix.

super seed mix Stir sunflower seeds and pepitas in a small frying pan over medium heat for 2 minutes or until lightly golden. Add sesame seeds, poppy seeds, chia seeds and linseeds; stir for 30 seconds or until all are toasted. Remove from pan; cool. Stir in currants and goji berries. Makes 1 cup.

tips *When in season, you can use pears instead of apples. Super seed mix can be made ahead. Store seed mix in an airtight container or jar in the fridge for up to 3 months.*

I AM
GLUTEN-FREE
HIGH IN FIBRE &
OMEGA-3 FATTY ACIDS

STRAWBERRY & ALMOND

sweet frittata

PREP + COOK TIME **30 MINUTES** SERVES **4**

250g (8 ounces) strawberries, hulled

1 tablespoon coconut sugar

1 vanilla bean

6 free-range eggs

2 tablespoons coconut sugar, extra

⅓ cup (40g) ground almonds

10g (½ ounce) butter

100g (3 ounces) firm ricotta,
   crumbled coarsely

⅓ cup (55g) dry-roasted almonds,
   chopped coarsely

1 Thinly slice half the strawberries; cut remaining strawberries in half. Combine halved strawberries with coconut sugar in a small bowl. Reserve sliced strawberries.

2 Split vanilla bean lengthways; using the tip of a knife, scrape the seeds. Reserve pod for another use (see tips).

3 Place vanilla seeds, eggs, extra coconut sugar and ground almonds in a medium bowl; whisk until combined.

4 Preheat grill (broiler) to high.

5 Melt butter in a 24cm (9½-inch) non-stick ovenproof frying pan over medium heat. Add egg mixture, top with sliced strawberries, ricotta and half the chopped almonds. Reduce heat to low; cook, for 8 minutes or until half set. Place pan under grill for a further 8 minutes or until ricotta is lightly browned and mixture just set.

6 Serve immediately topped with halved strawberries and remaining chopped almonds. Drizzle with some honey and sprinkle with black chia seeds, if you like.

tips *The unused vanilla pod can be wrapped and frozen for up to 1 year. Use in recipes where a vanilla bean is called for. You can use macadamias and hazelnuts instead of the almonds, if you like.*

I AM

GLUTEN-FREE

ANTIOXIDANT RICH

SUGAR-FREE

WITH PASSIONFRUIT YOGHURT

PREP + COOK TIME **25 MINUTES** SERVES **4**

Microwaving the couscous after it has absorbed the water produces a lovely light and fluffy couscous.

I AM
VEGETARIAN
ANTIOXIDANT RICH
LOW FAT

1 cup (200g) wholemeal couscous
2 teaspoons extra virgin olive oil
1 teaspoon mixed spice
¼ teaspoon allspice
¼ cup (90g) honey
1 cup (250ml) boiling water
½ cup (50g) walnuts, toasted
¾ cup (200g) greek-style yoghurt
2 tablespoons passionfruit pulp
2 medium oranges (480g), peeled,
    sliced thinly
⅓ cup (50g) blueberries
¼ cup loosely packed fresh
    mint leaves

1 Combine couscous, oil, mixed spice, allspice, a pinch of salt, honey and the boiling water in a medium heatproof bowl; stand for 5 minutes or until liquid is absorbed, fluffing with a fork occasionally.
2 Cover couscous with plastic wrap. Microwave on HIGH (100%) for 30 seconds; fluff couscous with a fork to separate grains. Repeat process two or three times or until couscous is very fluffy. Stir in walnuts.
3 Meanwhile, combine yoghurt and passionfruit in a small bowl.
4 Serve couscous topped with orange slices, blueberries, yoghurt mixture and mint.

moroccan lamb

& CHICKPEA WRAPS

PREP + COOK TIME **15 MINUTES** SERVES **2**

200g (6 ounces) lamb fillets

125g (4 ounces) canned chickpeas
(garbanzo beans), rinsed, drained

60g (2 ounces) drained char-grilled
capsicum (bell pepper),
sliced thinly

½ small red onion (50g),
chopped finely

1 large tomato (220g), chopped finely

¼ cup loosely packed fresh
mint leaves

2 tablespoons lemon juice

1 teaspoon olive oil

¼ cup (70g) low-fat plain yoghurt

¼ teaspoon harissa paste

6 butter (boston) lettuce leaves

2 rye mountain breads (50g)

1 Cook lamb on a heated oiled grill plate (or grill or barbecue) until cooked as desired. Cover lamb; rest for 5 minutes, then slice thickly.

2 Meanwhile, combine chickpeas, capsicum, onion, tomato, mint, juice and oil in a large bowl; stir to combine.

3 Combine yoghurt and harissa in a small bowl.

4 Divide yoghurt mixture, lettuce, lamb and chickpea mixture between wraps. Roll firmly to enclose filling.

tips There are many types of mountain bread available; choose your favourite for this recipe. Harissa is a very hot chilli paste that varies in strength between brands. Reduce the amount of harissa to suit your taste if you are not used to fiery heat. To take to work, transport the wrap in an airtight container; keep refrigerated.

I AM
LOW GI
IRON & PROTEIN RICH
NUT-FREE

ZUCCHINI & FREEKEH
chicken soup

PREP + COOK TIME **1 HOUR** SERVES **4 (MAKES 8 CUPS)**

½ cup (100g) cracked greenwheat
   freekeh

1 tablespoon olive oil

1 medium leek (350g), white part
   only, halved, sliced thinly

4 cloves garlic, sliced thinly

1.25 litres (5 cups) water

4 chicken thigh cutlets (800g),
   trimmed

150g (4½ ounces) green beans,
   trimmed, cut into 2cm
   (¾-inch) lengths

1 large zucchini (150g), sliced thinly

½ cup (60g) frozen peas

2 tablespoons chopped fresh
   flat-leaf parsley

1 Place freekeh in a medium
saucepan of water; bring to the boil.
Reduce heat to low; simmer, partially
covered, for 15 minutes or until
almost tender. Drain.

2 Meanwhile, heat oil in a large
saucepan over medium heat; cook
leek, stirring, for 4 minutes until
softened. Add garlic; cook, stirring,
for 2 minutes.

3 Add the water and chicken; bring
to the boil. Reduce heat to low; cook,
covered, for 30 minutes or until
chicken is cooked. Remove chicken
from stock, discard skin and bones;
shred meat. Return shredded chicken
to pan with beans and freekeh,
then season; cook, uncovered, for
5 minutes. Add zucchini and peas;
cook for 3 minutes until tender.

4 Ladle soup into bowls; serve
topped with parsley.

tip For a more intense flavour,
use homemade chicken stock
instead of water.

I AM
EGG-FREE
PROTEIN RICH
LOW GI

falafel scotch eggs
WITH GREEN TAHINI

PREP + COOK TIME **30 MINUTES (+ REFRIGERATION)** SERVES **4**

400g (12½ ounces) canned chickpeas (garbanzo beans), drained, rinsed

400g (12½ ounces) canned cannellini beans, drained, rinsed

¼ cup (35g) plain (all-purpose) flour

2 green onions (scallions), chopped

1 tablespoon ras el hanout

4 free-range eggs

¼ cup (35g) sesame seeds

vegetable oil, for shallow-frying

2 baby cos (romaine) lettuce (180g), quartered

250g (8 ounces) heirloom cherry tomatoes, halved

GREEN TAHINI

1 cup chopped fresh mint

½ cup (140g) greek-style yoghurt

¼ cup (60ml) lemon juice

¼ cup (70g) tahini

1 tablespoon cider vinegar

½ small clove garlic, crushed

1 Process chickpeas, cannellini beans, flour, green onion and ras el hanout to form a coarse paste. Season. Refrigerate for 30 minutes or until firm.

2 Meanwhile, place eggs in a small saucepan with enough cold water to cover. Bring to the boil. Reduce heat; simmer, uncovered, for 4 minutes for soft boiled. Drain; rinse under cold water then peel. Pat eggs dry with paper towel.

3 Shape a quarter of the chickpea mixture around each egg. Sprinkle with sesame seeds to lightly coat. Refrigerate for 30 minutes.

4 Heat oil in a medium frying pan over medium heat; shallow-fry scotch eggs for 5 minutes, turning on all sides until golden and crisp. Drain on paper towel.

5 Make green tahini.

6 Serve scotch eggs with lettuce and tomatoes; drizzle with green tahini. Season to taste.

green tahini Blend ingredients until smooth. Thin with a little water if necessary. Season.

tip For a gluten-free option, use chickpea flour (besan) or rice flour instead of plain (all-purpose) flour.

I AM
VEGETARIAN
PROTEIN RICH
HIGH FIBRE

open rye sandwich

WITH SMOKED TROUT & CHERRY SALAD

PREP + COOK TIME **25 MINUTES** SERVES **2**

Smoked trout is available at most supermarkets in various sized filleted portions. These sandwiches are best assembled just before serving.

I AM
PROTEIN RICH
HIGH IN OMEGA 3
HIGH FIBRE

2 tablespoons raw buckwheat

1 smoked trout (300g), skinned, boned, flaked coarsely

150g (4½ ounces) fresh cherries, pitted, squashed

½ small red onion (50g), sliced thinly

¾ cup loosely packed fresh dill

1 tablespoon lemon juice

1 tablespoon extra virgin olive oil

4 slices rye bread (180g)

1 medium avocado (250g)

1 Place buckwheat in a small dry frying pan; cook, stirring, over high heat for 1 minute or until browned lightly.

2 Combine trout, cherries, onion, dill, juice and 3 teaspoons of the oil in a large bowl; season.

3 Toast bread until browned lightly; spread avocado on slices. Spoon trout mixture on bread; top with buckwheat and remaining oil.

GREEN
smoothie soup

PREP + COOK TIME **40 MINUTES** SERVES **4**

Green smoothie soup can be made up to 3 days ahead; keep, covered, in the fridge. Refrigerate ginger mixture in a separate container. Soup can be frozen for up to 3 months.

½ cup (125ml) extra virgin olive oil

1 medium leek (350g), white part only, chopped finely

1 clove garlic, crushed

2 teaspoons finely grated fresh ginger

150g (4½ ounces) broccoli, chopped coarsely

1 small pear (180g), chopped coarsely

2 tablespoons ground almonds

1 litre (4 cups) salt-reduced chicken stock

80g (2½ ounces) baby spinach leaves

5cm (2-inch) piece fresh ginger (25g), extra, peeled, cut into thin matchsticks

¼ cup (20g) natural flaked almonds

1 Heat 2 tablespoons of the oil in a large saucepan over low heat; cook leek, garlic and grated ginger, stirring, for 8 minutes or until leek is soft. Increase heat to medium, add broccoli, pear and ground almonds; cook, stirring, for 2 minutes or until broccoli and pear are hot and vegetables are coated in almonds.

2 Add stock; bring to the boil. Reduce heat; simmer, covered, for 10 minutes or until broccoli is tender. Stir in spinach; stand for 10 minutes.

3 Blend or process soup, in batches, until smooth. Return soup to pan; stir over heat until hot. Season.

4 Meanwhile, heat remaining oil in a medium frying pan over high heat; cook extra ginger, stirring occasionally, for 1 minute or until golden. Drain on paper towel; season. Add flaked almonds to same pan; cook, stirring, for 30 seconds or until browned lightly. Drain on paper towel.

5 Ladle soup into serving bowls, top with toasted flaked almonds and crisp ginger.

I AM
DAIRY-FREE
VITAMIN RICH
LOW CARB

WITH MIXED HERB SALAD

PREP + COOK TIME **40 MINUTES** SERVES **4**

10 free-range eggs

500g (1 pound) cooked, peeled
   beetroot (beets), chopped coarsely

¼ cup coarsely chopped fresh dill

½ cup (55g) coarsely chopped
   roasted walnuts

2 tablespoons olive oil

MIXED HERB SALAD

1 tablespoon sunflower seeds

3 teaspoons black chia seeds

½ small red onion (50g), sliced thinly

⅔ cup loosely packed fresh flat-leaf
   parsley leaves

⅔ cup loosely packed fresh
   mint leaves

2 tablespoons small fresh
   tarragon leaves

2 tablespoons fresh dill sprigs

1 tablespoon extra virgin olive oil

1 tablespoon lemon juice

1 Preheat oven to 180°C/350°F.
Grease 8 holes of two 6-hole
(¾-cup/180ml) texas muffin pans;
line bases with baking paper.

2 Whisk eggs in a medium bowl.
Stir in beetroot, dill, walnuts and
oil until combined; season. Divide
mixture into pan holes.

3 Bake frittatas for 20 minutes or
until a sharp knife inserted into the
centre comes out clean.

4 Meanwhile, make mixed herb salad.

5 Serve frittatas with salad.

mixed herb salad Heat a large
frying pan over medium heat; cook
seeds, stirring, for 2 minutes or until
toasted. Place seeds in a medium
bowl with remaining ingredients;
toss gently to combine.

*tip Frittatas are great to pack for
work or school lunch.*

I AM
GLUTEN-FREE
PROTEIN RICH
LOW CARB

BROCCOLI & PRAWN

fried rice

PREP + COOK TIME **30 MINUTES** SERVES **4**

¼ cup (60ml) reduced-salt soy sauce

2 tablespoons lime juice

1 tablespoon finely grated
fresh ginger

1 fresh long red chilli, sliced thinly

1 clove garlic, crushed

500g (1 pound) large uncooked
prawns (shrimp)

1 tablespoon virgin coconut oil

2 free-range eggs, beaten lightly

500g (1 pound) broccoli, cut into
florets, stems chopped

4 green onions (scallions),
sliced thinly

1 medium carrot (120g),
grated coarsely

1 tablespoon reduced-salt soy sauce,
extra

½ cup (75g) roasted cashews,
chopped coarsely

⅓ cup loosely packed fresh
coriander (cilantro) leaves

lime cheeks, to serve

1 Whisk soy sauce, juice, ginger, chilli and garlic in a medium bowl. Peel and devein prawns, leaving tails intact; cut in half lengthways. Add prawns to bowl; toss to combine in soy mixture.

2 Heat 1 teaspoon of the coconut oil in a wok over high heat. Pour egg into wok; cook, tilting wok, until almost set. Remove omelette from wok; roll tightly, slice thinly.

3 Place broccoli in a food processor; pulse until finely chopped and it resembles rice.

4 Heat remaining coconut oil in wok over high heat. Add green onion and carrot; stir-fry for 5 minutes or until tender. Add prawn mixture; stir-fry for 5 minutes until just cooked. Add broccoli and extra soy sauce; stir-fry for 2 minutes.

5 Serve fried rice topped with cashews, coriander, omelette and lime cheeks.

tip Fried rice is best made just before serving.

I AM
PROTEIN RICH
MINERAL RICH
LOW CARB

SALAD BOWL

PREP + COOK TIME **30 MINUTES** SERVES **4**

Store dressing in a small separate airtight container. You will need 2 cups of cooked brown rice.

400g (12½ ounces) canned black beans, drained, rinsed
2 green onions (scallions), chopped finely
2 tablespoons lime juice
2 baby cos (romaine) lettuce hearts, quartered
200g (6½ ounces) shredded red cabbage
4 baby radishes (120g), trimmed, sliced thinly
1 tablespoon extra virgin olive oil
250g (8-ounce) packet microwave brown rice
1 cup (280g) greek-style yoghurt
2 teaspoons chipotle chilli sauce
250g (8 ounces) mini roma (egg) tomatoes
1 medium avocado (250g), sliced
½ cup loosely packed fresh coriander (cilantro) sprigs
lime wedges, to serve

SPICED PEPITAS

½ cup (100g) pepitas (pumpkin seeds)
1 tablespoon olive oil
1 tablespoon pure maple syrup
½ teaspoon cayenne pepper

1 Combine beans, green onion and juice in a small bowl; season to taste.
2 Place lettuce, cabbage, radish and oil in a large bowl; toss gently to combine.
3 Heat rice in microwave according to packet directions.
4 Make spiced pepitas.
5 Combine yoghurt and chilli sauce in a small jug.
6 Divide rice, bean mixture and cabbage salad among bowls. Top with tomatoes, avocado, spiced pepitas and coriander. Serve with yoghurt dressing and lime wedges.

spiced pepitas Stir ingredients in a hot frying pan until pepitas are popped and lightly browned. Cool.

I AM
EGG-FREE
PROTEIN RICH
LOW GI

Farro is the Italian name for 'emmer', an ancient wheat variety and one of the first grains ever to be cultivated. It's available in wholegrain form, retaining the majority of nutrients and fibre.

Hulled millet is a small gluten-free grain with a hard hull that is removed before using. It has a slightly nutty, corn-like flavour. It is a popular cereal in Africa and India where it is often used to make flatbread.

Spelt is another ancient grain making a comeback. It is high in fibre, protein, vitamins and minerals, and has a mild nutty flavour.

Barley is rich in fibre, and has been shown to be effective in reducing blood cholesterol. Pearl barley, pictured, has had the husk removed, then been hulled and polished so only the 'pearl' of the grain remains. After dehulling, it still has a low GI.

ancient grains

Grown for centuries by people around the world, many ancient grains fell by the wayside as ease of harvesting, uniform growth and a grain that resulted in the right kind of flour to make bread, pasta or other baked goods grew more popular. Now, however, they're making a comeback.

Teff (teff flour pictured) is a tiny grain high in resistant starch, which promotes the growth of beneficial bacteria in the gut. It is gluten-free, and is especially high in calcium, which is terrific for those on dairy-free diets.

Freekeh is an ancient grain made from roasted young green wheat. Nutritionally it has a low GI, four times the fibre of brown rice, and is higher in protein than regular wheat.

RAW VEGETABLE
noodle salad

PREP + COOK TIME **15 MINUTES** SERVES **6 (AS A SIDE)**

A spiralizer is a kitchen gadget that cuts vegetables to resemble noodles. If you don't have one, you can coarsely grate the vegetables or use a mandoline or V-slicer. This salad is perfect served at a barbecue. It can be easily doubled or tripled to serve a crowd.

2 medium zucchini (240g)

2 medium carrots (240g)

2 medium purple carrots (240g)

½ small daikon (200g)

½ cup firmly packed fresh flat-leaf parsley leaves

2 tablespoons finely chopped fresh chives

CREAMY MUSTARD DRESSING

½ cup (140g) greek-style yoghurt

2 tablespoons wholegrain mustard

2 tablespoons extra virgin olive oil

1 tablespoon lemon juice

1 Make creamy mustard dressing.

2 Using a vegetable spiralizer, cut zucchini, carrots and daikon into thick noodles.

3 Place vegetable 'noodles' in a large bowl with herbs and dressing; toss gently to combine.

creamy mustard dressing Whisk ingredients in a medium bowl until combined; season to taste.

I AM

LOW FAT

VEGETARIAN

RAW

CAULIFLOWER

burgers

PREP + COOK TIME **40 MINUTES (+ REFRIGERATION)** MAKES **4**

350g (11 ounces) beetroot (beets),
   peeled, grated coarsely

1 small red onion (100g),
   sliced thinly

1 teaspoon salt flakes

¼ cup (60ml) red wine vinegar

1 tablespoon light brown sugar

2 tablespoons chopped fresh thyme

250g (8 ounces) cauliflower,
   chopped coarsely

140g (4½-ounce) piece cheddar

½ cup (100g) canned cannellini
   beans, drained, rinsed

1 cup (70g) fresh breadcrumbs

2 tablespoons chopped fresh
   flat-leaf parsley

2 teaspoons finely grated lemon rind

2 tablespoons chopped skinless
   hazelnuts, toasted

1 free-range egg white, beaten lightly

2 tablespoons vegetable oil

8 large butter (boston) lettuce leaves

125g (4 ounces) cherry heirloom
   tomatoes, halved

LEMON MAYONNAISE

⅓ cup (100g) whole-egg mayonnaise

2 teaspoons finely grated lemon rind

2 teaspoons lemon juice

1 Place beetroot, onion, salt, vinegar, sugar and thyme in a medium saucepan; bring to the boil. Reduce heat; simmer, uncovered, stirring occasionally, for 20 minutes or until beetroot is tender and slightly sticky. Cool.

2 Meanwhile, boil, steam or microwave cauliflower until tender. Drain; cool. Thinly slice 90g (3 ounces) of the cheddar; grate remaining cheddar.

3 Place cauliflower and beans in a food processor, pulse until coarsely chopped (do not over process). Transfer to a large bowl. Add ¼ cup (15g) of the breadcrumbs, the grated cheddar, parsley, rind and nuts; season, stir to combine. Shape cauliflower mixture into four patties. Refrigerate for 30 minutes.

4 Make lemon mayonnaise.

5 Dip patties in egg white; coat patties in remaining breadcrumbs.

6 Heat oil in a large frying pan over medium-high heat; cook patties for 4 minutes each side or until browned and crisp. Drain on paper towel. Immediately top with sliced cheese for cheese to melt.

7 Place each patty in a lettuce leaf; top with tomato and a generous spoonful of the beetroot mixture (you will only use half the mixture, see tips). Drizzle with lemon mayonnaise; top with remaining lettuce leaf.

lemon mayonnaise Whisk ingredients in a small bowl until combined; season to taste.

tip Refrigerate leftover beetroot mixture in an airtight container for up to 1 week.

I AM
LOW CARB
VEGETARIAN
VITAMIN RICH

pea & prawn patties

WITH WATERCRESS SALAD

PREP + COOK TIME **45 MINUTES (+ REFRIGERATION)** SERVES **4**

1½ cups (180g) frozen peas

1 clove garlic, peeled

250g (4 ounces) peeled uncooked
   medium king prawns (shrimp),
   chopped coarsely

1 tablespoon fresh tarragon leaves,
   chopped coarsely

½ teaspoon finely grated lemon rind

1 tablespoon ground almonds

2 cups (235g) firmly packed
   trimmed watercress

1 medium fennel bulb (300g),
   sliced thinly

1 stalk celery (150g), trimmed,
   sliced thinly on the diagonal

¼ cup (40g) roasted whole blanched
   almonds, chopped coarsely

1 tablespoon fresh tarragon leaves,
   extra

2 tablespoons dill sprigs

2 tablespoons olive oil

MUSTARD & LEMON DRESSING

1½ tablespoons dijon mustard

1 tablespoon lemon juice

2 tablespoons olive oil

1 Boil, steam or microwave peas and
garlic together until the peas are
tender; drain.

2 Blend or process garlic and 1 cup
of the peas with prawns, chopped
tarragon, rind and ground almonds
until combined; season. Using oiled
hands, roll level tablespoons of
mixture into 16 balls; flatten slightly.
Cover; refrigerate for 1 hour. (The
patties are quite sticky, however they
will not fall apart during cooking.)

3 Meanwhile, make mustard and
lemon dressing.

4 Place watercress, fennel, celery,
blanched almonds, extra tarragon,
dill and remaining peas in a large
bowl with half the dressing; toss
to combine.

5 Heat oil in a large non-stick frying
pan over medium heat; cook patties,
in batches, for 2 minutes each side
or until golden and cooked through.
Remove from pan; cover to keep warm.

6 Serve patties with watercress salad,
drizzled with remaining dressing.

mustard & lemon dressing
Whisk ingredients in a small bowl
until combined; season to taste.

*tips Patties can be made up to 1 day
ahead; store in an airtight container
in the fridge. Use a mandoline or
V-slicer to slice the fennel very thinly.*

I AM
LOW CARB
PROTEIN RICH
LOW CALORIE

CHAR-GRILLED PERSIMMONS, AVOCADO
& watercress salad

PREP + COOK TIME **20 MINUTES (+ STANDING)** SERVES **4 (AS A SIDE)**

You can purchase two types of persimmons: a soft, astringent one and a firm, non-astringent sweet variety also known as fuji fruit. We used the sweet variety in this recipe. When persimmons are out of season, use pears instead.

I AM
HIGH FIBRE
HIGH IN VITAMIN C
EGG-FREE

2 medium persimmons (fuji) (860g), sliced thickly
2 tablespoons olive oil
1 large avocado (320g), chopped
2 cups (60g) picked watercress sprigs
¼ cup (35g) sunflower seeds, toasted

BUTTERMILK DRESSING
⅓ cup (80ml) buttermilk
1 teaspoon honey
2 teaspoons chopped fresh tarragon
½ clove garlic, crushed

1 Make buttermilk dressing.
2 Toss persimmons in olive oil to coat; season.
3 Cook persimmons, on a heated oiled grill plate (or grill or barbecue) over high heat for 1 minute each side or until grill marks appear.
4 Arrange avocado, persimmon and watercress on a large platter; sprinkle with sunflower seeds and drizzle with dressing. Season. Serve immediately.

buttermilk dressing Place ingredients in a screw-top jar; shake well. Season to taste.

Raspberry vinegar may be either light, made from fresh raspberries steeped in a white wine vinegar; or dark, made from a reduction of red wine vinegar and raspberry juice.

Apple cider vinegar is touted as being a cure-all for pretty much everything from sore throats to detoxing the body. Unfortunately, there is very little evidence to back up any of these claims, and some have been completely disproven.

White wine vinegar is made from a blend of white wines.

Coconut vinegar is made from the fermented sap (or nectar) from the blossoms of the coconut palm trees.

Sherry vinegar is a traditional wine vinegar made from the sherry grape grown in the southwest of Spain. It is aged in oak casks, where it develops a rich mellow, sweet-sour flavour.

Red wine vinegar is based on fermented red wines. They have a more robust flavour than vinegars based on white wines.

vinegar

Vinegar is produced as a result of fermentation of a certain food (apples, coconut, berries, etc) by a bacteria or other microorganism. This process converts the sugars in the food to alcohol, and then to vinegar, which literally means 'sour wine'.

The magic of vinegar is best expressed when used to create a vinaigrette. It will take a salad from bland to brilliant with just a splash and a gentle toss. Simply remember the all-important ratio of 3 parts oil to 1 part vinegar, and you have the start of a delicious dressing. Next, add any desired flavours that will complement the dish - a squeeze of citrus, a dash of honey, some chopped herbs or minced shallots; the combinations are endless.

Vino cotto is the result of slowly cooking grape must (the freshly pressed grape juice from young dark grapes containing the skins, seeds and stems of the fruit) until it reduces to a thick syrup. It is then aged to develop its rich flavours.

SALMON & GREEN LENTIL
niçoise salad

PREP + COOK TIME **35 MINUTES** SERVES **4**

To save time, use 400g (12½ ounces) canned drained lentils and 400g (12½ ounces) canned quality red salmon.

¾ cup (150g) dried french-style green lentils, rinsed

½ medium white onion (75g), halved

1 bay leaf

3 small kumara (orange sweet potatoes) (250g), cut into 5mm (¼-inch) round slices

olive oil cooking spray

4 x 100g (3-ounce) salmon fillets, skin on

4 free-range eggs

200g (6½ ounces) green beans, trimmed

1 small radicchio (150g), leaves separated

OLIVE DRESSING

¼ cup (60ml) extra virgin olive oil

2 tablespoons finely chopped kalamata olives

2 tablespoons finely chopped red onion

1½ tablespoons red wine vinegar

2 teaspoons wholegrain mustard

2 teaspoons pure maple syrup

1 Preheat oven to 200°C/400°F.

2 Bring a medium saucepan of salted water to the boil. Add lentils, onion and bay leaf; reduce heat to low, simmer, uncovered, for 20 minutes or until just tender. Drain well. Remove and discard onion and bay leaf.

3 Meanwhile, place kumara, in a single layer, over two-thirds of a baking-paper-lined oven tray; spray with oil, season. Bake for 10 minutes. Add salmon to tray; spray with oil, season. Bake a further 7 minutes or until salmon and kumara are just cooked through. Remove from tray.

4 Place eggs in a medium saucepan with enough cold water to cover; bring to the boil. Reduce heat; simmer, uncovered, for 4 minutes for soft boiled, adding beans for the final minute of cooking. Drain; refresh eggs and beans under cold running water. Peel eggs.

5 Make olive dressing.

6 Divide lentils and radicchio among serving plates; drizzle with half the dressing. Top with beans, kumara, salmon and halved eggs; drizzle with remaining dressing.

olive dressing Place ingredients in a screw-top jar; shake well. Season to taste.

I AM
PROTEIN RICH
HIGH IN OMEGA 3
NUT-FREE

kale caesar salad

WITH CHICKPEA CROÛTONS

PREP + COOK TIME **20 MINUTES** SERVES **4**

4 free-range eggs

500g (1 pound) kale, trimmed,
    chopped coarsely

1 tablespoon olive oil

½ teaspoon sea salt

½ cup (40g) shaved parmesan

micro radish leaves, to serve

CHICKPEA CROÛTONS

400g (12½ ounces) canned chickpeas
    (garbanzo beans), drained, rinsed

1 tablespoon olive oil

1 teaspoon smoked paprika

¼ cup (40g) smoked almonds,
    chopped

BUTTERMILK DRESSING

⅓ cup (80ml) buttermilk

2 teaspoons lemon juice

1 teaspoon dijon mustard

1 large anchovy fillet, chopped finely

½ clove garlic, crushed

1 Make chickpea croûtons.

2 Meanwhile, place eggs in a medium saucepan with enough cold water to cover; bring to the boil. Reduce heat; simmer, uncovered, for 4 minutes for soft boiled. Drain; refresh under cold running water. Peel eggs.

3 Make buttermilk dressing.

4 Place kale, oil and salt in a large bowl; rub well to soften the leaves, it will lose about half its volume. Add chickpea croûtons and half the dressing; toss gently to combine. Serve topped with halved eggs, parmesan, micro leaves and remaining dressing.

chickpea croûtons Combine ingredients in a medium bowl. Cook chickpea mixture in a large frying pan over high heat, stirring, for 8 minutes, or until crisp. Cool.

buttermilk dressing Place ingredients in a screw-top jar; shake well.

tip You could use baby kale leaves if you prefer, as they are not as tough as regular kale.
serving suggestion Add some sliced smoked chicken.

I AM
IRON RICH
HIGH IN VITAMIN A
LOW GI

super green salad
WITH GREEN GODDESS DRESSING

PREP + COOK TIME **20 MINUTES** SERVES **4**

¾ cup (25g) puffed millet

⅓ cup (45g) shelled pistachios, chopped coarsely

175g (5½ ounces) broccolini, trimmed, sliced lengthways

200g (6½ ounces) snow peas, trimmed

1 lebanese cucumber (130g), sliced lengthways

1 medium avocado (250g), sliced

⅔ cup (70g) mixed crunchy sprouts

⅔ cup (30g) alfalfa sprouts

micro mint, to serve

GREEN GODDESS DRESSING

¼ cup (70g) greek-style yoghurt

¼ cup (60g) sour cream

1 small clove garlic, crushed

¼ cup coarsely chopped fresh flat-leaf parsley

¼ cup coarsely chopped fresh chives

1 tablespoon chopped fresh tarragon

1 tablespoon lemon juice

1 Preheat oven to 180°C/350°F.

2 Spread millet and pistachios on an oven tray. Bake for 5 minutes, stirring halfway through cooking, or until millet is crisp. Cool on tray.

3 Meanwhile, place broccolini and snow peas in a colander in the sink. Bring a jug of water to the boil. Pour boiling water over vegetables to lightly blanch. Rinse under cold water; drain well.

4 Make green goddess dressing.

5 Arrange the broccolini and snow peas with cucumber and avocado on a serving platter; top with millet mixture and sprouts. Serve drizzled with dressing. Sprinkle with micro mint.

green goddess dressing Blend ingredients in a blender until smooth. Season to taste.

tip Salad is best assembled close to serving.

I AM
LOW CARB
VEGETARIAN
EGG-FREE

lamb fillet salad

WITH SPINACH PESTO DRESSING

PREP + COOK TIME **35 MINUTES** SERVES **4**

The oil from the marinated goat's cheese adds an extra depth of flavour to this dish. The cheese we used was marinated in a mixture of olive oil, garlic, thyme and chilli.

8 lamb fillets (550g)

1 clove garlic, crushed

1 tablespoon olive oil

4 large flat mushrooms (320g)

1 small red onion (100g),
   cut into thin wedges

3 medium heirloom tomatoes (450g),
   quartered

1 medium radicchio (200g),
   leaves separated

25g (¾ ounce) baby rocket
   (arugula) leaves

½ cup (100g) soft marinated goat's
   cheese, reserve 2 tablespoons of
   the marinating oil (see note above)

¼ cup fresh micro cress

SPINACH PESTO DRESSING

½ cup (130g) baby spinach pesto

¼ cup (60ml) olive oil

1 Combine lamb, garlic and oil in a medium bowl; season.

2 Cook mushrooms and onion on a heated oiled grill plate (or grill or barbecue) until browned and just tender; season. Remove from heat; cover to keep warm.

3 Cook lamb on heated oiled grill plate for 10 minutes or until cooked as desired. Remove from heat; rest, covered, for 5 minutes before slicing.

4 Meanwhile, make spinach pesto dressing.

5 Place mushrooms and onion in a large bowl with tomato, radicchio, rocket and reserved marinating oil; toss gently to combine. Season.

6 Add lamb to salad; toss to combine. Arrange salad on a large serving platter. Top with crumbled cheese; drizzle with dressing and sprinkle with micro cress.

spinach pesto dressing Place ingredients in a small screw-top jar; shake well to combine.

I AM
HIGH IN IRON
PROTEIN RICH
LOW CARB

KUMARA TURKEY

burger

PREP + COOK TIME **1 HOUR (+ REFRIGERATION)** MAKES **6**

The kumara needs to be about 12cm (4¾ inches) in diameter, as it will serve as the 'bun' for the burgers.

1 large kumara (orange sweet potato) (500g), unpeeled

cooking-oil spray

⅓ cup (25g) quinoa flakes

¼ cup (60ml) milk

1 small zucchini (90g), grated coarsely

1 small purple carrot (70g), grated coarsely

1 small red onion (100g), grated coarsely

400g (12½ ounces) minced (ground) free-range turkey or chicken

1 tablespoon finely chopped fresh flat-leaf parsley

2 tablespoons olive oil

1 large tomato (220g), sliced thinly

100g (3 ounces) trimmed watercress

1 small red onion (100g), extra, sliced thinly

1 tablespoon sesame seeds, toasted

GREEN TAHINI

¼ cup (70g) tahini

2 tablespoons fresh flat-leaf parsley leaves

2 tablespoons lemon juice

1 tablespoon olive oil

1 small clove garlic, crushed

1 Preheat oven to 200°C/400°F. Oil and line two large oven trays with baking paper.

2 Cut kumara into 12 x 1.5cm (¾-inch) thick rounds; discard tapered ends. Place kumara slices, in a single layer, on oven trays; spray with cooking oil. Roast for 20 minutes or until tender. Cover to keep warm.

3 Meanwhile, make green tahini.

4 Combine quinoa flakes and milk in a small bowl; stand for 10 minutes.

5 Combine zucchini, carrot, onion, turkey, parsley and quinoa mixture in a medium bowl; season. Using damp hands, shape turkey mixture into six 8cm (3¼-inch) patties. Cover, refrigerate for 30 minutes.

6 Heat oil in a large non-stick frying pan over medium heat; cook patties for 4 minutes on each side or until golden and cooked through.

7 Place patties on six kumara rounds; top with tomato, green tahini, watercress, extra onion and remaining kumara rounds. Sprinkle with sesame seeds.

green tahini Process ingredients until smooth; season to taste.

I AM
LOW CARB
GLUTEN-FREE
EGG-FREE

Pickles are vegetables that have been fermented; this allows them to be stored in jars for many months. Particular bacteria convert the sugars in the food to lactic acid, and this acts as a preservative. Fermented foods promote good gut health and powers our immune systems.

Natural yoghurt is the healthiest option; read the ingredients list to find one with only milk and cultures, and nothing else added.

Sourdough bread is made using a bacterial culture called the 'mother', rather than using yeast to rise the dough. This gives a slight acidity to the bread, which in turn lowers the glycaemic index. The starch present is therefore broken down more slowly and has a gentler effect on blood glucose levels.

Kimchi, traditional to Korea, is a spicy fermented side dish of vegetables, often using cabbage.

White or shiro miso is a combination of fermented rice and soy beans. It's salty, but quite mild in taste.

Miso, Japan's famous bean paste, is made from fermenting soy beans with a particular fungus, salt and other ingredients including rice, beans, barley and other grains. Red miso is fermented from barley and soy beans.

fermented foods

Traditional foods were fermented as a means of preservation before refrigeration. And, while they boost the levels of good bacteria in the gut, some are high in salt, so are not suitable for people with kidney or blood pressure problems.

Kefir is a fermented milk drink that tastes a little like yoghurt. The levels of probiotic bacteria are much higher than most commercial yoghurts. For people with lactose-intolerance, kefir is a great dairy option, as the bacteria break down the lactose leaving only a trace in the end product.

Olives picked fresh from the tree are bitter and unpalatable. But for many centuries, countries in the Mediterranean, including Greece and Italy, have picked their olives and fermented them with bacteria and yeast.

Sauerkraut (meaning sour cabbage) is Germany's favourite pickled cabbage; it is low in fat, high in vitamin C and fibre, but also tends to be high in salt.

PRAWN & SQUID KELP
noodle salad

PREP + COOK TIME **45 MINUTES** SERVES **4**

900g (1¾ pounds) kelp noodles
   (see tips)
500g (1 pound) squid hoods
500g (1 pound) uncooked medium
   prawns (shrimp), peeled,
   deveined, tails intact
2 tablespoons peanut oil
2 limes, cut into cheeks
¼ cup (60ml) peanut oil, extra
¼ cup (60ml) rice wine vinegar
1 tablespoon sambal oelek
1 tablespoon fish sauce
2 tablespoons grated palm sugar
½ medium green papaya (500g),
   cut into long thin matchsticks
1 medium red onion (170g),
   sliced thinly
1 cup micro shiso (baby perilla leaves)
1 fresh purple chilli, sliced thinly

1 Cook noodles in a large saucepan
of boiling water for 10 minutes; drain.
2 Meanwhile, cut squid hoods in
half lengthways. Using a sharp knife,
score inside surface in a crisscross
pattern at 1cm (½-inch) intervals.
Halve squid, then cut each strip
diagonally into thirds.
3 Combine squid, prawns and oil in
a large bowl; season.
4 Cook squid and prawns on a
heated oiled grill plate (or grill or
barbecue) over high heat, squid for
2 minutes and prawns for 3 minutes
or until just cooked.
5 Place lime cheeks, cut-side down,
on heated grill plate for 2 minutes
or until charred.
6 Whisk extra oil, vinegar, sambal
oelek, fish sauce and palm sugar in
a small jug.

7 Place noodles and seafood in a
large bowl with papaya, onion and
dressing; toss gently to combine.
8 Serve salad topped with herbs,
chilli and charred lime.

*tips After cooking, kelp noodles do
not go tender like regular noodles,
but retain their crunch. A ½ cup
serving of kelp noodles provides
approximately 12% of the RDI of
calcium, 13% of the RDI of iron and
45% of the RDI of vitamin K.*

I AM
DAIRY-FREE
PROTEIN RICH
LOW CARB

FENNEL, APPLE & PISTACHIO
chicken salad

PREP + COOK TIME **25 MINUTES (+ COOLING)** SERVES **4**

When poaching chicken, it is easy to overcook and make it tough. The secret to keeping it tender and moist, is to finish off the cooking in the gentle residual heat of the pan. This method also works well when you are cooking fish.

2 cups (500ml) chicken stock

2 cups (500ml) water

4 thin slices lemon

4 cloves garlic, bruised (see tips)

6 fresh thyme sprigs

2 x 200g (6½-ounce) free-range
   chicken breasts

½ cup (125ml) lemon juice

1 tablespoon dijon mustard

⅓ cup (80ml) extra virgin olive oil

1 small fennel (130g), sliced thinly

1 medium apple (150g), sliced thinly

1 cup (40g) trimmed watercress

1 cup firmly packed fresh flat-leaf
   parsley leaves

1 cup firmly packed torn fresh mint

1 medium avocado (250g),
   sliced thinly

½ cup (60g) unsalted shelled
   pistachios, chopped coarsely

1 Place stock, the water, lemon slices, garlic and thyme in a medium saucepan over medium heat. Add chicken; bring to the boil. Reduce heat; simmer for 4 minutes. Cover pan, turn off heat; set aside to cool to room temperature. Remove chicken; shred coarsely. (Reserve poaching liquid for another use; see tips).

2 Whisk juice and mustard in a small bowl until combined; gradually whisk in oil until combined. Season to taste.

3 Combine fennel, apple, watercress, herbs and avocado in a large bowl. Add chicken and dressing; toss to combine. Season to taste. Serve salad topped with pistachios.

tips To bruise garlic, place the flat side of a cook's knife on the unpeeled clove; using the heel of your other hand push down on the knife to flatten the garlic. Remove the skin. Store the reserved poaching liquid in the refrigerator for up to 3 days.

I AM
SUGAR-FREE
HIGH IN GOOD FATS
LOW CARB

EDAMAME, GRAPE &
grapefruit salad

PREP + COOK TIME **45 MINUTES (+ STANDING)** SERVES **4**

1 cup (200g) frozen shelled edamame
 (soy beans), thawed
2 small ruby red grapefruit (700g)
150g (4½ ounces) seedless
 green grapes
½ small red onion (50g), sliced thinly
75g (2½ ounces) snow pea sprouts,
 trimmed
75g (2½ ounces) red veined
 sorrel leaves
⅓ cup loosely packed fresh
 coriander (cilantro) leaves
⅓ cup loosely packed fresh
 thai basil leaves
2 tablespoons fresh micro or
 baby mint leaves
2 fresh kaffir lime leaves,
 shredded finely
¼ cup (60ml) lime juice
1 tablespoon peanut oil

1 Boil, steam or microwave edamame
until just tender; drain. Refresh in a
bowl of iced water; drain.
2 Use a small sharp knife to cut the
top and bottom from each grapefruit.
Cut off the rind with the white pith,
following the curve of the fruit. Cut
grapefruit crossways into thick slices.
3 Place edamame and grapefruit
in a medium bowl with remaining
ingredients, season; toss gently to
combine.

tips *Edamame are fresh soy beans
in the pod; available frozen from
Asian food stores and major
supermarkets. Grapes contain high
levels of manganese, the "memory
mineral", which nourishes the nervous
system and assists in the formation
of healthy red blood cells; they also
contain ellagic acid that may have
anti-carcinogenic effects.*

I AM
VEGAN
HIGH IN VITAMIN C
HIGH FIBRE

TURKEY LARB
lettuce cups

PREP + COOK TIME **30 MINUTES (+ COOLING)** SERVES **4**

1 tablespoon jasmine rice

1 tablespoon virgin coconut oil

3 cloves garlic, chopped finely

1 lemon grass stalk, white part only,
   sliced thinly

3 kaffir lime leaves, shredded finely

500g (1 pound) minced (ground)
   turkey

1 small fennel (130g), sliced thinly

8 butter (boston) lettuce leaves

1 fresh long green chilli,
   sliced thinly

½ cup loosely packed micro
   radish leaves

½ cup loosely packed small
   fresh mint leaves

VIETNAMESE DRESSING

¼ cup (60ml) fish sauce

¼ cup (60ml) lime juice

2 tablespoons grated palm sugar

1 Make vietnamese dressing.

2 Cook rice in a small frying pan over medium-high heat, stirring, for 3 minutes or until lightly toasted. Pound rice in a mortar and pestle until coarsely crushed.

3 Heat coconut oil in a large non-stick frying pan over medium heat, add garlic, lemon grass and lime leaves; cook, stirring, for 30 seconds or until fragrant.

4 Increase heat to high, add turkey; cook, stirring to break up lumps, for 7 minutes or until cooked. Add half the dressing; cook, stirring, for 1 minute.

5 Spoon turkey mixture and fennel into lettuce leaves; top with chilli, herbs and crushed rice. Serve lettuce cups with remaining dressing.

vietnamese dressing Stir ingredients in a small bowl until sugar dissolves.

tips Tomato, carrot and cucumber can also be used in this recipe. The cooked mince can be frozen for up to 3 months. If you don't have coconut oil use olive oil instead. **serving suggestion** *Serve with steamed rice.*

I AM
LOW CARB
PROTEIN RICH
LOW FAT

Green lentil sprouts are related to the famous French lentils du puy; these tiny green-blue lentils have a nutty and earthy flavour. Their hardy texture allows them to be boiled rapidly without disintegrating.

Fenugreek is a crunchy, aromatic sprout with a mild sweet curry flavour. It contains B vitamins, folic acid, calcium, iron and zinc, and many more.

Quinoa and amaranth are quite similar seeds. They are fast-growing, high in protein, vitamins A, B, C and E and minerals, such as iron, potassium and calcium.

Sunflower sprouts are similar to alfalfa sprouts; they have a sweet nutty flavour and a crunchy texture.

Yellow mustard sprouts have a delicate mustard flavour and crunchy texture.

Wheat sprouts have a sweet taste. They are quick and easy to grow at home.

Green lentil sprouts are also an excellent source of essential nutrients; they have a mildly peppery flavour.

Tiny **black beluga lentils** have a rich earthy flavour and a soft texture.

Chickpea sprouts have a nutty flavour and crunchy texture. They are high in protein and carbohydrate, and contain vitamins A, B, C and folic acid, and calcium, iron, magnesium and potassium.

Chia seeds have a light nutty taste; they are full of fibre, and are a good source of calcium.

You can sprout a whole host of seeds like alfalfa, and legumes such as beans and lentils at home. See glossary, page 480, for information on growing your own sprouts. Don't forget to soak and cook the sprouts, which makes them safe to eat.

Mung bean sprouts are full of iron, calcium, selenium, zinc and B-group vitamins.

This combination of **alfalfa, radish** and **broccoli sprouts** is high in vitamins, minerals and essential trace elements.

FIVE-GRAIN

salad

PREP + COOK TIME **45 MINUTES** SERVES **6**

⅓ cup (70g) black quinoa, rinsed

⅔ cup (160ml) cold water

⅓ cup (65g) couscous

⅓ cup (80ml) boiling water

⅓ cup (65g) barley

⅓ cup (65g) wholegrain greenwheat
    freekeh

⅓ cup (65g) brown rice

3 medium oranges (720g)

1 medium red apple (150g),
    unpeeled, sliced thinly

1 small red onion (100g),
    sliced thinly

1 cup loosely packed fresh
    flat-leaf parsley leaves

½ cup loosely packed fresh
    mint leaves

⅓ cup (80ml) olive oil

200g (6½ ounces) goat's fetta,
    crumbled

½ cup (80g) brazil nuts,
    chopped coarsely

1 Place quinoa and the cold water in a small saucepan; bring to the boil. Reduce heat to low; simmer, uncovered, for 15 minutes, stirring occasionally, or until most of the water is absorbed. Remove from heat; cover, stand for 5 minutes.

2 Meanwhile, combine couscous with the boiling water in a large heatproof bowl. Cover; stand for 5 minutes or until liquid is absorbed, fluffing with a fork occasionally.

3 Cook barley, freekeh and rice in a large saucepan of boiling water for 25 minutes or until tender. Drain; rinse under cold water, drain well.

4 Remove rind from oranges with a zester (see tips). Cut the top and bottom from each orange. Cut off the white pith, following the curve of the fruit. Hold fruit over a bowl to catch the juices; cut down both sides of the white membrane to release each segment. Reserve juice.

5 Place all grains, rind and orange segments in a large bowl with apple, onion and herbs; toss to combine. Season.

6 Place oil and 2 tablespoons of the reserved juice in a screw-top jar; shake well. Season.

7 Add dressing to salad with half the fetta; toss gently to combine. Serve salad on a platter topped with brazil nuts and remaining fetta.

tips If you don't have a zester to create thin strips of orange rind, simply peel long, wide pieces of rind from the oranges, without the white pith, then cut them lengthways into thin strips. The salad can be prepared ahead of time; add dressing just before serving.

I AM
HIGH FIBRE
HIGH IN VITAMINS C & B
LOW GI

TOFU & CARROT
kimchi lettuce wraps

PREP + COOK TIME **35 MINUTES (+ STANDING)** SERVES **4**

¼ cup (60ml) soy sauce

1½ tablespoons caster (superfine)
    sugar

2 cloves garlic, crushed

½ teaspoon sesame oil

400g (12½ ounces) firm tofu, drained,
    cut into 1cm (½-inch) slices

1 medium red onion (170g),
    cut into thin wedges

2 baby cos (romaine) lettuce (260g),
    leaves separated

1 medium nashi (200g), halved,
    cored, sliced thinly

2 teaspoons toasted sesame seeds

CARROT KIMCHI

2 medium carrots (240g), cut into
    long thin strips

250g (8 ounces) baby radishes,
    trimmed, sliced thinly

4 green onions (scallions),
    sliced thinly

2 cloves garlic, crushed

2 teaspoons soy sauce

2 teaspoons caster (superfine) sugar

1 teaspoon chilli flakes

1 Make carrot kimchi.

2 Meanwhile, stir soy sauce, sugar, garlic and oil in a medium bowl until sugar dissolves. Add tofu; toss to coat in marinade. Stand for 15 minutes.

3 Cook tofu and onion on a heated oiled grill plate (or grill or barbecue) over high heat for 4 minutes, or until golden brown and grill marks appear on both sides. Transfer tofu and onion to a plate; cover to keep warm.

4 Arrange lettuce on a large platter; top with tofu, onion, nashi and kimchi. Sprinkle with sesame seeds.

carrot kimchi Place ingredients in a medium bowl; toss well to combine. Stand for 15 minutes.

tips Kimchi is traditionally left to ferment but this quick version mimics the flavours in a fraction of the time. You can buy small tubs of kimchi from most Asian grocers, if you prefer. Use a julienne peeler, or a mandoline or V-slicer with julienne attachment to cut the carrot into long thin strips. Lettuce wraps are best eaten in one bite, so make them small and manageable.

I AM
VEGAN
HIGH IN VITAMIN A
PROTEIN RICH

BABY CARROT &
black rice salad

PREP + COOK TIME **45 MINUTES** SERVES **6**

⅔ cup (130g) black rice

400g (12½ ounces) multi-coloured
   baby carrots, trimmed

250g (8 ounces) baby rocket
   (arugula) leaves, torn

1 cup loosely packed fresh
   mint leaves

1 cup (160g) almonds, roasted,
   chopped coarsely

PRESERVED LEMON DRESSING

1 tablespoon finely chopped
   preserved lemon rind (see tips)

⅓ cup (80ml) lemon juice

½ cup (125ml) olive oil

1 clove garlic, crushed

2 teaspoons fennel seeds, toasted,
   crushed lightly

2 teaspoons ground cumin

1 teaspoon sweet paprika

¼ teaspoon cayenne pepper

1 teaspoon honey

1 Cook rice in a large saucepan
of boiling water, uncovered, for
30 minutes or until tender; drain.
Rinse under cold running water;
drain well.

2 Meanwhile, make preserved
lemon dressing.

3 Using a mandoline or V-slicer,
thinly slice the carrots.

4 Place carrots and rice in a large
bowl with rocket, mint, almonds and
dressing; toss gently to combine.

preserved lemon dressing
Remove and discard flesh from
preserved lemon wedges; rinse
rind well, then chop finely. Place
chopped rind in a large screw-top
jar with remaining ingredients;
shake well. Season to taste.

*tips Preserved lemons are
available at delicatessens and
some supermarkets. Remove and
discard the flesh; rinse the rind
well, then chop finely. If you don't
have a mandoline, use a vegetable
peeler to peel the carrots lengthways
into ribbons. To toast fennel seeds,
stir seeds in a dry frying pan over
medium heat for 2 minutes or until
fragrant. The dressing can be made
2 days ahead; refrigerate in the jar.*

I AM
VEGETARIAN
HIGH IN VITAMIN C
HIGH FIBRE

SPRING GREENS & FETTA

bruschetta

PREP + COOK TIME **40 MINUTES** SERVES **4**

170g (5½ ounces) asparagus, trimmed, cut into 2cm (¾-inch) lengths

1 cup (120g) frozen broad (fava) beans, peeled

½ cup (60g) frozen peas

8 x 1cm (½-inch) slices sourdough bread (280g)

1 tablespoon olive oil

1 clove garlic, crushed

1 tablespoon lemon juice (see tips)

90g (3 ounces) drained marinated fetta, crumbled

2 tablespoons small fresh mint leaves

1 teaspoon lemon rind strips (see tips)

ROCKET & ALMOND PESTO

60g (2 ounces) rocket (arugula) leaves

1 cup firmly packed fresh basil leaves

½ cup (70g) slivered almonds, roasted

1 clove garlic, crushed

1 teaspoon finely grated lemon rind

⅓ cup (25g) finely grated parmesan

½ cup (125ml) olive oil

1 Cook asparagus in a medium saucepan of boiling water for 2 minutes. Add beans and peas; simmer for 2 minutes. Drain; refresh in a bowl of iced water. Drain well.

2 Make rocket and almond pesto.

3 Place bread on a heated oiled grill plate (or grill or barbecue) for 1 minute each side or until lightly charred. Spread ⅓ cup pesto over toasted bread slices.

4 Heat oil in a medium frying pan over medium-high heat; cook garlic for 1 minute. Add asparagus, beans and peas; cook for 1 minute or until hot. Stir in juice just before serving; season to taste.

5 Spoon vegetable mixture onto toasted bread; top with fetta, mint and rind.

rocket & almond pesto Process rocket, basil, almonds, garlic, rind, parmesan and 1 tablespoon of the oil until coarsely chopped. With motor operating, add remaining oil in a thin, steady stream until mixture is smooth; season.

tips *It will be easier to remove the rind from the lemon before you squeeze the juice. To create the thin strips of lemon rind, use a zester if you have one. If you don't have one, peel two long, wide pieces of rind from the lemon, without the white pith, then cut them lengthways into thin strips. For a large crowd, use small slices of baguette and serve as canapés. This recipe makes 1 cup of rocket and almond pesto; leftover pesto can be served on grilled fish or chicken or tossed through hot pasta. Pesto can also be frozen, in small tightly-sealed containers, for up to 3 months.*

I AM
VEGETARIAN
VITAMIN RICH
HIGH IN FOLATE

3pm slump

BLISS

balls

PREP TIME **20 MINUTES** MAKES **42 (14 OF EACH FLAVOUR)**

APRICOT & TAHINI

½ cup (100g) dried apricots

¼ cup (30g) linseed (flaxseed) meal

1 cup (160g) almonds

¼ green apple (30g), unpeeled, grated coarsely

1 tablespoon raw honey, rice malt syrup or pure maple syrup

1 tablespoon hulled tahini

¼ teaspoon orange blossom water, optional

½ cup (40g) shredded coconut

FIG & HAZELNUT

1 cup (140g) roasted skinned hazelnuts

100g (3 ounces) dried figs

¼ cup (30g) linseed (flaxseed) meal

¼ green apple (30g), grated coarsely

¼ teaspoon ground cinnamon

2 tablespoons white chia seeds

DATE & CACAO NIBS

100g (3 ounces) fresh dates, pitted

1 cup (160g) almonds

¼ cup (35g) cacao nibs

¼ green apple (30g), grated coarsely

2 teaspoons dutch-processed cocoa

2 teaspoons dutch-processed cocoa, extra

1 For apricot and tahini balls: process apricots, linseed meal, almonds and apple for 1 minute or until mixture is the consistency of breadcrumbs. Add honey, tahini and orange blossom water; process a further minute or until the mixture clings together when pressed.

2 Roll tablespoons of the mixture into balls; wet your hands every third or fourth ball to stop the mixture from sticking. Coat balls in coconut.

3 Make fig and hazelnut balls, then date and cacao balls.

fig & hazelnut Process hazelnuts with figs, linseed meal, apple and cinnamon for 2 minutes or until mixture starts to clump together. Roll tablespoons of the mixture into balls then coat in chia seeds.

date & cacao nibs Process dates with almonds, cacao nibs, apple and cocoa for 2 minutes or until mixture starts to clump together. Roll tablespoons of the mixture into balls then dust with extra cocoa.

I AM

SUGAR-FREE

LOW IN SATURATED FATS

PROTEIN RICH

APRICOT & CARDAMOM

muesli slice

PREP + COOK TIME **40 MINUTES** MAKES **18**

1 cup (150g) dried apricots

2 cups (185g) quinoa flakes

½ cup (70g) quinoa flour

½ cup (75g) sunflower seeds

½ cup (80g) coarsely chopped
   raw almonds

1 teaspoon ground cardamom

1 teaspoon gluten-free baking powder

1 tablespoon finely grated orange rind

⅓ cup (70g) virgin coconut oil

⅓ cup (115g) honey

3 free-range eggs, beaten lightly

2 teaspoons vanilla extract

2 tablespoons sugar-free apricot jam,
   melted, strained

1 Preheat oven to 160°C/325°F. Grease a 16cm x 26cm x 4cm (6½-inch x 10½-inch x 1½-inch) slice pan; line with baking paper.

2 Roughly chop half the apricots; place in a large bowl. Cut remaining apricots in half lengthways; set aside.

3 Add quinoa flakes and flour, seeds, nuts, cardamom, baking powder and rind to chopped apricots in bowl; stir to combine.

4 Place oil and honey in a small saucepan over medium heat; bring to the boil, stirring until melted and combined.

5 Add hot mixture to dry ingredients with eggs and extract; mix well to combine. Spread into pan, levelling mixture with the back of a spoon. Top with apricot halves; press down lightly into the mixture.

6 Bake slice for 20 minutes or until golden and a skewer inserted into the centre comes out clean. Brush hot slice with apricot jam; cool in the pan. Cut into slices to serve.

tip For a variation, you can use walnuts, pecans, macadamias or cashews instead of almonds.

I AM
SUGAR-FREE
HIGH IN VITAMIN E
GLUTEN-FREE

HOMEMADE CHOCOLATE HAZELNUT SPREAD

PREP TIME 10 MINUTES

MAKES 2 CUPS

1½ cups (210g) roasted hazelnuts, skins removed

¼ cup (25g) cacao powder

¼ teaspoon sea salt flakes

½ cup (125ml) unsweetened almond milk

⅓ cup (80ml) pure maple syrup

1 tablespoon vanilla extract

1 tablespoon virgin coconut oil

1 Blend together ingredients for 5 minutes, scraping down the sides occasionally, until smooth.

2 Spoon spread into a small airtight container. Store in the fridge for up to 1 month.

tips Use as a filling for cakes or cookies, or spread onto bread. To roast and peel your own hazelnuts, spread nuts on an oven tray and roast at 180°C/350°F for 8 minutes or until golden. Rub warm nuts in a clean tea towel to remove skins; cool.

I AM

VEGAN

DAIRY- & SUGAR-FREE

PALEO

RAW TURKISH DELIGHT BARK

PREP TIME 10 MINUTES (+ REFRIGERATION)

SERVES 10

1 cup (200g) virgin coconut oil
½ cup (50g) cacao powder
pinch sea salt
⅓ cup (115g) rice malt syrup
⅓ cup (50g) coarsely chopped
   raw almonds
⅓ cup (50g) dried cherries
¼ cup (4g) dried edible rose petals

1 Grease a 20cm x 30cm (8-inch
x 12-inch) slice pan; line base and
sides with baking paper, extending
paper 5cm (2-inches) over long
sides of pan.
2 Place the oil, sifted cacao and
salt in a medium bowl. Whisk to
combine. Gradually add the syrup,
whisking to combine.
3 Spread mixture evenly into pan.
Scatter with nuts, cherries and
rose petals. Refrigerate until set.
Break into shards to serve.

tips *Don't worry if the bark has
a slight whitish look to it, this is
simply the coconut oil, but it won't
affect the taste. Because of the low
melting point of the coconut oil, the
bark should always be stored in the
fridge otherwise it will be too soft
to handle.*

I AM
VEGAN
GLUTEN-FREE
SUGAR-FREE

SUGAR-FREE
chocolate almond balls

PREP + COOK TIME **30 MINUTES (+ REFRIGERATION)** MAKES **20**

We used 99.8% sugar-free chocolate, available from health food stores and pharmacies. These balls will keep in an airtight container in the refrigerator for up to 2 weeks.

100g (3 ounces) sugar-free dark chocolate, chopped finely

½ cup (140g) 100% almond spread (no added sugar)

100g (3 ounces) sugar-free dark chocolate, chopped finely, extra

1 tablespoon flaked almonds, chopped, toasted

1 Place chocolate into a medium heatproof bowl over a medium saucepan of simmering water (don't let water touch base of bowl); stir until melted and smooth. Remove bowl from heat.

2 Stir almond spread into melted chocolate until smooth and well combined. Spread mixture onto a baking-paper-lined oven tray. Refrigerate for 15 minutes or until firm.

3 Spoon teaspoons of mixture onto another baking-paper-lined oven tray. Refrigerate 10 minutes. Roll into balls; refrigerate for a further 20 minutes or until firm.

4 Melt extra chocolate until smooth. Dip balls, one at a time, into melted chocolate; allow excess chocolate to drain, then return to tray. Sprinkle with flaked almonds. Refrigerate for 30 minutes or until firm.

tip You can also melt the chocolate in the microwave. Place in a microwave-safe dish, then microwave on HIGH (100%) in 30-second bursts, stirring until melted and smooth.

I AM
LOW CARB
LOW CALORIE
HIGH PROTEIN

NORI SESAME

chips

PREP + COOK TIME **20 MINUTES** MAKES **60 PIECES**

The nori sheet edges will have a rippled effect when cooking. Keep nori chips in an airtight container for up to 2 weeks.

10 yaki nori sheets (25g)
1½ tablespoons salt-reduced
 soy sauce
2½ teaspoons sesame oil
1½ tablespoons white sesame seeds

1 Preheat oven to 150°C/300°F. Line three large oven trays with baking paper.
2 Place two sheets of nori, shiny-side up, on each tray. (If two sheets don't fit on one tray, cook one at a time.)
3 Combine soy sauce and sesame oil in a small bowl. Brush half the soy mixture on nori sheets on trays; sprinkle with half the sesame seeds.
4 Bake nori for 8 minutes or until crisp. Transfer to wire racks to cool.
5 Repeat with remaining nori sheets, soy mixture and sesame seeds, re-using trays and baking paper.
6 Cut each sheet into six pieces before serving.

tip Seaweeds contain alginic acid, which binds with heavy metals to eliminate them from the body.

I AM
VEGAN
MINERAL RICH
LOW CARB

SEED & NUT
snack bars

PREP + COOK TIME **45 MINUTES (+ REFRIGERATION)** MAKES **24**

On cooling, the peanut butter mixture becomes firm and starts to set. You may need to use your hands when incorporating into the other ingredients. When adding chocolate in the choc-chip variation ensure peanut butter mixture is cool otherwise the chocolate will melt.

½ cup (80g) almonds (natural almonds), chopped coarsely

½ cup (50g) walnuts, quartered

¼ cup (40g) white sesame seeds

¼ cup (50g) pepitas (pumpkin seeds)

¼ cup (35g) sunflower seeds

¾ cup (210g) crunchy peanut butter (see tips)

⅔ cup (160ml) rice malt syrup

2 cups (40g) puffed millet

2 tablespoons white chia seeds

2 tablespoons linseeds (flaxseeds)

1 Preheat oven to 180°C/350°F. Grease a 20cm x 30cm (8-inch x 12-inch) slice pan. Line base and long sides with baking paper, extending the paper 5cm (2 inches) over sides.

2 Place almonds, walnuts, sesame seeds, pepitas and sunflower seeds on a large oven tray in a single layer. Bake 10 minutes or until browned lightly and fragrant. Transfer to a large heatproof bowl.

3 Meanwhile, stir peanut butter and rice malt syrup in a small saucepan over low heat until combined.

4 Add syrup mixture to nut mixture with puffed millet, chia seeds and linseeds; stir until well combined. Press mixture firmly into pan. Refrigerate for 4 hours or overnight.

5 Remove slice from pan; cut into 24 bars.

FLAVOUR VARIATIONS

choc-chip Stir 50g (1½oz) chopped sugar-free dark chocolate into mixture before pressing into pan. Drizzle top with 50g (1½oz) melted sugar-free dark chocolate.

coconut Omit the pepitas and sunflower seeds and add ¾ cup (60g) shredded unsweetened coconut. Sprinkle the top with ¼ cup (20g) toasted shredded unsweetened coconut.

tips You can use any type of nut butter or sunflower butter instead of peanut butter. For a crisper bar, bake at 180°C/350°F for 10 minutes or until lightly browned. Cool in pan.

I AM
GLUTEN FREE
MINERAL RICH
LOW CARB

Green tea is a good source of antioxidants, and studies have shown a reduced risk of several cancers and heart disease with the consumption of green tea.

Maca powder is claimed to help with menstrual problems and chronic fatigue and to act as an aphrodisiac; there is some evidence of the latter, but no evidence for the others. It is a rich source of vitamins C and B6, iron and calcium.

Olive oil is rich in healthy monounsaturated fats and antioxidants. It can help to lower blood pressure, reduce abdominal fat, and lowers the risk of heart disease and some cancers.

Edamame beans are fresh green baby soy beans. Soy is high in protein and is a good source of fibre. It also provides two of the essential fatty acids, and vitamins and minerals.

Pomegranates are rich in fibre, vitamin C, and polyphenols, credited in helping the prevention of heart disease and cancer.

Whey protein is a popular supplement in the gym, and evidence has shown that if consumed immediately after a strength-training workout, it leads to better muscle repair than other forms of protein.

Wheatgrass is usually sold as a 'shot' of juice or as a dried powder to add to your own smoothies at home. Unlike wheat, wheatgrass is gluten free. It is certainly nutrient-rich, but no more so than green vegies. A shot of wheatgrass juice will give you a good dose of plant iron and vitamin C to help absorb it.

food trends

The latest trends in food may be more hype than healthy, with many claims not being scientifically substantiated. However, some pack a nutritional punch with loads of vitamins, minerals and fibre.

Goji berries, like most berries, are rich in antioxidants, high in fibre, and stand out for their vitamins A and C, and iron content.

Spirulina is rich in protein and contains all the essential amino acids. It is also a good source of iron, making it a great supplement for vegans and vegetarians.

There is no scientific evidence supporting **bee pollen's** claim of boosting the immune system. There have been, however, documented cases of severe anaphylactic reactions, see glossary, page 480.

COCONUT

chocolate bars

PREP + COOK TIME **30 MINUTES (+ FREEZING & REFRIGERATION)** MAKES **16**

We used 99.8% sugar-free chocolate, available from health food stores and pharmacies. These bars can be stored in an airtight container in the refrigerator for up to 1 week.

2½ cups (190g) shredded coconut

2 teaspoons stevia

⅔ cup (160ml) coconut cream

2 teaspoons vanilla extract

300g (6 ounces) sugar-free dark chocolate, chopped finely

50g (1½ ounces) butter

I AM
SUGAR-FREE
HIGH IN GOOD FATS
LOW CARB

1 Combine coconut, stevia, coconut cream and half the extract in a medium bowl. Divide mixture into 16 portions; shape each portion into a 6cm (2½-inch) log. Place logs on a baking-paper-lined oven tray. Freeze for 1 hour or until firm.

2 Place chocolate and butter in a small microwave-safe bowl. Microwave on HIGH (100%) in 30-second bursts, stirring, until melted and smooth. Add remaining extract; stir until smooth. Cool to room temperature.

3 Dip bars, one at a time, into chocolate mixture to evenly coat; allow excess to drain, then return to tray. Refrigerate for 30 minutes or until firm.

tip Stevia comes from the leaf of a plant, so is promoted as a natural sweetener. It is processed into a white powder that can be used in a similar way to sugar. It has a minimal effect on blood glucose levels and has no kilojoules, so it can be a useful way to reduce your sugar intake. Coconut contains 'medium chain saturated fats', which are burned more readily for energy than other fats, so are less likely to be stored as fat.

CAULIFLOWER, QUINOA &

asparagus bites

PREP + COOK TIME **50 MINUTES (+ SOAKING & COOLING)** MAKES **12**

These bites will keep in an airtight container in the fridge for up to 3 days.

2 tablespoons white quinoa

350g (11 ounces) cauliflower, chopped

300g (9½ ounces) asparagus,
   trimmed, chopped coarsely

3 free-range eggs, beaten lightly

¼ teaspoon ground nutmeg

½ cup (50g) grated mozzarella

⅓ cup (50g) finely grated parmesan

1 green onion (scallion), sliced thinly

1 Preheat oven to 180°C/350°F. Grease a 12-hole (⅓ cup/80ml) muffin pan. Cut out twelve 12cm (4¾-inch) squares from baking paper; line holes with squares.

2 Rinse quinoa in cold water; drain. Soak quinoa in ¼ cup (60ml) water in a small saucepan for 15 minutes. Place over heat; bring to the boil. Reduce heat; simmer, covered, for 5-8 minutes or until water is absorbed. Remove from heat; stand 10 minutes. Fluff with a fork. Cool.

3 Meanwhile, boil, steam or microwave cauliflower and asparagus, separately, until tender; drain. Refresh asparagus in cold water; cool. Reserve asparagus tips.

4 Combine egg, nutmeg, cheeses and green onion in a large bowl. Season. Add cauliflower, asparagus and quinoa; mix well. Spoon mixture evenly into holes. Top with reserved asparagus tips.

5 Bake for 20 minutes or until golden brown. Leave in pan for 5 minutes; transfer to a wire rack to cool.

I AM
GLUTEN-FREE
HIGH IN FOLATE
VEGETARIAN

ROASTED SESAME
edamame beans

PREP + COOK TIME **25 MINUTES** SERVES **4**

500g (1 pound) edamame (soy beans),
    peeled (see tip)
2 teaspoons olive oil
2 teaspoons black sesame seeds
2 teaspoons white sesame seeds
½ teaspoon sesame oil
½ teaspoon salt flakes

1 Preheat oven to 220°C/425°F. Line an oven tray with baking paper.
2 Place ingredients in a medium bowl; stir to combine. Spread mixture onto tray.
3 Bake for 15 minutes or until golden.

tip You can use fresh or frozen (thawed) edamame; available from Asian food stores and some supermarkets. To quickly thaw the beans, place in a heatproof bowl, top with hot water; stand for 1 minute. Drain, then peel away skins

I AM
VEGAN
MINERAL RICH
LOW CARB

PEA, CHICKPEA &
hazelnuts falafel

PREP + COOK TIME **30 MINUTES (+ REFRIGERATION)** SERVES **4 (MAKES 12)**

½ cup (60g) frozen peas, thawed

125g (4 ounces) canned chickpeas
   (garbanzo beans), drained, rinsed

50g (1½ ounces) fetta, crumbled

2 tablespoons coarsely chopped
   fresh mint

1 fresh long green chilli, seeded,
   chopped finely

1 free-range egg

¼ cup (25g) ground hazelnuts

1 tablespoon white sesame seeds

¼ cup (30g) finely chopped hazelnuts

vegetable oil, for shallow-frying

1 medium lemon (140g),
   cut into wedges

MINT YOGHURT

½ cup (140g) greek-style yoghurt

1 tablespoon lemon juice

1 tablespoon finely chopped
   fresh mint

1 Place peas, chickpeas, fetta, mint, chilli, egg and ground hazelnuts in a food processor; pulse until coarsely chopped and combined. Season. Shape tablespoons of mixture into balls; flatten slightly. Toss falafel in combined sesame seeds and chopped hazelnuts. Place falafel on a baking-paper-lined oven tray. Refrigerate for 30 minutes.

2 Meanwhile, make mint yoghurt.

3 Heat oil in a medium frying pan over medium-high heat; shallow-fry falafel, in batches, for 5 minutes or until golden brown. Drain on paper towel.

4 Serve falafel with mint yoghurt and lemon wedges.

mint yoghurt Combine ingredients in a small bowl.

I AM
LOW CARB
VEGETARIAN
HIGH FIBRE

APPLE & ALMOND

friands

PREP + COOK TIME **45 MINUTES** MAKES **9**

*These friands can be made a
day ahead. Store in an airtight
container.*

2 cups (240g) ground almonds
¼ cup (35g) self-raising flour
1 teaspoon baking powder
1 tablespoon stevia
1 teaspoon ground cinnamon
4 free-range egg whites,
   beaten lightly
120g (4 ounces) butter, melted
1 medium red apple (150g),
   grated coarsely
¼ cup (20g) flaked almonds

1 Preheat oven to 200°C/400°F.
Grease a 9-hole oval (⅓ cup/80ml)
friand pan.
2 Combine ground almonds, flour,
baking powder, stevia and cinnamon
in a large bowl. Add egg white,
butter and apple; stir to combine.
Spoon mixture evenly into holes.
Top with flaked almonds.
3 Bake friands for 18-20 minutes
or until a skewer inserted in centre
comes out clean. Leave friands in
pan for 5 minutes before turning,
top-side up, onto a wire rack to cool.

*tip Stevia comes from the leaf of a
plant, so is promoted as a natural
sweetener. It is processed into a white
powder that can be used in a similar
way to sugar. It has a minimal effect
on blood glucose levels and has no
kilojoules, so it can be a useful way to
reduce your sugar intake*

I AM
LOW CARB
PROTEIN RICH
SUGAR-FREE

KALE

chips

PREP + COOK TIME **25 MINUTES (+ COOLING)** SERVES **8**

These kale chips will keep in an airtight container for up to 2 weeks.

450g (14½ ounces) kale
1 tablespoon extra virgin olive oil
½ teaspoon crushed sea salt flakes

I AM
LOW FAT
HIGH FIBRE
LOW CARB

1 Preheat oven to 190°C/375°F; place three large oven trays in the oven while preheating.
2 Remove and discard kale stems from leaves. Wash leaves well; pat dry with paper towel or in a salad spinner. Tear kale leaves into 5cm (2-inch) pieces; place in a large bowl, then drizzle with oil and sprinkle with salt. Using your hands, rub oil and salt through the kale. Spread kale, in a single layer, on trays.
3 Bake kale for 10 minutes. Remove any pieces of kale that are already crisp. Return remaining kale to the oven for a further 2 minutes; remove any pieces that are crisp. Repeat until all the kale is crisp. Cool.

tip Kale is among the most nutrient-dense foods in existence; it's a vitamin, mineral and antioxidant powerhouse whilst being very low in calories. It has more calcium than milk, has more iron than meat, is one of the best sources of vitamin C (1 cup of kale has more vitamin C than 1 whole orange) and is a rich source of vitamins A, K and B-group and it contains omega-3 fatty acid alpha-linolenic acid.

SUGAR-FREE CHOC-CRANBERRY

snack bars

PREP + COOK TIME **50 MINUTES (+ COOLING)** MAKES **16 BARS**

We used 99.8% sugar-free chocolate, available from health food stores and pharmacies. When measuring honey, lightly spray the measuring cup with oil first and the honey will slide out more easily.

2½ cups (50g) puffed rice

½ cup (60g) pecan nuts, chopped

⅓ cup (65g) pepitas (pumpkin seeds)

¼ cup (35g) dried unsweetened cranberries, chopped coarsely

2 tablespoons LSA (see tip)

1 tablespoon white sesame seeds

½ cup (180g) honey

1 teaspoon vanilla extract

½ teaspoon salt flakes

45g (1½ ounces) sugar-free dark chocolate, chopped coarsely

1 Preheat oven to 150°C/300°F. Grease a 20cm (8-inch) square cake pan; line base and two opposite sides with baking paper, extending the paper 5cm (2 inches) over the sides.
2 Combine puffed rice, nuts, pepitas, cranberries, LSA and sesame seeds in a large bowl.
3 Place honey, extract and salt in a small saucepan over medium heat; cook, stirring, for 2 minutes or until mixture just comes to a simmer. Pour honey mixture over dry ingredients; stir through until evenly coated. Cool for 5 minutes. Add chocolate; stir until combined. Transfer mixture to pan; pressing down firmly with the back of a spoon.
4 Bake for 30 minutes or until golden brown. Cool in pan. Cut into 16 bars.

tip LSA is a ground mixture of linseeds, sunflower seeds and almonds. It is available from supermarkets and health food stores.

I AM
GLUTEN-FREE
SUGAR-FREE
LOW CARB

CHEESE & HERB
balls

PREP TIME **20 MINUTES (+ REFRIGERATION)** MAKES **12**

125g (4 ounces) cream cheese,
    at room temperature
75g (2½ ounces) fresh goat's cheese,
    at room temperature
⅓ cup finely chopped fresh
    flat-leaf parsley
1 tablespoon finely chopped
    fresh chives

1 Combine cream cheese and goat's cheese in a medium bowl.
2 Roll 2 level teaspoons of mixture into balls. Roll balls in combined herbs. Place balls on a baking-paper-lined oven tray. Refrigerate for 1 hour.

tips These cheese balls can be stored in an airtight container in the refrigerator for up to 1 week. Parsley is packed with nutrients and is an excellent source of vitamins A, C and K. It also contains volatile oils that have been found to neutralise some carcinogens and flavonoids that act as powerful antioxidants.

I AM
LOW CARB
GLUTEN-FREE
CALCIUM RICH

SWEET POTATO CHIPS

PREP + COOK TIME
30 MINUTES
SERVES 8

Sweet potato and kumara chips will stay fresh in an airtight container for up to 2 days.

2 small purple-skinned white
    sweet potato (320g)
2 small kumara (orange sweet
    potato) (500g)
vegetable oil, for deep-frying

1 Scrub vegetables lightly and wash well; pat dry. Trim ends of vegetables. Using a mandoline or V-slicer, slice vegetables thinly lengthways into 1mm slices.
2 Preheat the oil in a large saucepan to 150°C/300°F. Deep-fry white sweet potato, in batches, until beginning to brown around the edges. Remove from oil with a slotted spoon; drain well on paper towel. When cooled, if any chips are not completely crisp, deep-fry again for 30 seconds; drain on paper towels. Repeat with kumara.
3 Sprinkle chips lightly with salt before serving.

I AM
LOW CARB
HIGH IN VITAMINS A & C
HIGH FIBRE

LITTLE BANANA COCONUT CAKES

PREP + COOK TIME
40 MINUTES
MAKES **24**

You will need 1 large overripe banana for this recipe.

4 free-range egg whites
60g (2 ounces) butter, melted
⅓ cup (50g) coconut sugar
⅔ cup (80g) ground almonds
⅓ cup (50g) wholemeal
   self-raising flour
⅓ cup (100g) mashed overripe
   banana (see note above)
½ cup (25g) flaked coconut
½ teaspoon ground cinnamon

1 Preheat oven to 180°C/350°F. Grease two 12-hole (1-tablespoon/20ml) mini muffin pans.
2 Using a fork, lightly whisk egg whites in a medium bowl until combined. Add butter, coconut sugar, ground almonds and flour; stir until combined. Stir in banana.
3 Spoon mixture into holes; top with flaked coconut.
4 Bake cakes for 15 minutes or until browned and cooked. Turn cakes top-side up onto wire rack to cool. Serve sprinkled with cinnamon.

tip These can be kept in an airtight container for up to 2 days or frozen for up to 3 months.

GINGER & SESAME

seed logs

PREP TIME **15 MINUTES (+ REFRIGERATION)** MAKES **26**

1 cup (100g) walnuts

1 cup (140g) macadamias

1 cup (90g) rolled oats

400g (12½ ounces) fresh medjool
   dates, pitted

1½ teaspoons ground ginger

½ teaspoon sea salt

½ cup (75g) sesame seeds

1 Process nuts and oats in a food
processor until finely chopped. Add
dates, ginger and salt; process until
mixture forms a paste.

2 Shape level tablespoons of mixture
into 5cm (2-inch) long logs; place
on a baking-paper-lined oven tray.
Refrigerate for 15 minutes.

3 Meanwhile, stir sesame seeds in
a frying pan over medium heat for
2 minutes or until lightly toasted.
Cool to room temperature.

4 Roll logs in sesame seeds; place
on a tray. Refrigerate for 2 hours or
until firm.

*tips Medjool dates are available
from the fresh food section of major
supermarkets. Store seed logs in
an airtight container in the fridge
for up to 2 weeks or freeze for up to
3 months.*

I AM
VEGAN
SUGAR-FREE
MINERAL RICH

CHILLI

miso soup

PREP + COOK TIME **15 MINUTES** SERVES **2**

¼ cup (75g) dashi miso paste
3 cups (750ml) water
150g (4½ ounces) silken tofu, cut into 1cm (½-inch) cubes
3 green onions (scallions), sliced thinly on the diagonal
1 fresh long red chilli, sliced thinly on the diagonal
2 toasted nori (seaweed) sheets, each cut into eight pieces
2 teaspoons black sesame seeds

1 Whisk dashi miso paste and water in a small saucepan.
Bring to a simmer over medium heat.
2 Meanwhile, divide tofu, green onion, chilli and nori
between two bowls.
3 Pour miso soup into bowls; sprinkle with sesame seeds.
Serve immediately.

I AM
VEGAN
HIGH IN CALCIUM
PROTEIN RICH

ROASTED SWEET & SOUR
chickpeas & beans

PREP + COOK TIME **1 HOUR** SERVES **4 (MAKES 2½ CUPS)**

2 x 400g (12½ ounces) canned
  chickpeas (garbanzo beans)

2 x 400g (12½ ounces) canned
  butter beans

1 tablespoon extra virgin olive oil

1 tablespoon finely grated lime rind

2 teaspoons ground cumin

2 teaspoons ground coriander

1 teaspoon chilli flakes

1 tablespoon coconut sugar

1 Preheat oven to 220°C/425°F. Line an oven tray with baking paper.

2 Drain then rinse chickpeas and beans; place in a medium heatproof bowl. Cover with boiling water; drain. Dry on paper towel. (This will ensure that the chickpeas and beans will dry and crisp during roasting.)

3 Place chickpeas and beans on tray. Bake for 50 minutes, stirring occasionally, or until golden and crisp.

4 Transfer roasted chickpeas and beans to a medium bowl. Add oil, rind, cumin, coriander, chilli flakes and coconut sugar. Season generously with salt and freshly ground black pepper; toss until well coated.

tips You can use dried legumes instead of canned chickpeas: soak them overnight first and cook for 1½ hours in boiling water. Experiment with different spices and herbs to flavour how you like it. Store the roasted mix in an airtight container or jar for up to 4 days.

I AM
SUGAR-FREE
PROTEIN RICH
HIGH FIBRE

CHIA & TOMATO GUACAMOLE
with sumac crisps

PREP + COOK TIME **20 MINUTES** SERVES **4**

cooking oil spray

4 rye mountain breads (100g)

1½ teaspoons ground sumac

2 medium avocados (500g),
    chopped coarsely

⅓ cup (80ml) lime juice

1 small red onion (100g),
    chopped finely

⅓ cup (60g) semi-dried tomatoes,
    chopped finely

¼ cup fresh coriander (cilantro),
    chopped coarsely

½ teaspoon smoked paprika

1½ tablespoons black or white
    chia seeds

2 fresh long red chillies,
    sliced thinly

1 Preheat oven to 200°C/400°F. Line three oven trays with baking paper; spray with cooking oil.

2 Cut each sheet of mountain bread into 16 triangles. Place in a single layer on trays; spray with oil. Sprinkle with sumac; season with salt and pepper. Bake for 5 minutes or until golden and crisp.

3 Place avocado and juice in a medium bowl; mash lightly with a fork. Stir in red onion, tomato, coriander, paprika, 1 tablespoon chia seeds and three-quarters of the chilli. Season to taste with salt.

4 Place guacamole in a serving bowl; top with remaining chilli and remaining chia seeds. Serve with sumac crisps.

tips *Guacamole can be stored, covered, in the fridge for up to 2 days. Sumac crisps will keep in an airtight container at room temperature for up to 1 week. Avocados are an excellent source of pantothenic acid (also known as vitamin B5); pantothenic acid is essential to support health. Without pantothenic acid and its incorporation in coenzyme A, our bodies would be unable to use fats, carbohydrates or proteins for energy use and would be unable to make hormones vital for metabolic processes.*

I AM
VEGAN
RICH IN GOOD FATS
HIGH FIBRE

Fresh **small red thai** and fresh **long red and green chillies**.

The spicy heat of **chillies** comes from the chemical 'capsaicin'. In sufficient quantities this can give a little boost to your metabolism, but that means a whole lot of chilli! It may, however, be more effective as an anti-inflammatory agent and to clear stuffy, blocked sinuses.

Ginger root has a whole host of studied beneficial effects from lowering cholesterol to boosting immunity and easing indigestion and immunity.

Star anise, a hard, star-shaped seed pod of the anise bush, adds a wonderful flavour in Asian cooking.

Saffron has been studied for its potential benefit in relieving premenstrual syndrome and menstrual discomfort.

Finely grate **nutmeg** as you need it, as store-bought ground nutmeg loses its flavour rapidly.

Fresh turmeric is said to have anti-inflammatory properties.

Turmeric can be bought as the whole root (right), or ground as a bright orange powder. Traditionally used in curries, it's increasingly recognised for its health benefits. It is rich in curcumin, shown to have anti-cancer and anti-inflammatory properties.

spices

Traditionally, spices were used to treat digestive disorders, and many are still used for this: ginger remains a popular treatment for nausea and vomiting. Spices are also a rich source of antioxidants.

Ground fennel is more beneficial if crushed from seeds just before using. Commercially ground fennel rapidly loses its potency.

Fennel seeds come from the fennel plant native to the Mediterranean region. The seeds seem to be helpful in relieving indigestion and bloating.

Cinnamon, from the inner bark of a group of trees, has a long history as both a flavouring and for its medicinal value. It is a rich source of antioxidants and has anti-bacterial and anti-viral effects.

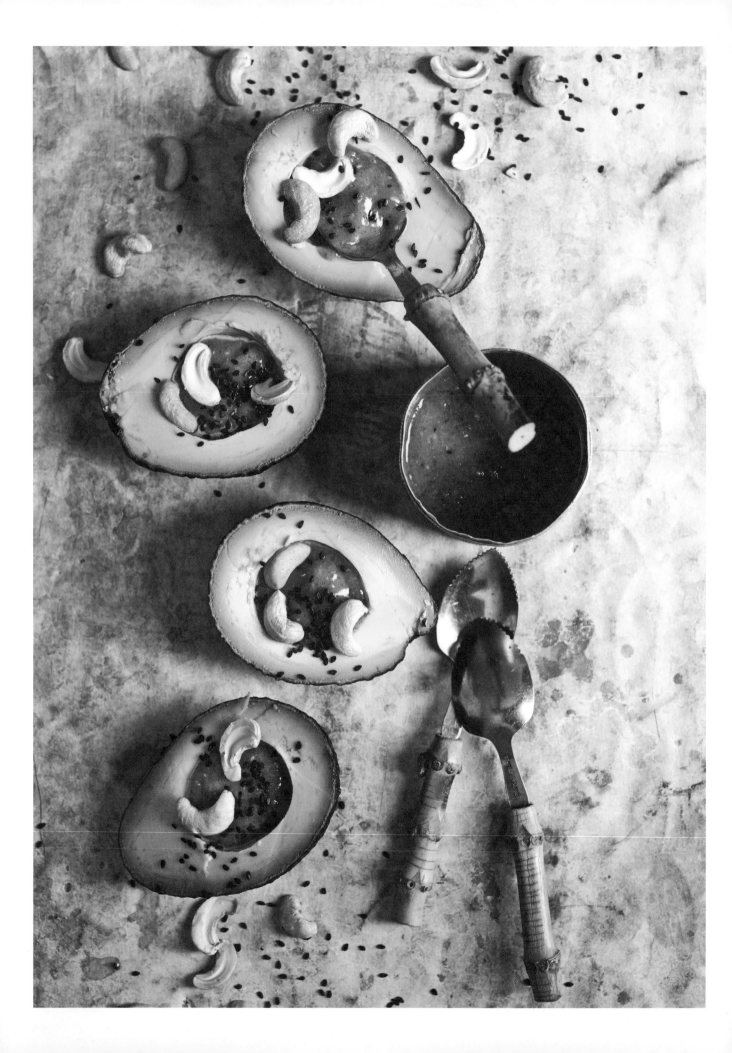

miso almond butter

WITH AVOCADO

PREP + COOK TIME **15 MINUTES** SERVES **4**

1½ tablespoons white (shiro)
   miso paste
2 tablespoons almond butter
2 tablespoons olive oil
½ teaspoon sesame oil
1 tablespoon mirin
1 tablespoon water
2 medium avocados (500g)
⅓ cup (50g) roasted cashews,
   chopped coarsely
½ teaspoon black sesame seeds

1 Stir miso, almond butter, oils, mirin and the water in a medium jug until smooth; season to taste.
2 Cut unpeeled avocados in half; discard stones. Spoon dressing into avocado hollow; sprinkle with cashews and sesame seeds. Serve immediately.

tips Use any of your favourite healthy dressings or dips for this quick and easy snack. The miso almond butter will keep in an airtight container and can also be used as a dressing for salads.

I AM
VEGAN
SUGAR-FREE
FIBRE RICH

FROZEN GREEN

power bites

PREP + COOK TIME **10 MINUTES (+ FREEZING)** MAKES **25**

3 ripe medium bananas (600g)

¼ cup (30g) ground almonds

½ cup (70g) chopped pitted dates

½ cup (80g) currants

¾ cup (90g) coarsely chopped pecans

¼ cup (35g) sesame seeds

¼ cup (25g) cacao powder

2 tablespoons coconut butter, melted

½ cup (40g) quinoa flakes

1 tablespoon spirulina powder

2 tablespoons barley malt syrup

25 mini wooden popsicle sticks

¼ cup (20g) shredded coconut

¼ cup (30g) coarsely chopped pecans, extra

1 Mash banana in a large bowl with a fork. Add ground almonds, dates, currants, pecans, sesame seeds, cacao, coconut butter, quinoa flakes, spirulina powder and syrup; stir until well combined.

2 Spoon mixture into 25 ice-cube tray holes (2-tablespoon capacity). Insert popsicle sticks; freeze for 5 hours or until set.

3 Stir shredded coconut in a small frying pan over medium heat for 5 minutes or until golden. Transfer immediately to a small bowl; cool. Stir in extra pecans until combined.

4 Carefully ease power bites from holes; dip in coconut mixture. Store in an airtight container in the freezer until ready to eat.

tips Coconut butter is the blended flesh of coconut. Spirulina is a cyanobacterium (sometimes referred to as blue-green algae although this is not technically correct) that grows in lakes. It is sold as a powder or as tablets. Spirulina powder is rich in protein – a tablespoon provides 4g of protein – and contains all of the essential amino acids. It is also a very good source of iron, making it a great supplement for vegans and vegetarians. It's rich in B group vitamins, copper and manganese, and is a source of the plant omega-3 fat, alpha-linolenic acid (ALA). Coconut butter and spirulina are both available from health food stores. Bites can be stored in the freezer for up to 1 month.

I AM

VEGAN

SUGAR-FREE

PROTEIN RICH

WITH CHILLI YOGHURT

PREP + COOK TIME **40 MINUTES** SERVES **8**

Socca, also known as farinata, is a traditional Italian and Provençal pancake made from chickpea flour. You will need an ovenproof frying pan for this recipe.

1 medium brown onion (150g), unpeeled

½ cup (125ml) olive oil

1½ cups (180g) chickpea (besan) flour

1 teaspoon salt flakes

1¼ cups (310ml) lukewarm water

2 teaspoons chopped fresh rosemary

1 tablespoon small fresh rosemary sprigs

¼ cup (20g) finely grated parmesan

CHILLI YOGHURT

½ cup (140g) greek-style yoghurt

1 teaspoon raw honey

1 tablespoon coarsely chopped fresh flat-leaf parsley

¼ teaspoon chilli flakes

1 Preheat oven to 200°C/400°F. Line an oven tray with baking paper.

2 Cut onion into eight wedges; separate layers. Place onion in a medium bowl with 1 tablespoon of the olive oil; toss to coat. Season. Place onion on tray; bake for 20 minutes or until browned.

3 Place chickpea flour, salt, the water, chopped rosemary and ¼ cup of the olive oil in a medium bowl; whisk until smooth. Season with cracked black pepper. Set aside for 5 minutes.

4 Make chilli yoghurt.

5 Increase oven to 250°C/480°F. Heat a large heavy-based ovenproof frying pan over a medium-high heat. Add remaining oil, heat for a few seconds, pour in batter, top with onion and rosemary sprigs. Cook for 1 minute; transfer to oven, bake for 10 minutes or until golden and socca pulls away from the side of the pan.

6 Serve socca cut into wedges, topped with parmesan and chilli yoghurt.

chilli yoghurt Combine ingredients in a small bowl.

tips Reheat socca between sheets of baking paper in a sandwich press. Store socca in an airtight container in the fridge for up to 3 days or freeze for up to 1 month.

I AM
NUT-FREE
SUGAR-FREE
GLUTEN-FREE

CREAMY CARROT

miso dip

PREP + COOK TIME **20 MINUTES** SERVES **4**

2 sheets original mountain
  bread (50g)

cooking oil spray

2 medium carrots (260g),
  chopped coarsely

1 small clove garlic, chopped

1 medium shallot (25g),
  chopped coarsely

2 tablespoons white (shiro) miso paste

¼ cup (60ml) avocado or vegetable oil

2 teaspoons sesame oil

2 tablespoons rice wine vinegar

1 tablespoon water

1 teaspoon black sesame seeds

1 tablespoon micro coriander
  (cilantro) leaves

1 Preheat oven to 200°C/400°F.
2 Place mountain bread on two
oven trays, spray both sides with
cooking oil; season with salt. Bake
for 4 minutes or until golden and
crisp. Break into large pieces.
3 Blend or process carrot, garlic,
shallot, miso, oils, vinegar and the
water for 30 seconds or until mixture
is smooth; season to taste.
4 Serve dip sprinkled with sesame
seeds and coriander, with mountain
bread crisps.

*tips Mountain bread crisps will
keep in an airtight container for
up to 3 days. Dip will keep in an
airtight container in the fridge for
up to 3 days; stir before serving.*

I AM
VEGAN
RICH IN BETA-CAROTENE
SUGAR-FREE

GREEN POWER
mini frittatas

PREP + COOK TIME **35 MINUTES** MAKES **8**

2 teaspoons olive oil

1 small leek (200g), sliced thinly

½ clove garlic, crushed

3 cups (120g) firmly packed baby
    spinach leaves, chopped finely

5 free-range eggs

½ cup (125ml) pouring cream

1 tablespoon finely chopped
    fresh mint

1 tablespoon finely chopped
    fresh basil

1 tablespoon finely chopped
    fresh dill

100g (3 ounces) goat's fetta,
    crumbled

1 Preheat oven to 180°C/350°F. Line
8 holes of a 12-hole (⅓ cup/80ml)
muffin pan with paper cases.

2 Heat oil in a medium saucepan
over medium heat; cook leek, stirring,
for 3 minutes. Add garlic; cook for
2 minutes or until leek is soft. Add
spinach; cook, stirring, 30 seconds
or until wilted. Remove from heat.
Set aside.

3 Whisk eggs, cream and herbs in a
medium jug; season.

4 Divide spinach mixture into pan
holes; pour in egg mixture, then top
with fetta.

5 Bake frittatas for 20 minutes or
until set. Leave in pan for 5 minutes
before serving warm or at room
temperature.

*tip Store frittatas in an airtight
container in the fridge for up to
5 days or freeze for up to 1 month.*

I AM
VEGETARIAN
ANTIOXIDANT RICH
LOW CARB

CACAO & DATE
caramel slice

PREP TIME **25 MINUTES (+ REFRIGERATION & FREEZING)** MAKES **16**

½ cup (115g) fresh dates, pitted

1 cup (130g) roasted almonds

1½ tablespoons virgin coconut oil, melted

¼ teaspoon fine sea salt flakes

DATE CARAMEL

1 cup (230g) fresh dates, pitted

½ cup (125ml) pure maple syrup

⅓ cup (95g) natural crunchy peanut butter

¼ cup (60ml) melted virgin coconut oil

CACAO TOPPING

¼ cup (20g) raw cacao powder

¼ cup (60ml) melted virgin coconut oil

2 teaspoons pure maple syrup

1 Line a 19cm (7¾-inch) square pan with baking paper.

2 Process dates, almonds and coconut oil until smooth. Press mixture evenly onto the base of the pan. Refrigerate for 1 hour or until set.

3 Make date caramel; spread mixture evenly over base mixture in pan. Freeze for 1 hour or until firm.

4 Make cacao topping. Working quickly, pour topping over date caramel mixture; sprinkle with salt. Refrigerate for 1 hour or until set.

5 Use a hot sharp knife to cut slice into 16 pieces.

date caramel Process ingredients for 2 minutes or until very smooth.

cacao topping Whisk ingredients in a medium bowl until smooth.

tips Make cacao topping just before you are ready to use it or it may begin to set. The slice will keep in an airtight container in the fridge for up to 1 week.

I AM
VEGAN
SUGAR-FREE
GLUTEN-FREE

Lemon thyme has a lemony scent due to the high level of citral, which is an oil also found in lemon, orange, verbena and lemon grass. Crush the leaves before using.

Rosemary is a rich source of antioxidants, and has beneficial effects on brain and eye health.

Flat-leaf parsley is packed with nutrients including carotenoids, which reduce the risk of macular degeneration of the eye, a common cause of blindness.

Mint has strong antioxidant properties, and has been studied for its positive effects on the gut. It's also a well-known breath freshener.

Berries and cream mint is so-named because its leaves have a sweet berry and mint flavour.

Sage has been shown to help reduce the loss of minerals from bone and to help boost long-term memory retention.

Bay leaf has been used for its antioxidant, anti-bacterial, anti-inflammatory and anti-fungal properties.

Oregano is packed full of antioxidants.

herbs

Coriander's fresh leaves have good antioxidant properties and are a rich source of vitamin K.

Using herbs brings a wealth of benefits; they give an added depth of flavour to food, boost your intake of beneficial plant compounds, including antioxidants, and many have particular medicinal effects.

Thyme is another herb with good antioxidant properties. It also has shown to be beneficial in maintaining strong bones.

Basil has anti-inflammatory effects, as well as containing vitamin A, folate, vitamin C and several minerals. Thai basil, with its aniseed flavour, is found in Asian dishes.

BERRY

moon rocks

PREP TIME **15 MINUTES (+ FREEZING)** SERVES **4**

250g (8 ounces) small strawberries,
    with stems on
175g (5½ ounces) blackberries
125g (4 ounces) raspberries
400g (12½ ounces) greek-style
    yoghurt
1½ tablespoons raw honey
1 vanilla bean, split lengthways,
    seeds scraped
⅔ cup (90g) finely chopped pistachios

1 Place all berries, separated in a single layer, on a tray; freeze for 30 minutes.
2 Combine yoghurt, honey, vanilla seeds and half the pistachios in a medium bowl. Add ½ cup of the frozen raspberries to the bowl, crush against the side of the bowl with a wooden spoon.
3 Using a toothpick, dip frozen berries, one at a time into the yoghurt mixture; place berries on a baking-paper-lined tray. Freeze for 3 hours until coating is set. Cover remaining yoghurt mixture; refrigerate.
4 Repeat dipping coated berries in remaining yoghurt mixture for a second coat; sprinkle with remaining pistachios. Freeze for 5 hours or overnight until frozen. Store in an airtight container in the freezer.

tips *Swap mango or pineapple chunks for berries. Use any leftover yoghurt for breakfast or on its own as a delicious snack. Store berry moon rocks in the freezer for up to 2 weeks.*

I AM
SUGAR-FREE
HIGH IN ANTIOXIDANTS
CALCIUM RICH

CACAO & HAZELNUT
cookies

PREP + COOK TIME **30 MINUTES** MAKES **18**

½ cup (80g) firmly packed fresh
  dates, pitted

2 cups (200g) ground hazelnuts

1½ cups (225g) wholemeal
  spelt flour

¼ cup (50g) chia seeds

1 teaspoon ground cinnamon

pinch sea salt flakes

¼ cup (50g) virgin coconut oil,
  at room temperature

½ cup (170g) rice malt syrup

1 free-range egg

2 teaspoons vanilla extract

½ cup (50g) cacao nibs

1 Preheat oven to 160°C/325°F. Line two oven trays with baking paper.

2 Place dates in a small heatproof bowl, cover with boiling water; stand for 5 minutes. Drain.

3 Process dates, ground hazelnuts, flour, seeds, cinnamon, salt, oil, syrup, egg and extract until well combined. Stir in cacao nibs.

4 Using damp hands, roll 2-tablespoonfuls of mixture into a ball, place on tray; flatten with the palm of your hand into a 4cm (1½-inch) round. Using the back of a damp fork, mark each cookie.

5 Bake cookies for 15 minutes or until a cookie can be gently pushed without breaking. Cool on trays.

tip Cacao nibs are created in the early stages of chocolate production; cocoa beans are dried then roasted, after which they are crushed into what is termed 'nibs'. The nibs are then ground to separate the cocoa butter and cocoa solids. Nibs are both textural and chocolatey with no sweetness. Buy from health food stores and specialist food stores.

I AM
SUGAR-FREE
PROTEIN RICH
LOW GI

BASIC CRACKERS

PREP + COOK TIME **45 MINUTES**
(+ REFRIGERATION & COOLING) MAKES **12**

Preheat oven to 180°C/350°F. Pulse 1½ cups natural
ground almonds, 1 free-range egg, 30g (1oz) chopped
cold butter and ½ teaspoon salt in a food processor until
mixture comes together. Knead lightly until smooth.
Roll dough between baking paper into a 20cm x 30cm
(8-in x 12-in) rectangle. Refrigerate for 30 minutes.
Remove top sheet of baking paper; cut dough into
12 rectangles. Lift dough on paper onto an oven tray.
Using the back of a knife, make an indent at centre
of each rectangle; prick all over with a fork. Bake for
20 minutes or until golden. Leave on tray for 5 minutes;
cool on a wire rack.

TRIO OF SEEDS

PREP + COOK TIME **45 MINUTES**
(+ REFRIGERATION & COOLING) MAKES **12**

Preheat oven to 180°C/350°F. Place ingredients for basic
crackers in a food processor with 1 tablespoon each of
linseeds, sunflower seeds and pepitas; pulse until mixture
comes together. Knead lightly until smooth. Roll dough
between baking paper into a 25cm x 40cm (10-in x 16-in)
rectangle. Refrigerate for 30 minutes. Remove top sheet
of baking paper. Lift dough on paper onto an oven tray.
Bake for 20 minutes or until golden. Leave on tray for
5 minutes; cool on a wire rack. Break into 12 pieces.

FENNEL & POPPY SEEDS

PREP + COOK TIME **45 MINUTES**
(+ REFRIGERATION & COOLING) MAKES **24**

Preheat oven to 180°C/350°F. Place ingredients for basic crackers in a food processor with 2 teaspoons each of fennel seeds and poppy seeds; pulse until mixture comes together. Knead lightly until smooth. Roll dough between baking paper into a 20cm x 30cm (8-in x 12-in) rectangle. Refrigerate for 30 minutes. Remove top sheet of baking paper. Cut dough into 12 x 10cm (4-in) squares; cut squares diagonally into triangles. Lift dough on paper onto an oven tray. Brush with water, sprinkle with ¼ teaspoon sea salt flakes. Bake for 20 minutes or until golden. Leave on tray 5 minutes; cool on a wire rack.

ROSEMARY & PARMESAN

PREP + COOK TIME **45 MINUTES**
(+ REFRIGERATION & COOLING) MAKES **15**

Preheat oven to 180°C/350°F. Place ingredients for basic crackers in a food processor with ¼ cup finely grated parmesan and 2 tablespoons finely chopped fresh rosemary; pulse until mixture comes together. Knead lightly until smooth. Roll dough between baking paper into a 25cm x 40cm (10-in x 16-in) rectangle. Refrigerate for 30 minutes. Remove top sheet of baking paper. Lift dough on paper onto an oven tray. Bake for 20 minutes or until golden. Leave on tray for 5 minutes; cool on a wire rack. Break into 15 pieces.

DINNERS

 spelt pizza

WITH KUMARA, PEPITAS & GOAT'S CHEESE

PREP + COOK TIME **1 HOUR 45 MINUTES (+ STANDING)** SERVES **4**

2 teaspoons (7g) dried yeast

½ teaspoon salt

2 cups (300g) plain (all-purpose)
spelt flour

1 cup (250ml) warm water

⅓ cup (80ml) olive oil

3 medium brown onions (600g),
halved, sliced thinly

2 cloves garlic, crushed

800g (1½ pounds) kumara (orange
sweet potato), sliced thinly

⅓ cup (65g) pepitas (pumpkin seeds)

1 fresh long green chilli, seeded,
chopped finely

200g (7 ounces) soft goat's cheese,
crumbled

20g (¾ ounce) baby rocket
(arugula) leaves

1 Combine yeast, salt and flour in a
large bowl; make a well in the centre.
Stir in the water and 2 tablespoons
of the oil until mixed well. Knead
dough on a floured surface for
5 minutes until smooth and elastic.
Place dough in an oiled bowl;
cover with plastic wrap. Stand for
30 minutes or until doubled in size.
2 Heat remaining oil in a large
frying pan over medium-high heat;
cook onion and garlic, stirring
occasionally, for 5 minutes.
Reduce heat to low; cook, stirring
occasionally, for 20 minutes or until
onion is light golden. Cool.
3 Preheat oven to 220°C/425°F. Oil
two 30cm (12-inch) pizza or oven trays.
4 Divide dough in half, roll each half
into a 25cm (10-inch) round; place on
tray. Spread onion mixture between
pizza bases; top with kumara, slightly
overlapping the slices, and pepitas.

5 Bake pizzas for 15 minutes,
swapping trays halfway through
cooking time, or until crust is
golden. Serve topped with chilli,
cheese and rocket.

*tips Use a mandoline or V-slicer
to easily cut the kumara into thin
slices. For extra protein, add
2 tablespoons chia seeds to the
pizza dough.*

I AM
VEGETARIAN
EGG-FREE
HIGH FIBRE

tandoori lamb cutlets

WITH GREEN ONION ROTI

PREP + COOK TIME **40 MINUTES (+ REFRIGERATION)** SERVES **4**

12 french-trimmed lamb
  cutlets (600g)
1 tablespoon tandoori paste
2 lebanese cucumbers (260g)
400g (12½ ounces) red radishes,
  sliced thinly
1 tablespoon white vinegar
1 tablespoon caster (superfine)
  sugar
1 cup loosely packed fresh mint leaves
1 cup loosely packed fresh coriander
  leaves (cilantro)

GREEN ONION ROTI

1 teaspoon cumin seeds
1 green onion (scallion), sliced thinly
1 cup (150g) chickpea (besan) flour
¼ teaspoon xantham gum
2 tablespoons buttermilk
2 tablespoons water
1 tablespoon vegetable oil
chickpea (besan) flour, extra,
  for dusting
2 tablespoons ghee, melted

1 Combine lamb and paste in a
large bowl. Cover, refrigerate for
30 minutes.
2 Meanwhile, make green onion roti.
3 Using a vegetable peeler, cut
cucumber lengthways into thin
ribbons. Combine cucumber with
radish, vinegar and sugar in a
medium bowl; toss until sugar
dissolves. Stand for 5 minutes to
allow vegetables to pickle; drain.
Add mint and coriander to bowl;
toss to combine.
4 Cook lamb on a heated oiled
grill plate (or grill or barbecue)
for 2 minutes each side or until
cooked as desired. Cover lamb;
stand for 5 minutes before serving
with cucumber salad and roti.

green onion roti Cook seeds in a
small dry frying pan, over medium
heat, stirring for 1 minute or until
fragrant. Stir seeds, onion, flour
and xantham gum in a large bowl
to combine; season. Add buttermilk,

the water and oil; stir to form a firm
dough. Divide dough into eight
balls. Lightly flour work surface
with extra chickpea flour; using a
rolling pin, roll each ball into 2mm
(⅛-inch) thick, 12cm (4¾-inch)
rounds. Brush a heated small frying
pan with ghee; cook roti, over high
heat, for 1 minute each side or until
lightly golden and cooked through.
Transfer to a plate, cover with foil to
keep warm. Repeat with remaining
roti dough and ghee.

*tips Brush roti with garlic oil
for a garlic flavour. Roti can be
made a day ahead. To reheat,
warm in a heated dry frying pan,
or wrap roti in foil and place in
a 180°C/350°F oven for about
10 minutes or until heated through.*

I AM
EGG-FREE
GLUTEN-FREE
PROTEIN RICH

lamb kofta

WITH WHITE BEANS

PREP + COOK TIME **40 MINUTES (+ COOLING)** SERVES **4**

400g (12½ ounces) canned white
  beans, drained, rinsed

1 tablespoon lemon juice

2 tablespoons fresh oregano leaves

2 tablespoons olive oil

½ cup (35g) fresh breadcrumbs

2 tablespoon milk

600g (1¼ pounds) minced
  (ground) lamb

1 teaspoon ground allspice

⅓ cup fresh oregano leaves, extra,
  chopped coarsely

100g (3 ounces) fetta, crumbled

1 baby cos (romaine) lettuce,
  trimmed, leaves separated

BEETROOT TZATZIKI

200g (6½ ounces) beetroot (beets),
  peeled, grated coarsely

1 cup (280g) greek-style yoghurt

2 tablespoons chopped fresh mint

1 clove garlic, crushed

1 tablespoon finely grated
  lemon rind

1 Make beetroot tzatiki.

2 Combine white beans, juice,
oregano and half the oil in a
medium bowl. Season to taste.

3 Place breadcrumbs and milk in
a medium bowl; stand for 3 minutes
or until milk has been absorbed.
Add lamb, allspice and extra
oregano; season. Using your hands,
work mixture until well combined.
Add fetta; stir until combined. Roll
heaped tablespoonful measures of
lamb mixture into kofta shapes.

4 Heat remaining oil in a large non-
stick frying pan over medium-high
heat; cook kofta, turning occasionally,
for 10 minutes or until browned and
cooked through.

5 Serve kofta on lettuce with bean
mixture and tzatziki.

beetroot tzatziki Combine
ingredients in a medium bowl;
season to taste.

*tip Cooked or uncooked kofta can
be frozen for up to 3 months. Thaw
in the fridge. Thread kofta shapes
onto wooden skewers, if you like.*

I AM
PROTEIN RICH
HIGH IN CALCIUM
EGG-FREE

WITH ZUCCHINI & ASPARAGUS SALAD

PREP + COOK TIME **40 MINUTES** SERVES **4**

The salad can be dressed up to 30 minutes before serving. You will need about 5 tablespoons of dukkah.

2 x 200g (6½-ounce) skinless salmon fillets, halved crossways

2 green onions (scallions), trimmed, sliced thinly, reserve trimmings

5cm (2-inch) strip lemon rind

4 whole black peppercorns

1 cup (250ml) water

¾ cup (150g) couscous

1 tablespoon olive oil

¼ cup coarsely chopped fresh flat-leaf parsley

2 free-range eggs, beaten lightly

45g (1½-ounce) packet lemon and herb dukkah, plus extra to serve

⅓ cup (80ml) olive oil, extra

1 medium zucchini (120g)

170g (5½ ounces) asparagus, trimmed

½ teaspoon finely grated lemon rind

1 tablespoon lemon juice

⅔ cup (190g) greek-style yoghurt

1 Place salmon, reserved green onion trimmings, rind, peppercorns and the water in a medium saucepan; bring to the boil. Remove from heat; stand for 10 minutes. Remove salmon from poaching liquid to a plate; remove and discard green onion trimmings, rind and peppercorns.

2 Bring poaching liquid back to the boil. Remove from heat; stir in couscous. Stand; covered for 5 minutes or until liquid is absorbed. Separate grains with a fork.

3 Place couscous in a medium bowl with oil; mix well. Add flaked salmon, green onion, parsley and half the egg; season. With wet hands, shape mixture into eight patties; place on a baking-paper-lined oven tray.

4 Place remaining egg and dukkah in separate small bowls. Dip patties in egg, draining off excess; coat in dukkah.

5 Heat half the extra oil in a large frying pan over medium heat; cook patties, in two batches, for 3 minutes each side or until golden and heated through. Drain on paper towel.

6 Use a mandoline or V-slicer to thinly slice zucchini and asparagus into ribbons. Place in a medium bowl with combined rind, juice and remaining extra oil; toss gently.

7 Serve patties with salad, yoghurt and extra dukkah.

I AM
PROTEIN RICH
HIGH IN OMEGA 3
POTASSIUM RICH

Chicken breast fillet is good for poaching, or cut into stir-fry strips.

Beef rump steak, a tasty cut from the lower back, is also sold as medallions.

TO-DAYS PRICE 4/8 PER LB.

Venison backstrap comes from deer. It is lean and tender.

VENISON TENDERLOIN

Chicken drumstick has darker and more flavorful meat than breast fillet.

Kangaroo is a very lean cut of meat.

Beef kidneys should be bought fresh. Skin, slice lengthways and remove the tough inner core before cooking.

Pork neck roll is cut from the shoulder. It is also known as scotch roast.

Pork loin chop is a tender, tasty and quite lean cut once the fat is removed.

meat

Grass-fed animals and game meats, including venison, crocodile, kangaroo and rabbit, are terrific healthy choices as they tend to be leaner, with lower levels of saturated fats and higher levels of anti-inflammatory omega-3 fats.

Once cheap, lamb shanks now feature prominently on menus at high-end restaurants. When slow-cooked they are deliciously tender.

Lamb backstrap is a very tender cut. When left on the bone it is known as loin, and is rolled and tied for roasting.

pea & barley risotto

WITH GARLIC PRAWNS

PREP + COOK TIME **1 HOUR** SERVES **4**

1 tablespoon olive oil
1 fresh long red chilli, chopped finely
2 cloves garlic, chopped finely
2 shallots (50g), chopped finely
1 cup (200g) pearl barley
1 litre (4 cups) chicken stock
1 cup (250ml) water
1 tablespoon finely grated lemon rind
½ cup (60g) frozen peas
150g (4½ ounces) sugar snap peas, trimmed, halved lengthways
2 tablespoons olive oil, extra
400g (12½ ounces) peeled uncooked prawns (shrimp), tails intact, butterflied
2 cloves garlic, extra, crushed
snow pea tendrils and thin strips lemon rind, to serve (optional)

1 Heat oil in a large saucepan over medium-low heat, add chilli, garlic and shallots; cook, stirring, for 3 minutes or until tender. Add barley; cook, stirring for 2 minutes or until lightly toasted. Add half the stock; bring to the boil. Reduce heat to low; cook, stirring occasionally, for 18 minutes or until the liquid has been absorbed. Add remaining stock and the water; cook, stirring occasionally for a further 18 minutes or until most of the liquid has been absorbed. Add rind, peas and sugar snap peas; cook, stirring, for 3 minutes or until vegetables are tender. Season.

2 Meanwhile, heat extra oil in a medium frying-pan over high heat; cook prawns and extra garlic, stirring, for 5 minutes or until prawns are just cooked. Season.

3 Serve barley risotto topped with prawns, snow pea tendrils and lemon rind strips.

tip *Risotto is best made just before serving.*

I AM
LOW FAT
PROTEIN RICH
LOW GI

KOREAN BEEF & CORN

soft tacos

PREP + COOK TIME **40 MINUTES (+ STANDING & REFRIGERATION)** SERVES **4**

6 wombok (napa cabbage) leaves
    (450g), trimmed, cut into
    large pieces
2 tablespoons sea salt flakes
2 tablespoons rice vinegar
2 teaspoons korean chilli paste
    (gochujang)
2 tablespoons rice malt syrup
1 teaspoon sesame oil
½ medium brown onion (75g),
    grated coarsely
2 cloves garlic, grated finely
¼ cup (60ml) soy sauce
¼ cup (60ml) rice malt syrup, extra
1 tablespoon sesame oil, extra
750g (1½ pounds) beef flank (skirt)
    steak, butterflied to 1.5cm
    (¾-inch) thick
2 corn cobs (800g), trimmed,
    husk and silks removed
1 large avocado (320g), sliced thinly
8 x 15cm (6-inch) corn tortillas
    (200g), warmed
micro herbs, to serve (optional)

1 To make the spicy kimchi, wash wombok then toss with salt in a colander. Place colander over a bowl; stand for 30 minutes. Rinse wombok well to remove the salt; pat dry with paper towel. Combine rice vinegar, chilli paste, syrup and oil in a large bowl. Add wombok; toss well to coat. Set aside.
2 Meanwhile, combine onion, garlic, soy sauce, extra syrup and extra oil in a medium bowl; season. Add steak; mix well to coat. Cover; refrigerate for 1 hour.
3 Cook corn on an oiled grill plate (or grill or barbecue) over high heat for 10 minutes, turning occasionally, or until lightly charred. Remove from heat. When cool enough to handle, cut kernels from cobs.

4 Drain steak; discard marinade. Cook steak on an oiled grill plate (or grill or barbecue) over medium-high heat for 3 minutes each side for medium rare or until cooked to your liking. Remove from heat; rest, covered, for 5 minutes. Slice thinly.
5 Divide spicy kimchi, corn, avocado and steak among tortillas; top with micro herbs.

tip If you can't get flank or skirt steak, rump steak can also be used.

I AM
DAIRY-FREE
PROTEIN RICH
HIGH FIBRE

sticky chicken drumsticks

WITH FENNEL & FRESH FIGS

PREP + COOK TIME **55 MINUTES (+ REFRIGERATION)** SERVES **4**

To bruise garlic, press the side of a large cook's knife on each clove until it splits. When fresh figs are out of season, soak halved dried figs in boiling water for 15 minutes and use instead.

I AM
GLUTEN-FREE
PROTEIN RICH
DAIRY-FREE

1kg (2 pounds) chicken drumsticks
3 baby fennel bulbs (390g), sliced
    thickly, fronds reserved
8 cloves garlic, unpeeled, bruised
2 tablespoons fresh rosemary leaves
1 teaspoon finely grated lemon rind
¼ cup (90g) honey
¼ cup (60ml) extra virgin olive oil
2 tablespoons honey, extra
30g (1 ounce) baby rocket
    (arugula) leaves
6 medium fresh figs (360g),
    torn in half
2 tablespoons lemon juice

1 Combine chicken, sliced fennel, garlic, rosemary, rind, honey and half the oil in a large dish. Cover; refrigerate for 2 hours.
2 Preheat oven to 220°C/425°F. Line a large oven tray with baking paper.
3 Transfer chicken, sliced fennel, garlic and rosemary to tray, in a single layer; discard marinade. Drizzle chicken with extra honey; season. Roast, brushing occasionally with pan juices, for 40 minutes or until chicken is cooked through.
4 Meanwhile, combine 1 tablespoon of the remaining oil with rocket, figs and juice in a medium bowl; season.
5 Serve chicken mixture with rocket salad and reserved fennel fronds; drizzle with remaining oil.

barbecued kangaroo steaks

WITH BEETROOT SALAD

PREP + COOK TIME **50 MINUTES** SERVES **4**

We used the small leaves from the bunch of beetroot, but you can use mixed baby salad leaves instead.

1kg (2 pounds) baby beetroot (beets)

8 shallots (200g), unpeeled

¼ cup (60ml) extra virgin olive oil

4 x 180g (5½-ounce) kangaroo steaks

1 tablespoon finely chopped
   fresh rosemary

200g (6½ ounces) baby beetroot
   (beets) leaves

¼ cup (25g) roasted walnuts,
   chopped coarsely

ROSEMARY YOGHURT DRESSING

½ cup (140g) greek-style yoghurt

1 teaspoon finely chopped fresh
   rosemary leaves

1 tablespoon honey

1 tablespoon dijon mustard

1 tablespoon extra virgin olive oil

1 Make rosemary yoghurt dressing.

2 Place beetroot and shallots in the centre of two large pieces of foil, drizzle with 1 tablespoon of the oil; season. Fold foil into parcels to completely enclose vegetables. Place parcels on one side of a heated oiled grill plate (or grill or barbecue) over medium heat for 35 minutes, turning every 10 minutes, or until beetroot and shallots are tender.

3 Meanwhile, coat steaks in remaining oil; sprinkle with rosemary. Season. Cook steaks on the other side of the grill plate; cook for 2 minutes each side or until cooked as desired. Remove from heat; rest, covered, for 5 minutes.

4 Peel beetroot and shallots, then cut in half; place in a medium bowl with leaves and nuts. Toss to combine.

5 Serve sliced steak with salad, drizzled with dressing.

rosemary yoghurt dressing

Place ingredients in a screw-top jar; shake well. Season. Refrigerate until needed.

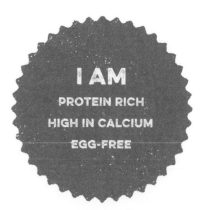

I AM
PROTEIN RICH
HIGH IN CALCIUM
EGG-FREE

WITH CARROT-TOP SALSA VERDE

PREP + COOK TIME **2 HOURS 30 MINUTES** SERVES **4**

Storing baby carrots with the leaves attached reduces their keeping time dramatically. Cut the tops off as soon as you can. wrap the tops in damp paper towel; refrigerate until needed.

⅓ cup (80ml) olive oil

1kg (2 pounds) boned lamb neck, cut into 5cm (2-inch) pieces

1 medium brown onion (150g), chopped finely

1 trimmed celery stalk (100g), chopped finely

3 cloves garlic, crushed

1.25 litres (5 cups) chicken stock

400g (12½ ounces) baby (dutch) carrots with tops, trimmed, tops reserved

1 medium swede (225g), cut into six wedges

½ cup (70g) roasted hazelnuts, chopped coarsely

CARROT-TOP SALSA VERDE

1½ cups loosely packed fresh flat-leaf parsley leaves

1½ tablespoons loosely packed fresh lemon thyme leaves

1 tablespoon drained capers

1 small clove garlic, crushed

1 teaspoon light brown sugar

½ cup (125ml) extra virgin olive oil

1½ tablespoons white wine vinegar

1 Heat 2 tablespoons of the oil in a large heavy-based saucepan over high heat; cook lamb, in batches, for 5 minutes, turning occasionally, until browned all over. Remove from pan. (If the base of the pan starts to burn, add 2 tablespoons water and stir to lift the meat sticking on the base of the pan.)

2 Reduce heat to medium, add remaining oil to pan; cook onion, celery and garlic, stirring occasionally, for 10 minutes or until softened. Return lamb to pan with stock; bring to the boil. Reduce heat to low; simmer, covered, for 2 hours or until meat is tender.

3 Meanwhile, wash reserved carrot-tops; you need ½ cup firmly packed tops for salsa verde, and extra to serve.

4 Make carrot-top salsa verde.

5 Increase pan heat to high; return to the boil. Add carrots and swede; simmer, uncovered, for 15 minutes or until liquid has thickened slightly. Season. Serve topped with hazelnuts, salsa verde and extra carrot-tops.

carrot-top salsa verde

Blend or process ingredients with the reserved ½ cup carrot-tops (from step 3), until well combined; season. Refrigerate until needed.

I AM
LOW CARB
PROTEIN RICH
PALEO

salmon pho

WITH KELP NOODLES

PREP + COOK TIME **30 MINUTES** SERVES **4**

Have your broth very hot for serving, as the heat of the soup will cook the salmon in the serving bowl.

3 litres (12 cups) fish stock

2 star anise

2 teaspoons finely grated fresh ginger

1 cinnamon stick

2 coriander roots, bruised

454g (14½ ounces) kelp noodles

1½ cups (120g) bean sprouts

¼ cup loosely packed fresh
    coriander (cilantro) leaves

¼ cup loosely packed fresh
    mint leaves

¼ cup loosely packed fresh
    thai basil leaves

2 green onions (scallions), sliced
    thinly on the diagonal

2 fresh long red chillies, sliced thinly
    on the diagonal

¼ cup (60ml) fish sauce

750g (1½ pounds) sashimi grade
    salmon, skinless, boned, cut
    into 5mm (¼-inch) slices

1 medium lemon (140g), cut into
    6 wedges

1 Place stock, star anise, ginger, cinnamon and coriander roots in a large saucepan; bring to the boil. Reduce heat to low; simmer for 10 minutes.

2 Meanwhile, cook noodles in another large saucepan of boiling water for 10 minutes or until softened slightly; drain well.

3 Combine sprouts, herbs, green onion and chilli in a medium bowl.

4 Strain broth though a fine sieve into another large saucepan. Bring to the boil over high heat; stir in fish sauce.

5 Divide noodles and salmon among soup bowls; ladle hot broth into bowls and top with sprout mixture. Serve with lemon wedges.

tips Kelp noodles are high in iodine and are gluten-free and low carb; they can be found in health food stores and some Asian supermarkets. You can use mung bean thread noodles or glass rice vermicelli noodles instead, if you like.

I AM
LOW CARB
HIGH IN OMEGA 3
PALEO

WITH GINGER & LIME

PREP + COOK TIME **20 MINUTES** SERVES **4**

You can use 2kg (4 pounds) of mussels if you can't find pipis, and use regular basil instead of thai basil, if you prefer.

1kg (2 pounds) pipis

1 cup (250ml) salt-reduced vegetable or chicken stock

3 fresh kaffir lime leaves, torn

1kg (2 pounds) small black mussels, scrubbed, beards removed

2 tablespoons vegetable oil

2 cloves garlic, crushed

1 fresh long red chilli, chopped finely

20g (¾-ounce) piece fresh ginger, cut into thin matchsticks

4 fresh kaffir lime leaves, extra, shredded

1 tablespoon fish sauce

1 tablespoon oyster sauce

1 cup loosely packed fresh coriander (cilantro) leaves

1 cup loosely packed fresh thai basil leaves

1 Soak pipis in a large bowl of cold water for 3 minutes; drain well.

2 Heat a wok over high heat, add pipis, stock and lime leaves; cook, covered, stirring occasionally, for 5 minutes or until pipis begin to open. Remove pipis with tongs as they open, discard pipis that remain closed. Repeat process with mussels.

3 Strain stock through a fine sieve into a small heatproof bowl; discard solids. Reserve stock.

4 Heat oil in wok over high heat; cook garlic, chilli, ginger and extra lime leaves, stirring occasionally, for 1 minute or until fragrant. Add sauces and 1 cup (250ml) of the reserved stock; cook, stirring, for 2 minutes or until thickened slightly. Add pipis and mussels; cook, stirring for 1 minute or until heated through. Stir in herbs, serve immediately.

serving suggestion Serve with cooked thai red rice or black rice, both can be found at Asian supermarkets.

I AM
LOW CARB
HIGH IN IRON
PALEO

#

WITH SILKY CAULIFLOWER SAUCE

PREP + COOK TIME **40 MINUTES** SERVES **4**

The creamy cauliflower sauce can also be served with grilled seafood or chicken. Or reduce the milk to ¼ cup for a thicker cauliflower mash rather than a puree.

1kg (2 pounds) cauliflower, cut into florets

1 cup (250ml) vegetable stock

2 cloves garlic, peeled

2 tablespoons extra virgin olive oil

¾ cup (45g) multigrain breadcrumbs

1 fresh long red chilli, seeded, chopped finely

1 clove garlic, extra, crushed

¼ cup chopped fresh flat-leaf parsley

1 tablespoon finely grated lemon rind

375g (12 ounces) dried spelt fettuccine pasta

½ cup (40g) grated parmesan

2 tablespoons extra virgin olive oil, extra

1½ cups (375ml) milk

¾ cup (60g) grated parmesan, extra

1 tablespoon lemon juice

1 Place three-quarters of the cauliflower in a medium saucepan with stock and garlic; bring to the boil. Reduce heat; simmer, covered, for 10 minutes or until cauliflower is tender.

2 Meanwhile, cut remaining cauliflower into tiny florets. Heat oil in a large frying pan over high heat, add florets; cook stirring, for 2 minutes until lightly golden. Add breadcrumbs, chilli and extra garlic; cook, stirring for 2 minutes, or until breadcrumbs are golden and crisp. Remove from heat; stir in parsley and rind.

3 Cook pasta in a large saucepan of boiling salted water following packet instructions. Drain well; return to pan with parmesan and extra oil.

4 Blend cauliflower stock mixture with milk until very smooth. Stir in extra parmesan and juice. Season.

5 Spoon cauliflower sauce over pasta; serve topped with toasted cauliflower crumbs.

I AM

HIGH IN FOLATE

HIGH IN MAGNESIUM

PROTEIN RICH

red lentil dhal

WITH CASHEW TOPPING

PREP + COOK TIME **40 MINUTES** SERVES **4**

1 tablespoon ghee

1 large red onion (300g),
   chopped finely

4 cloves garlic, chopped finely

20g (¾-ounce) piece fresh ginger,
   chopped finely

10g (½-ounce) piece fresh turmeric,
   grated (see tips)

2 teaspoons garam masala

1 cup (200g) dry red lentils

2 medium tomatoes (300g), chopped

2 fresh long green chillies,
   sliced thinly

1 litre (4 cups) water

750g (1½ pounds) cauliflower,
   cut into florets

1 medium parsnip (250g),
   chopped finely

600g (1¼ ounces) rainbow chard,
   cut into 3cm (1¼-inch) pieces

½ cup (140g) greek-style yoghurt

4 pappadums (8g)

CASHEW TOPPING

1 tablespoon ghee

⅓ cup (50g) unsalted roasted cashews

2 teaspoons mustard seeds

1 teaspoon fennel seeds

¼ cup fresh curry leaves

1 Heat ghee in a large heavy-based saucepan over high heat, add onion, garlic and ginger; cook, stirring for 4 minutes, or until onion is golden brown. Add turmeric and garam masala; cook, stirring for 30 seconds or until fragrant.

2 Add lentils, tomato, chilli and the water; bring to the boil. Reduce heat; simmer, covered, for 15 minutes or until tender.

3 Add cauliflower and parsnip; simmer, covered, for 10 minutes or until cauliflower is just tender. Season.

4 Meanwhile, make cashew topping.

5 Add chard to dhal; simmer, covered, for 2 minutes or until just wilted.

6 Serve dhal topped with cashew topping and yoghurt, along with pappadums.

cashew topping Heat ghee in a small frying pan over medium heat, add nuts; cook, stirring for 2 minutes, or until golden and toasted. Stir in seeds and curry leaves; cook, stirring, for 1 minute or until leaves are crisp.

tips Ghee is clarified butter, you can use butter or vegetable oil instead. Use ½ teaspoon ground turmeric instead of fresh tumeric, if you prefer.

I AM
VEGETARIAN
PROTEIN RICH
HIGH FIBRE

beef curry

WITH TURMERIC RICE

PREP + COOK TIME **3 HOURS** SERVES **4**

3 shallots (75g), chopped coarsely

5 cloves garlic, chopped coarsely

6 fresh small red chillies

30g (1-ounce) piece fresh ginger,
  chopped finely

1 lemon grass stalk, white part only,
  sliced thinly

1 tablespoon tamarind puree

1 tablespoon virgin coconut oil

1kg (2 pounds) lean beef bolar
  blade roast or beef skirt steak,
  cut into 3cm (1¼-inch) pieces

1.5 litres (6 cups) water,
  approximately

½ cup (140g) greek-style yoghurt

fresh red chilli, sliced and fresh
  coriander (cilantro) leaves,
  to serve

TURMERIC RICE

1 tablespoon virgin coconut oil

1½ cups (300g) basmati rice, rinsed

2 teaspoons mustard seeds

½ teaspoon ground turmeric

2 cups (500ml) chicken stock

COCONUT SAMBAL

¼ cup (10g) flaked coconut, toasted

1 lebanese cucumber (130g), seeded,
  chopped finely

1 small red onion (100g),
  chopped finely

1 tablespoon lime juice

1 Process shallots, garlic, chilli,
ginger, lemon grass and tamarind
until smooth.

2 Heat coconut oil a large heavy-
based saucepan over medium
heat, add paste; cook, stirring for
3 minutes, or until fragrant.

3 Add beef to pan with enough of the
water to completely cover beef; bring
to the boil. Reduce heat; simmer,
uncovered, for 2½ hours. Liquid
will slowly evaporate and beef will
become very tender. Add more water
during cooking if necessary. Shred
beef with two forks.

4 Make turmeric rice, then coconut
sambal.

5 Serve curry topped with yoghurt,
chilli and coriander, along with
turmeric rice and coconut sambal.

turmeric rice Heat coconut oil in
a medium saucepan over high heat,
add rice, seeds and turmeric; cook,
stirring, for 1 minute to coat rice
well. Add stock; bring to the boil.
Cover with a firm fitting lid; reduce
heat to low, simmer for 12 minutes
or until tunnels appear on surface
of rice. Remove from heat; stand,
covered, for 10 minutes. Fluff grains
with a fork.

coconut sambal Combine
ingredients in a small bowl.

*tip To save time buy ready made
rendang paste, available from the
Asian section of most supermarkets.*

I AM
NUT-FREE
PROTEIN RICH
LOW GI

CAVOLO NERO &
mushroom lasagne

PREP + COOK TIME **1 HOUR 30 MINUTES** SERVES **6**

1kg (2 pounds) fresh ricotta

1½ cups (120g) grated pecorino
cheese

1 cup (250ml) buttermilk

½ teaspoon ground nutmeg

1 tablespoon finely grated lemon rind

2 tablespoons olive oil

2 cloves garlic, crushed

4 green onions (scallions),
sliced thinly

500g (1 pound) small portobello
mushrooms, sliced thinly

400g (12½ ounces) cavolo nero
(tuscan cabbage), trimmed,
chopped

350g (11 ounces) fresh wholemeal
lasagne sheets

1 tablespoon olive oil, extra

½ cup (70g) hazelnuts,
chopped coarsely

1 medium lemon (140g), rind cut
into thin strips

1 fresh long green chilli,
sliced thinly

1 Combine ricotta, half the pecorino,
the buttermilk, nutmeg and grated
rind in a large bowl.

2 Heat oil in a large frying pan over
medium-high heat, add garlic, half the
green onion and 400g (12½ ounces)
of the mushrooms; cook, covered,
for 5 minutes or until mushrooms
start to soften. Add 300g (9½ ounces)
of the cavolo nero; stir until wilted.
Cool slightly.

3 Preheat oven to 180°C/350°F.

4 Grease a 3-litre (12 cup) ovenproof
dish. Spread base with ¼ cup of the
ricotta mixture. Top with a single
layer of lasagne sheets, trimming
to fit. Top with one-third of the
remaining ricotta mixture and half
the mushroom mixture. Continue
layering, ending with ricotta mixture.

5 Cover lasagne with foil. Bake for
25 minutes. Remove foil; bake a
further 20 minutes or until pasta is
cooked through and top is golden
brown.

6 Meanwhile, heat extra oil in a
medium frying pan over high heat;
cook remaining mushrooms and
remaining cavolo nero, stirring, for
3 minutes. Add remaining green
onion, the hazelnuts, rind strips
and chilli; toss to combine.

7 Serve lasagne topped with
mushroom mixture and remaining
pecorino.

*tips Lasagne can be made a
day ahead. Keep, covered, in the
refrigerator. Some cheeses may
contain animal rennet; check
labels carefully for non-animal
rennet. There are now many
vegetarian cheese varieties
available in supermarkets.*

I AM
VEGETARIAN
PROTEIN RICH
HIGH IN IRON

BLACK RICE

seafood paella

PREP + COOK TIME **1 HOUR** SERVES **4**

¼ cup (60ml) olive oil

1 medium white onion (150g),
    chopped finely

1½ teaspoons smoked paprika

1 small red capsicum (bell pepper)
    (150g), sliced thickly

2 cloves garlic, chopped finely

1 cup (200g) black rice, rinsed

400g (12½ ounces) canned
    cherry tomatoes

2 cups (500ml) vegetable stock

2 cups (500ml) water

8 large uncooked prawns (shrimp)
    (500g), peeled and deveined,
    tails intact

300g (9½ ounces) firm white
    fish fillets, cut into 4cm
    (1½-inch) pieces

4 scallops on shell (100g)

8 pipis (320g)

½ cup (60g) frozen peas

¼ cup loosely packed fresh flat-leaf
    parsley leaves

lemon wedges, to serve

1 Heat oil in a large frying pan
or paella pan over medium heat;
cook onion, stirring, for 3 minutes
or until softened. Add paprika,
capsicum, garlic and rice; cook,
stirring, for 2 minutes or until well
combined. Add tomatoes, stock and
the water; bring to the boil. Reduce
heat; simmer, uncovered, stirring
occasionally, for 40 minutes or
until most of the liquid has been
absorbed and rice is tender.

2 Arrange seafood and peas on rice
mixture; season. Cook, covered, for
5 minutes or until seafood is just
cooked through.

3 Serve paella topped with parsley
and lemon wedges.

*tip Recipe is best made just before
serving.*

I AM
LOW FAT
PROTEIN RICH
LOW GI

broccoli steaks
WITH QUINOA & RICOTTA

PREP + COOK TIME **20 MINUTES** SERVES **4**

½ cup (100g) white quinoa

700g (1½ pounds) broccoli, cut into
  1cm (½-inch) thick slices

2 small zucchini (180g), sliced thinly

1 tablespoon olive oil

80g (2½ ounces) ricotta, crumbled

2 tablespoons natural flaked almonds

2 tablespoons dried unsweetened
  cranberries

LEMON DRESSING

¼ cup (60ml) extra virgin olive oil

2 tablespoons lemon juice

1 teaspoon finely grated lemon rind

1 small clove garlic, crushed

1 Preheat oven to 180°C/350°F.

2 Rinse quinoa under cold water;
drain well. Spread on an oven tray.
Bake for 10 minutes, stirring halfway
through, or until toasted and golden.
Cool to room temperature.

3 Combine broccoli, zucchini and
oil in a large bowl until vegetables
are coated. Cook broccoli on a heated
oiled grill plate (or grill or barbecue)
over medium-high heat for 3 minutes,
each side or until just cooked.
Remove from heat; cover to keep
warm. Cook zucchini on heated oiled
grill plate for 1 minute each side.

4 Make lemon dressing.

5 Arrange vegetables on a serving
platter, top with ricotta, quinoa,
almonds and cranberries. Serve
drizzled with dressing.

lemon dressing Whisk ingredients
in a small bowl; season to taste.

tip *Add a pinch of crushed chilli
flakes to the quinoa for the final
minute of baking time.*

I AM
EGG-FREE
VEGETARIAN
LOW FAT

mountain rice salad

WITH HALOUMI

PREP + COOK TIME **50 MINUTES** SERVES **4**

Mountain rice blend is a combination of brown rice, black rice and red rice. You can use frozen peas instead of broad beans, if you like.

I AM
PROTEIN RICH
HIGH IN VITAMIN C
GLUTEN-FREE

¼ cup (60ml) red wine vinegar

1 tablespoon dijon mustard

¼ cup (60ml) olive oil

¼ cup (90g) honey

1 cup (200g) mountain rice blend

500g (1 pound) frozen broad (fava) beans, blanched, peeled

1 baby fennel (130g), trimmed, sliced thinly

400g (12½ ounces) heirloom tomatoes, cut into wedges

100g (3 ounces) champagne radishes, sliced thinly

½ cup coarsely chopped fresh dill

250g (8 ounces) haloumi cheese, cut into 1cm (½-inch) slices

1 Place vinegar, mustard and 2 tablespoons each of the oil and the honey in a screw-top jar; shake well to combine.

2 Cook rice in a large saucepan of boiling water for 20 minutes or until tender. Drain; rinse well. Transfer to a large bowl with half the dressing; mix well.

3 Add broad beans, fennel, tomatoes, radishes and half the dill to rice; toss to combine.

4 Heat remaining oil in a large non-stick frying pan over medium-high heat; cook haloumi for 3 minutes on each side or until golden brown. Drizzle with the remaining honey.

5 Serve rice salad on a large platter, topped with haloumi and honey juices; drizzle with remaining dressing and top with remaining dill.

Kale is rich in the carotenoids lutein and zeaxanthin (which have been shown to reduce the risk of age-related macular degeneration and cataracts), and is a good source of vitamins A, C and K, and calcium.

Sugar snap peas look just like peas, but are smaller, more tender and have an edible pod with sweet, juicy seeds (immature peas).

Cavolo nero, also known as tuscan cabbage, has good levels of vitamins A, C and K, folate and fibre. It doesn't lose its volume like silver beet or spinach when cooked, but may need longer cooking.

Buk choy (mature and baby) is part of the brassica family. Collectively, these reduce the risk of stomach, colon and lung cancers. It is rich in vitamins A and C and several B-group vitamins, and has small but significant amounts of iron and calcium.

Broccolini is a cross between broccoli and gai lan. You can eat the whole vegetable from stalk to floret. Like broccoli, it's rich in antioxidants that help fight oxidative damage that causes disease and aging.

Green beans are a good source of vitamins and minerals. Firm vegies have more fibre than leafy greens.

leafy greens

"Eat your greens" were actually wise words of wisdom from our mothers, but there were times when even the threat of no dessert, wasn't enough to get us to eat up. Now we know better... their multitude of protective functions against disease and aging make them powerhouses of health.

Brussels sprouts are in the same family as broccoli and have many of the same benefits, particularly in reducing the risk of cancers of the bowel.

Green peas are one of the best vegetable sources of fibre. They also have a good amount of protein, iron, zinc, folate and vitamin C. Green peas have a high sugar content, but this starts to deteriorate soon after picking.

pan-fried chicken

WITH ZUCCHINI & SALSA VERDE

PREP + COOK TIME **30 MINUTES** SERVES **4**

4 chicken breast fillets (680g),
    halved lengthways
1 tablespoon olive oil
5 medium zucchini (500g)
⅓ cup (25g) flaked almonds, toasted
100g (3 ounces) goat's fetta, crumbled
¼ cup fresh flat-leaf parsley leaves

SALSA VERDE
½ cup coarsely chopped fresh
    flat-leaf parsley
¼ cup coarsely chopped fresh basil
1 clove garlic, crushed
2 teaspoons drained baby capers,
    rinsed
1 teaspoon dijon mustard
¼ cup (60ml) olive oil
2 teaspoons red wine vinegar

1 Season chicken. Heat oil in a large frying pan over medium-high heat; cook chicken, in batches, for 4 minutes each side or until browned and cooked through. Remove from pan; cover to keep warm.
2 Using a vegetable spiralizer, cut zucchini into spirals.
3 Make salsa verde.
4 Serve chicken with zucchini topped with salsa verde, almonds, fetta and parsley.

salsa verde Combine herbs, garlic and capers in a small bowl; whisk in mustard, oil and vinegar until thickened.

tip A spiralizer is a kitchen gadget that cuts vegetables into long thin spirals. If you don't have one, you can use a mandoline or V-slicer.

I AM
LOW CARB
PROTEIN RICH
GLUTEN-FREE

veal cutlets

WITH BEETROOT SALAD & WHITE BEAN SAUCE

PREP + COOK TIME **1 HOUR 30 MINUTES** SERVES **4**

500g (1 pound) baby beetroot (beets),
 stems attached

4 x 200g (6½-ounce) veal cutlets

2 cloves garlic, crushed

1 tablespoon fresh thyme leaves

1 tablespoon lemon juice

1 tablespoon olive oil

170g (5½ ounces) asparagus,
 trimmed, halved lengthways

250g (8 ounces) frisee leaves,
 trimmed

½ cup (50g) roasted walnuts

120g (4 ounces) goat's cheese,
 crumbled

LEMON DRESSING

1 medium lemon (140g)

1 tablespoon olive oil

WHITE BEAN SAUCE

400g (12½ ounces) canned cannellini
 beans, drained, rinsed

½ cup (125ml) salt-reduced
 chicken stock

1 small clove garlic, crushed

½ teaspoon finely grated lemon rind

1 Preheat oven to 200°C/400°F.
2 Trim beetroot, leaving 3cm
(1¼ inches) of the stem attached;
discard roots. Wrap beetroot in foil.
Place beetroot on an oven tray.
Roast for 50 minutes or until tender.
When cool enough to handle;
remove skin. Cut beetroot in half.
3 Combine veal, garlic, thyme,
juice and oil in a large bowl;
stand 10 minutes.
4 Cook veal on a heated oiled
grill plate (or grill or barbecue)
for 3 minutes each side or until
browned and cooked as desired.
Cover; stand 5 minutes.
5 Meanwhile, boil, steam or
microwave asparagus until tender.
6 Make lemon dressing and white
bean sauce.
7 Place beetroot and asparagus in a
large bowl with frisee and dressing;
toss gently to combine. Top with
walnuts and cheese.
8 Serve veal with beetroot salad,
topped with bean sauce.

lemon dressing Using a zester or
small sharp knife, cut lemon rind
into long thin strips. Squeeze juice
from lemon; you need 2 tablespoons.
Place ingredients in a screw-top jar;
shake well.

white bean sauce Blend or process
ingredients until combined; season.
Transfer to a small saucepan over
medium heat; stir for 3 minutes or
until heated through.

I AM
PROTEIN RICH
HIGH IN VITAMINS A & C
LOW CARB

chicken tikka

WITH CAULIFLOWER RICE

PREP + COOK TIME **50 MINUTES** SERVES **4**

1 tablespoon peanut oil

800g (1½ pounds) chicken thigh
fillets, sliced thickly

1 medium brown onion (150g),
cut into wedges

1 large red capsicum (bell pepper)
(350g), chopped coarsely

250g (8 ounces) truss cherry
tomatoes

⅓ cup (100g) tikka curry paste

2 fresh long green chillies,
sliced thinly

300ml light cooking cream

1 small cauliflower (1kg),
stems finely chopped,
florets coarsely chopped

¾ cup loosely packed fresh
coriander (cilantro) leaves

RAITA

¾ cup (200g) greek-style yoghurt

1 lebanese cucumber (130g), seeded,
chopped finely

1 tablespoon finely chopped
fresh mint

1 Heat oil in a large deep frying
pan over medium-high heat; cook
chicken, in batches, until browned
all over. Remove from pan.

2 Add onion, capsicum and tomatoes
to same pan, reduce heat to medium;
cook, stirring, for 5 minutes or until
onion softens. Remove tomatoes
from pan; cover to keep warm. Add
paste and half the chilli to pan;
cook, stirring, for 2 minutes or until
fragrant. Return chicken to pan with
cooking cream; bring to the boil.
Reduce heat; simmer, uncovered,
for 10 minutes or until chicken is
cooked through. Remove from heat;
return tomatoes to mixture.

3 Meanwhile, process cauliflower
until finely chopped and it
resembles rice. Place cauliflower
in a large frying pan over medium
heat; cook, stirring occasionally,
for 10 minutes or until just tender.
Season to taste.

4 Make raita.

5 Top chicken with coriander
and remaining chilli. Serve with
cauliflower rice and raita.

raita Combine ingredients in a
small bowl; season.

*tip Cauliflower is an excellent
source of vitamin C, vitamin K,
B-group vitamins, folic acid and
pantothenic acid. It is a good
source of fibre, choline, biotin,
manganese and phosphorous.*

I AM
HIGH FIBRE
PROTEIN RICH
LOW CARB

jerk fish
WITH SLAW & AVOCADO CREAM

PREP + COOK TIME **40 MINUTES** SERVES **4**

800g (1½ pounds) firm white
    fish fillets
1½ tablespoons garlic powder
1½ teaspoons cayenne pepper
1 teaspoon ground cinnamon
1 teaspoon ground allspice
½ teaspoon dried thyme leaves
2 tablespoons olive oil
1 cup (280g) greek-style yoghurt
2 tablespoons harissa
2 radicchio (400g), leaves separated
lime wedges, to serve

SLAW

350g (11 ounces) white cabbage,
    shredded
2 cups loosely packed fresh
    coriander (cilantro) leaves
1 small red onion (100g), halved,
    sliced thinly
2 tablespoons sliced pickled
    jalapeño
¼ cup (60ml) freshly squeezed
    orange juice
1 clove garlic, crushed

AVOCADO CREAM

2 small avocados (400g), halved
⅓ cup (80g) sour cream
2 tablespoons lime juice

1 Cut fish fillets diagonally into
1.5cm (¾-inch) wide, 12cm (4¾-inch)
long strips. Combine garlic powder,
cayenne, cinnamon, allspice, thyme
and oil in a medium bowl; season.
Add fish; toss to coat well in mixture.
Cover; refrigerate until required.
2 Make slaw, then avocado cream.
3 Combine yoghurt and harissa in a
small bowl; season to taste.
4 Heat a large, non-stick frying
pan over high heat; cook fish, in
two batches, for 4 minutes or until
just cooked.
5 Fill radicchio leaves with slaw
and fish, top with avocado cream
and harissa yoghurt (drizzle with a
little extra harissa sauce if you like).
Serve with lime wedges.

slaw Place ingredients in a large
bowl; toss to combine. Season.

avocado cream Combine
ingredients in a small bowl;
season to taste.

*tips Fish can be prepared 4 hours
ahead to the end of step 1. Avocado
cream, harissa yoghurt and slaw
(without the orange juice) can also
be prepared 4 hours ahead; add juice
to slaw just before serving. Jerk is
both the name for a Jamaican dry or
wet spice seasoning, characterised
by allspice and chillies, and the
method of cooking over barbecue
coals. Traditionally the seasoning is
rubbed over chicken, pork and fish.*

I AM
LOW CARB
HIGH IN CALCIUM
GLUTEN-FREE

MUSHROOM, CAVOLO NERO &

quinoa risotto

PREP + COOK TIME **45 MINUTES** SERVES **4**

10g (½ ounce) dried porcini
   mushrooms
½ cup (125ml) boiling water
2 tablespoons olive oil
1 medium brown onion (150g),
   chopped finely
1 flat mushroom (80g),
   chopped coarsely
200g (6 ounces) swiss brown
   mushrooms, sliced thinly
2 cloves garlic, crushed
1 cup quinoa (200g), rinsed, drained
1.25 litres (5 cups) salt-reduced
   vegetable stock
1 sprig fresh thyme
100g (3 ounces) cavolo nero
   (tuscan cabbage), sliced thinly
120g (4 ounces) goat's cheese,
   crumbled
⅓ cup (25g) finely grated parmesan
4 free-range eggs

1 Place porcini mushrooms in a heatproof bowl with the boiling water. Stand for 5 minutes.
2 Meanwhile, heat oil in a medium frying pan over medium heat; cook onion, stirring, for 3 minutes or until soft. Add flat and swiss brown mushrooms; cook, stirring, for 3 minutes or until browned and tender. Add garlic; cook, stirring, for 1 minute or until fragrant.
3 Stir in quinoa, stock and thyme. Remove porcini mushrooms from water (reserve the soaking liquid); chop coarsely. Add porcini and soaking liquid to pan; bring to the boil. Simmer, uncovered, for 20 minutes until liquid is absorbed and quinoa is tender. Discard thyme. Add cavolo nero; stir until wilted. Remove pan from heat; stir in goat's cheese and half the parmesan.

4 Meanwhile, half-fill a large frying pan with water; bring to the boil. Break one egg into a cup, then slide into pan; repeat with remaining eggs. When all eggs are in pan, return water to the boil. Cover pan, turn off heat; stand for 4 minutes or until a light film of egg white sets over yolks. Remove eggs, one at a time, using a slotted spoon; place spoon on paper-towel-lined saucer to blot up any poaching liquid.
5 Serve risotto topped with eggs and remaining parmesan. Season with black pepper.

tip Cavolo nero is considered one of the most antioxidant-rich vegetables in the world.

I AM
GLUTEN-FREE
HGIH IN ANTIOXIDANTS
VITAMIN D RICH

chermoulla chicken

WITH PEA PUREE

PREP + COOK TIME **35 MINUTES** SERVES **4**

2 cloves garlic

2 shallots (50g)

1 fresh small red thai chilli

1 sprig fresh coriander (cilantro),
   stem and root attached

2 teaspoons ground cumin

1 teaspoon smoked paprika

1½ tablespoons extra virgin olive oil

8 x 125g (4-ounce) chicken
   thigh fillets

100g (3 ounces) snow pea tendrils

PEA PUREE

500g (1 pound) frozen baby peas,
   thawed

25g (¾ ounce) butter

¾ cup (180g) sour cream

1 Blend or process garlic, shallots, chilli, coriander, cumin, paprika and half the oil until almost smooth. Transfer mixture to a large bowl; add chicken, rub mixture all over chicken. Season.

2 Cook chicken on a heated, oiled grill plate (or grill or barbecue), until chicken is browned both sides and cooked through.

3 Meanwhile, make pea puree.

4 Serve chicken with pea puree and snow pea tendrils; drizzle with remaining oil, sprinkle with pepper.

pea puree Stir peas and butter in a medium saucepan, over medium heat, for 5 minutes or until peas are tender and butter is melted. Blend or process pea mixture with sour cream until smooth.

I AM
LOW CARB
PROTEIN RICH
HIGH FIBRE

Mussels have more iron than red meat! Shellfish is one of the best dietary sources of iodine, essential for brain development in children.

Bream, have a mild, sweet flavour and a moist, non-oily, flesh. The skin is also edible, so can be left on after cooking. A versatile fish, it lends itself to many different cooking methods, including poaching, pan-frying and barbecuing.

Whiting have a delicate, sweet flavour and medium-textured, flaky flesh. King George whiting (left) have dark spots on their side. School whiting (right) have a distinct silvery stripe running down the middle of their body.

Prawns (tiger, left and king, right) are highly perishable when raw (green) so are often frozen at sea when caught. If cooking, buy raw prawns, as cooked prawns will toughen if reheated.

fish

Fish, and other seafood, have been an important part of human diets since hunter-gatherer days. It is high in protein, is lean (with the exception of oily fish, and these have high levels of essential omega-3 fats), and is rich in many nutrients, including those often low in our diets, such as iodine.

Sardines are small, oily fish with fine, edible soft bones that are packed with calcium.

Red mullet, a species of goatfish, not mullet, is rich in omega-3 fatty acids, which have an anti-inflammatory effect in the body and are important for brain health.

PORK WITH BEETROOT MASH &

sprout salad

PREP + COOK TIME **45 MINUTES** SERVES **4**

500g (1 pound) baby beetroot (beet), trimmed, chopped coarsely

1 small kumara (orange sweet potato) (250g), chopped coarsely

1 tablespoon olive oil

4 pork mid-loin chops (1.2kg)

1 cup (250ml) pouring cream

100g (3 ounces) gorgonzola cheese

300g (9½ ounces) brussels sprouts, trimmed, shredded

50g (1½ ounces) small red-veined sorrel leaves

¼ cup (35g) hazelnuts, roasted, chopped coarsely

MUSTARD DRESSING

1 tablespoons wholegrain mustard

1 tablespoon extra virgin olive oil

2 teaspoons lemon juice

1 Boil, steam or microwave beetroot and kumara, separately, until tender; drain. Place beetroot and kumara in a large bowl; mash to combine. Season to taste.

2 Meanwhile, heat oil in a large frying pan over high heat; cook pork for 5 minutes each side or until cooked through. Remove from pan; cover to keep warm.

3 Discard oil from frying pan, add cream and cheese; cook, stirring, over medium heat until smooth. Bring to the boil. Reduce heat; simmer for 2 minutes or until sauce thickens.

4 Meanwhile, make mustard dressing.

5 Place brussels sprouts, sorrel and hazelnuts in a medium bowl with dressing; toss gently to combine.

6 Serve pork with mash and salad, drizzled with sauce.

mustard dressing Whisk ingredients in a small bowl to combine; season to taste.

I AM
PROTEIN RICH
HIGH IN FOLATE
HIGH IN IRON

honey soy pork

WITH PINK GRAPEFRUIT & SNOW PEA SALAD

PREP + COOK TIME **2 HOURS 45 MINUTES (+ REFRIGERATION)** SERVES **4**

2 cloves garlic, crushed

1 tablespoon olive oil

¼ cup (90g) honey

1 teaspoon finely grated fresh ginger

2 tablespoons soy sauce

2 tablespoons lime juice

800g (1½-pound) trimmed pork neck

**PINK GRAPEFRUIT &
SNOW PEA SALAD**

1 medium pink grapefruit (425g)

100g (3 ounces) snow peas, trimmed

⅓ cup (80ml) extra virgin olive oil

1 teaspoon finely grated lime rind

200g (6½ ounces) baby
   spinach leaves

6 green onions (scallions),
   sliced thinly

⅓ cup (40g) roasted unsalted
   cashews

1 Combine garlic, oil, honey, ginger, soy sauce and juice in a large bowl; add pork, turn to coat in marinade. Cover; refrigerate 3 hours or overnight, turning pork occasionally in marinade.

2 Preheat oven to 180°C/350°F.

3 Remove pork from marinade; reserve marinade. Wrap pork in three layers of foil, securing ends tightly; place in a baking dish. Bake for 2 hours 20 minutes or until cooked. Stand for 10 minutes. Shred meat coarsely; cover to keep warm in cooking juices.

4 Make pink grapefruit and snow pea salad.

5 Serve salad topped with pork.

pink grapefruit & snow pea salad
Segment grapefruit, by cutting off the rind along with the white pith. Cut between membranes, over a small bowl to catch any juice, releasing segments; you need ¼ cup (60ml) juice, reserve. Boil, steam or microwave snow peas until tender; refresh in iced water. Drain. Place reserved juice, oil and rind in a screw-top jar; shake well. Season to taste. Place grapefruit segments and snow peas in a large bowl with spinach, green onion and cashews; drizzle with dressing.

I AM
LOW CARB
HIGH IN VITAMIN C
PROTEIN RICH

herb-crusted salmon

WITH PICKLED VEG

PREP + COOK TIME **35 MINUTES (+ REFRIGERATION)** SERVES **8**

You will need to make the pickled veg a day ahead. You can also cook the salmon a day ahead, if you like.

2 tablespoons olive oil

1.3kg (2¾-pound) salmon fillet, skinned, pin-boned

¼ cup each finely chopped fresh dill, chervil, mint and chives

2 cups (50g) watercress sprigs

PICKLED VEG

2 cups (500ml) white wine vinegar

3 cups (750ml) water

2 tablespoons sea salt

¼ cup (50g) norbu (monk fruit sugar)

1 tablespoon pink peppercorns

4 bay leaves

½ cup fresh dill sprigs

3 fresh long red chillies, halved

170g (5½ ounces) asparagus, trimmed, halved

400g (12½ ounces) baby rainbow carrots, trimmed, scrubbed, halved lengthways

8 small radishes (120g), halved

250g (8 ounces) baby cucumbers, halved lengthways

HORSERADISH YOGHURT

1½ cups (420g) greek-style yoghurt

⅓ cup (90g) horseradish cream

1½ tablespoons finely chopped fresh dill

1 Make pickled veg.

2 Preheat oven to 180°C/350°F. Line a large oven tray with baking paper; drizzle with half the oil, season. Position salmon on tray to fit; rub with remaining oil, season.

3 Combine herbs in a small bowl; press onto salmon to thickly coat. Bake for 15 minutes for medium-rare or until cooked to your liking.

4 Meanwhile, make horseradish yoghurt.

5 Serve salmon with pickled veg, watercress and horseradish yoghurt.

pickled veg Place vinegar and the water in a deep glass or ceramic rectangular dish; stir in salt and norbu until dissolved. Add remaining ingredients, ensuring vegetables are completely covered (add extra water if necessary). Cover; refrigerate overnight.

horseradish yoghurt Whisk ingredients in a small bowl. Season. Refrigerate until required.

tips The pickled veg can be made up to 1 week ahead. Store in an airtight container in the fridge. You can use black peppercorns instead of pink, ocean trout instead of salmon and any combination of soft-leaf herbs you prefer including flat-leaf parsley and tarragon.

I AM
LOW CARB
RICH IN OMEGA-3
SUGAR-FREE

Bone broths

Hot broth is a great healthy alternative to tea or coffee. Broths can be made up to 3 days ahead, keep, covered, in the refrigerator, or frozen for up to 3 months.

FISH BROTH

PREP + COOK TIME **45 MINUTES**
(+ COOLING & REFRIGERATION) MAKES **2 LITRES (8 CUPS)**

Place 1.5kg (3lbs) fish bones, 3 litres (12 cups) water, 1 coarsely chopped onion, 2 coarsely chopped trimmed celery stalks, 6 stalks fresh flat-leaf parsley and 1 teaspoon black peppercorns in a large saucepan; bring to the boil. Reduce heat; simmer, uncovered, for 30 minutes. Strain stock through a muslin-lined sieve into a heatproof bowl; discard solids. Season with salt and 2 tablespoons lemon juice. Cool. Cover; refrigerate until cold. Skim and discard any surface fat before use.

CHICKEN BROTH

PREP + COOK TIME **6 HOURS 15 MINUTES**
(+ COOLING & REFRIGERATION) MAKES **3 LITRES (12 CUPS)**

Place 2kg (4lbs) chicken bones, 2 tablespoons cider vinegar, 2 coarsely chopped medium onions, 2 coarsely chopped trimmed celery stalks, 2 coarsely chopped medium carrots, 8 peeled cloves garlic, 6 stalks fresh flat-leaf parsley, 2 teaspoons black peppercorns and 5 litres (20 cups) water in a large saucepan; bring to the boil. Reduce heat; simmer, uncovered, for 6 hours, skimming the surface occasionally. Strain stock through a muslin-lined sieve into a heatproof bowl; discard solids. Season with sea salt. Cool. Cover; refrigerate until cold. Skim and discard surface fat before using.

BEEF BROTH

PREP + COOK TIME **9 HOURS 15 MINUTES** (+ COOLING & REFRIGERATION) MAKES **2 LITRES (8 CUPS)**

Preheat oven to 200°C/400°F. Roast 2kg (4lbs) beef bones on a large oven tray, uncovered, for 1 hour or until browned. Place bones in a large saucepan with 2 chopped unpeeled brown onions, 2 coarsely chopped trimmed celery stalks, 2 chopped carrots, 8 cloves peeled garlic, 2 tablespoons cider vinegar, 2 teaspoons black peppercorns and 5 litres (20 cups) water; bring to the boil. Reduce heat; simmer, uncovered, for 8 hours, skimming the surface occasionally. Strain stock through a muslin-lined sieve into a heatproof bowl; discard solids. Add extra water to make up 2 litres. Season with salt. Cool. Cover; refrigerate until cold. Skim and discard surface fat before using.

VEGETABLE BROTH

PREP + COOK TIME **2 HOURS 15 MINUTES** (+ COOLING & REFRIGERATION) MAKES **3 LITRES (12 CUPS)**

Place 4 coarsely chopped onions, 2 coarsely chopped large carrots, 8 coarsely chopped trimmed celery stalks, 2 coarsely chopped large parsnips, 8 peeled cloves garlic, 6 stalks fresh flat-leaf parsley, 2 teaspoons black peppercorns and 4 litres (16 cups) water in a large saucepan; bring to the boil. Reduce heat; simmer, uncovered, for 1½ hours. Add 200g (6½oz) coarsely chopped cup mushrooms and 4 coarsely chopped tomatoes; simmer, uncovered, for a further 30 minutes. Strain stock through a muslin-lined sieve into a heatproof bowl; discard solids. Season with salt. Cool. Cover; refrigerate until cold.

QUINOA CRUSTED
kale & fig tart

PREP + COOK TIME **1 HOUR 30 MINUTES (+ REFRIGERATION)** SERVES **6**

¾ cup (150g) tri-coloured quinoa, rinsed

1½ cups (120g) finely grated pecorino cheese

3 free-range eggs

1 teaspoon sea salt flakes

1 tablespoon olive oil

1 clove garlic, crushed

3 cups (70g) firmly packed coarsely chopped kale

¼ cup (60ml) water

1 tablespoon dijon mustard

¾ cup (180ml) pouring cream

10 medium figs (600g), torn in half

1 cup (40g) loosely packed rocket (arugula) leaves

¼ cup (35g) roasted hazelnuts, halved

YOGHURT DRESSING

⅓ cup (95g) greek-style yoghurt

1 teaspoon raw honey

2 teaspoons chopped fresh tarragon

½ clove garlic, crushed

1 Grease an 11cm x 35cm (4½-inch x 14-inch) rectangular loose-based tart tin.

2 Cook quinoa in a large saucepan of boiling water for 12 minutes or until tender; drain well. Cool.

3 Process quinoa and half the pecorino until quinoa is finely chopped. Add 1 egg and half the salt; process until mixture forms a coarse dough. Press mixture evenly over base and sides of tart tin. Refrigerate for 30 minutes or until firm.

4 Meanwhile, preheat oven to 200°C/400°F.

5 Bake tart shell for 30 minutes or until golden. Remove from oven; reduce temperature to 180°C/350°F.

6 Meanwhile, heat oil in a medium frying pan over medium heat; cook garlic for 30 seconds. Add kale; cook, stirring, for 30 seconds. Add the water; cook, covered, for 3 minutes. Remove from heat; stand, covered, for 1 minute. Cool; drain away any excess liquid.

7 Place kale mixture in a medium bowl with remaining eggs and salt, half the remaining pecorino, the mustard and cream; whisk to combine. Spread mixture evenly into tart shell; sprinkle with remaining pecorino.

8 Bake tart for 30 minutes or until filling is set. Place figs, cut-side up, on an oiled oven tray; bake alongside tart, for 30 minutes or until just soft.

9 Make yoghurt dressing.

10 Serve tart topped with figs, rocket and hazelnuts; drizzle with dressing.

yoghurt dressing Combine ingredients in a small bowl; season to taste.

I AM
GLUTEN-FREE
RICH IN CALCIUM
VEGETARIAN

ROASTED RHUBARB &
balsamic popsicles

PREP + COOK TIME **25 MINUTES (+ STANDING & FREEZING)** MAKES **6**

You need a six-hole ½-cup ice-block mould and six ice-block sticks for this recipe.

6 trimmed stalks rhubarb (330g), cut into 8cm (3¼-inch) lengths

1 vanilla bean, split lengthways, seeds scraped

1 tablespoon balsamic glaze

1 tablespoon raw honey or pure maple syrup

400ml coconut milk

¼ cup (90g) raw honey or pure maple syrup, extra

½ cup (80g) natural sliced almonds, chopped coarsely

CHOCOLATE COATING

½ cup (100g) virgin coconut oil

2 tablespoons cocoa powder

1 teaspoon vanilla extract

2 teaspoons raw honey or pure maple syrup

1 Preheat oven to 200°C/400°F. Line an oven tray with baking paper.

2 Place rhubarb, vanilla seeds and pod on oven tray; drizzle with balsamic glaze and honey. Roast for 15 minutes or until tender; stand until cool. Discard vanilla pod.

3 Process or blend rhubarb mixture with coconut milk and extra honey until smooth. Pour into ice-block mould. Cover mould with a double layer of plastic wrap (this will help keep the ice-block sticks upright). Pierce plastic with a small knife, then push an ice-block stick into each hole. Freeze for 4 hours or until frozen.

4 When you're ready to coat the popsicles, make chocolate coating.

5 Line an oven tray with baking paper; place in the freezer. Pour chocolate coating into a small, deep bowl. Place almonds in another small bowl. Dip popsicle mould very briefly in boiling water; remove popsicles. Dip the popsicles halfway into the chocolate coating, then dip into nuts. Place on chilled tray. Freeze for 5 minutes or until coating is set.

chocolate coating Stir ingredients in a small saucepan over low heat until oil is melted and mixture is combined. Remove from heat; stand at room temperature until cool.

tips If the chocolate coating mixture thickens too much while dipping the popsicles, place it in a microwave-safe bowl and microwave on MEDIUM (50%) for 10 seconds. Don't worry if the chocolate coating has a slight whitish look to it, this is simply the coconut oil and won't affect the taste.

I AM
SUGAR-FREE
HIGH IN VITAMIN C
DAIRY-FREE

banana & walnut cake

WITH CARAMEL SAUCE

PREP + COOK TIME **1 HOUR 45 MINUTES** SERVES **12**

185g (6 ounces) butter, softened, chopped

1 cup (245g) stevia

3 free-range eggs

2¼ cups (335g) self-raising flour

¼ teaspoon salt

¾ teaspoon bicarbonate of soda (baking soda)

1½ teaspoons ground cinnamon

2 cups (525g) mashed ripe banana

2 teaspoons vanilla extract

¾ cup (200g) sour cream

1 cup (100g) walnut halves, roasted, chopped

¼ cup (60ml) boiling water

3 teaspoons espresso coffee granules

CARAMEL SAUCE

⅔ cup (200g) rice malt syrup

125g (4 ounces) butter, softened, chopped

⅓ cup (80ml) thickened cream

1 Preheat oven to 180°C/350°F. Grease and line a deep 22cm (9-inch) round cake pan with baking paper.

2 Beat butter and stevia in a small bowl with an electric mixer until pale and fluffy. Beat in eggs, one at a time, until just combined. Transfer mixture to a large bowl. Stir sifted dry ingredients, banana, extract, sour cream, nuts and combined water and coffee into butter mixture. Spread mixture into pan.

3 Bake cake for 1¼ hours or until a skewer inserted into the centre comes out clean. Stand cake in pan for 5 minutes before turning, top-side up, onto a wire rack to cool.

4 Meanwhile, make caramel sauce; accompany cake with caramel sauce.

caramel sauce Place syrup in a small saucepan over medium heat, bring to the boil; boil for 12 minutes or until slightly dark golden in colour and the surface is covered with bubbles. Immediately add butter and cream; stir until smooth.

tips You will need approximately 4½ bananas to make 2 cups mashed banana. The cake can be made a day ahead; store in an airtight container at room temperature in a cool place.

I AM
VEGETARIAN
HIGH IN POTASSIUM
SUGAR-FREE

COCONUT & BERRY
chia pudding

PREP TIME **15 MINUTES (+ REFRIGERATION)** SERVES **6**

2½ cups (625ml) coconut milk

⅓ cup (55g) white chia seeds

1 teaspoon vanilla extract

2 tablespoons raw honey or
    pure maple syrup

1 medium banana (200g),
    chopped coarsely

1 tablespoon finely grated
    orange rind

3 cups (300g) mixed berries
    (see tips)

micro mint or small mint leaves,
    to serve

1 Place coconut milk, seeds, extract and honey in a large bowl. Cover; refrigerate for 1 hour or overnight until thick.

2 Blend or process coconut milk mixture with banana, rind and 2 cups of the berries. Spoon into six ¾-cup (180ml) serving glasses; refrigerate for 30 minutes or until pudding has thickened.

3 Serve puddings topped with remaining berries and mint.

tips Use whatever combination of berries you like, including cherries. If you have one, use a Thermomix or Vitamix to achieve a very smooth pudding consistency. Puddings can be made a day ahead; store, covered, in the fridge. Top with extra berries just before serving.

I AM
VEGAN
SUGAR-FREE
PALEO

DARK CHOCOLATE &

ricotta mousse

PREP + COOK TIME **20 MINUTES** SERVES **6**

Unlike most chocolate mousse recipes, this one can be served the minute it is made. If you do wish to make it a day ahead, refrigerate, covered, then bring to room temperature before serving. You could also top each serving with cherries.

⅓ cup (110g) rice malt syrup

1 tablespoon dutch-processed cocoa

2 tablespoons water

½ teaspoon vanilla extract

200g (6½ ounces) dark chocolate (70% cocoa), chopped

8 fresh dates (160g), pitted

½ cup (125ml) milk

2 cups (480g) ricotta

2 tablespoons pomegranate seeds

2 tablespoons chopped pistachios

1 Stir syrup, cocoa, the water and extract in a small saucepan over medium heat; bring to the boil. Remove from heat; cool.

2 Place chocolate in a small heatproof bowl over a small saucepan of simmering water (don't let the water touch the base of the bowl); stir until melted and smooth.

3 Process dates and milk until dates are finely chopped. Add ricotta; process until smooth. Add melted chocolate; process until well combined.

4 Spoon mousse into six ¾ cup (180ml) serving glasses. Spoon cocoa syrup on mousse; top with pomegranate seeds and nuts.

tips Fresh pomegranate seeds can sometimes be found in the fridge section of supermarkets or good green grocers. If unavailable, cut a whole pomegranate in half and scrape the seeds from flesh with your fingers while holding the pomegranate upside down in a bowl of cold water; the seeds will sink and the white pith will float. Pomegranate seeds will keep refrigerated for up to a week.

I AM
EGG-FREE
CALCIUM RICH
SUGAR-FREE

BLUEBERRY POPPY

seed crepes

PREP + COOK TIME **15 MINUTES** SERVES **4**

½ cup (120g) mascarpone

125g (4 ounces) blueberries

2 teaspoons finely grated
   orange rind

½ cup (75g) wholemeal spelt flour

2 teaspoons poppy seeds

1 free-range egg

⅔ cup (160ml) milk

2 teaspoons rice malt syrup

1 teaspoon vanilla extract

cooking oil spray

2 tablespoons rice malt syrup, extra

1 Place mascarpone, ⅓ cup of the blueberries and rind in a medium bowl; mash with a fork to combine.

2 Whisk flour, poppy seeds, egg, milk, syrup and extract in a small bowl.

3 Lightly spray a crêpe pan or heavy-based small frying pan with oil. Heat pan over medium heat; pour a scant ¼ cup of the batter into pan; swirl pan to coat base evenly. Cook crêpe for 2 minutes or until browned underneath. Turn, cook for a further 1 minute or until browned. Repeat with remaining crêpe batter to make a total of four crêpes.

4 Spread each crêpe with a slightly rounded tablespoon of mascarpone mixture; fold into triangles to enclose. Serve crêpes topped with remaining blueberries; drizzle with extra syrup. Sprinkle with strips of orange rind, if you like.

I AM
CALCIUM RICH
HIGH IN FOLATE
VITAMIN C RICH

EARL GREY & CHOCOLATE
vegan cheesecake

PREP + COOK TIME **20 MINUTES (+ STANDING & REFRIGERATION)** SERVES **10**

You need to start this recipe the day before serving. This vegan cheesecake is based on nuts, which provide a wonderful, natural richness and flavour. When figs are not in season, serve this cheesecake topped with fresh raspberries and flaked almonds.

4 cups (600g) raw unsalted cashews

8 earl grey tea bags

¼ cup (25g) cacao powder

1 cup (230g) fresh dates, pitted

1 cup (200g) virgin coconut oil

2 teaspoons vanilla extract

8 small figs (400g), torn in half

2 teaspoons cacao powder, extra

CHEESECAKE BASE

1 cup (170g) activated buckinis
 (buckwheat groats)

½ cup (80g) natural almonds

⅓ cup (35g) cacao powder

1 cup (230g) fresh dates, pitted

¼ cup (50g) virgin coconut oil

2 tablespoons warm water

1 teaspoon vanilla extract

1 Place cashews and tea bags in a large bowl, cover with cold water; stand for 24 hours.

2 Grease a 22cm (9-inch) (base measure) springform pan; line with baking paper.

3 Make cheesecake base. Using the back of a spoon, spread mixture evenly onto base of pan. Refrigerate for 15 minutes or until firm.

4 Drain cashews and tea bags, reserving ½ cup of the soaking liquid. Place cashews in the bowl of a food processor; empty tea leaves from tea bags onto cashews. Add reserved soaking liquid, cacao, dates, oil and extract; process until mixture is as smooth as possible. Spread filling mixture over chilled base. Refrigerate for at least 4 hours or until firm.

5 Before serving, top cheesecake with figs and dust with extra cacao.

cheesecake base Process buckinis, nuts and cacao powder until finely ground. With the motor operating, add dates, oil, the water and extract; process until well combined and the mixture sticks together when pressed.

tips Activated buckinis are buckwheat groats that have been soaked, washed, rinsed and dehydrated. The process is said to aid digestion. If you have one, use a high-speed blender such as a Vitamix when making the filling, to make the mixture very smooth. Use a hot, dry knife to slice the cheesecake cleanly.

I AM
VEGAN
HIGH IN VITAMIN E
PROTEIN RICH

CHAMOMILE & BUTTERMILK

panna cotta

PREP + COOK TIME **30 MINUTES (+ REFRIGERATION)** SERVES **4**

To unmould panna cotta, rub the outside of the mould with a hot kitchen cloth. Hold the mould upside down in your cupped hand, then shake it gently until panna cotta releases from the mould; carefully transfer to a serving plate.

1 cup (250ml) milk
¼ cup (50g) norbu (monk fruit sugar)
8 chamomile tea bags
2 teaspoons powdered gelatine
2 tablespoons water
1 cup (250m) buttermilk
1 medium lemon (140g), sliced thinly
¼ cup (90g) honey, warmed
1 tablespoon lemon juice
2 tablespoons almonds, toasted,
   chopped coarsely

1 Place milk, norbu and tea bags in a medium saucepan over low heat, stirring, for 2 minutes or until sugar dissolves and mixture comes almost to the boil. Remove from heat. Press tea bags against the side of the pan to extract flavour, add back to the mixture; stand for 10 minutes. Strain mixture; discard tea bags.
2 Sprinkle gelatine over the water in a small heatproof jug; stand jug in a small saucepan of simmering water. Stir mixture until gelatine dissolves; cool for 5 minutes. Add gelatine mixture and buttermilk to milk mixture; stir until combined.
3 Rinse four ⅔ cup (160ml) moulds with cold water, do not dry; place on an oven tray. Pour panna cotta mixture into moulds. Refrigerate 6 hours or overnight until set.
4 Preheat oven to 220°C/425°F. Grease a large oven tray; line with baking paper.

5 Place lemon slices, in a single layer, on tray; drizzle with honey and juice. Roast for 10 minutes, turning over halfway through cooking and basting occasionally with juices on tray until caramelised.
6 Serve panna cotta topped with lemon slices, almonds and any juices on the oven tray.

tip You can use other types of tea in this recipe such as peppermint or earl grey, if you like.

I AM
EGG-FREE
HIGH IN CALCIUM
LOW FAT

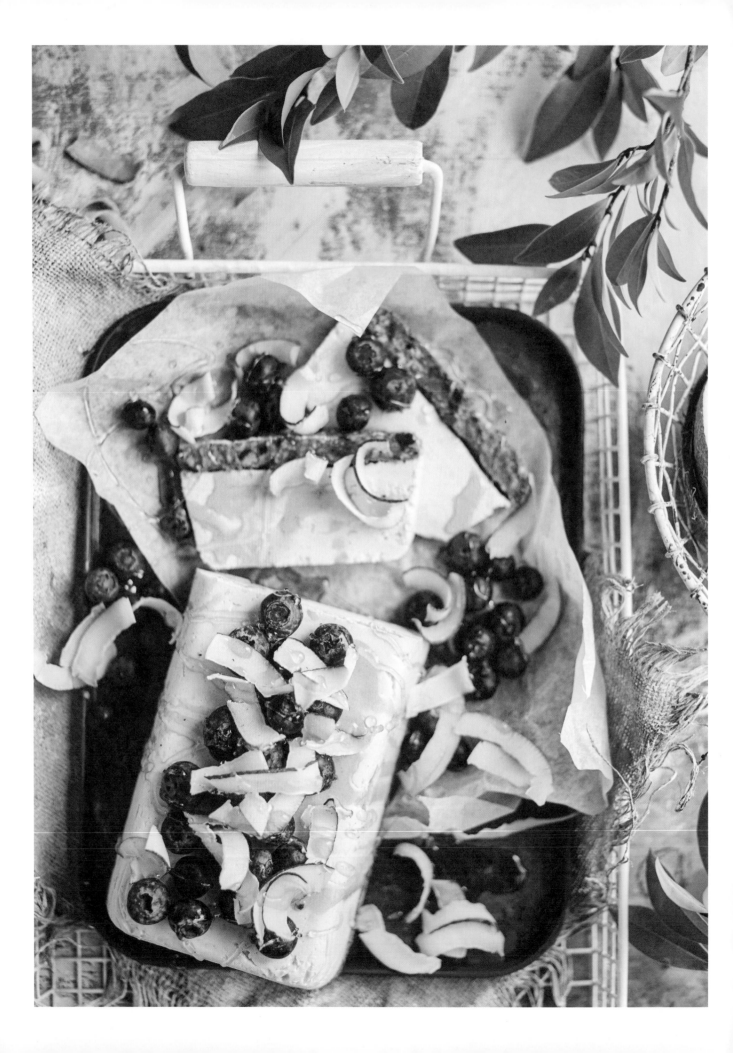

COCONUT & CHOC NUT

frozen terrine

PREP + COOK TIME **30 MINUTES (+ SOAKING & FREEZING)** SERVES **8**

Sugar-free chocolate is available from health food stores and pharmacies. Use lime instead of lemon. This terrine can be made 2 weeks ahead.

2½ cups (375g) raw cashews

1 cup (80g) desiccated coconut

½ cup (120g) virgin coconut oil,
    at room temperature

1 tablespoon finely grated lemon rind

½ cup (125ml) lemon juice

⅓ cup (80ml) pure maple syrup

1 cup (120g) pecans

⅓ cup (35g) ground hazelnuts

¼ cup (60g) virgin coconut oil, extra

50g (1½ ounces) sugar-free dark
    chocolate, chopped coarsely

125g (4 ounces) blueberries

½ cup (25g) flaked coconut, toasted

2 tablespoon pure maple syrup, extra

1 Soak cashews in cold water for 3 hours. Drain.

2 Grease and line the base and sides of a 9cm x 19.5cm (3¾-inch x 8-inch) loaf pan with baking paper, extending the paper 5cm (2 inches) above the edge.

3 Process drained cashews with desiccated coconut, coconut oil, rind, juice and maple syrup until smooth. Spoon cashew mixture into pan, pushing the mixture into the corners; smooth the surface. Freeze for 2 hours or until set.

4 Place pecans, ground hazelnuts, extra coconut oil, chocolate and half the extra maple syrup in the food processor; process until mixture is finely chopped.

5 Spread pecan mixture on cashew mixture to completely cover. Return to freezer for 1 hour or until firm.

6 Remove from freezer; stand at room temperature for 10 minutes before inverting onto a serving plate. Serve topped with blueberries and flaked coconut, drizzled with remaining extra maple syrup.

I AM
VEGAN
SUGAR-FREE
RAW

COCONUT RED RICE PUDDING
with papaya & lime

PREP + COOK TIME **50 MINUTES** SERVES **4**

This pudding would also be delicious served with sliced mango instead of papaya.

I AM
DAIRY-FREE
HIGH IN VITAMIN C
VEGAN

¾ cup (150g) red rice, rinsed

2 cups (500ml) coconut milk

¼ cup (70g) grated palm sugar

2 tablespoons coconut cream

½ medium papaya (500g), sliced

½ cup (25g) flaked coconut, toasted

1 lime, cut into cheeks

1 Cook rice in a small saucepan of boiling water for 30 minutes or until almost tender; drain.

2 Return rice to pan with coconut milk and sugar; bring to the boil. Cook, stirring occasionally, for 15 minutes or until rice is tender and liquid has thickened slightly.

3 Spoon rice into serving bowls, top with coconut cream, papaya and flaked coconut. Serve pudding with lime cheeks.

GINGER, PEAR &
pistachio crumbles

PREP + COOK TIME **1 HOUR 30 MINUTES** SERVES **6**

6 medium firm pears (1.4kg), peeled, chopped coarsely

125g (4 ounces) fresh or frozen raspberries

1 tablespoon finely grated fresh ginger

2 tablespoons cornflour (cornstarch) or arrowroot

¼ cup (60ml) pure maple syrup

1 tablespoon lemon juice

1 teaspoon vanilla extract

1 cup (140g) pistachios

1 cup (120g) pecans

1 cup (90g) rolled oats

¼ cup (60ml) olive oil

¼ cup (60ml) pure maple syrup, extra

1 teaspoon vanilla extract, extra

2 tablespoons freeze-dried or fresh pomegranate seeds (see tips)

2 cups (560g) coconut yoghurt

1 Preheat oven to 160°C/325°F.

2 Place pears, raspberries, ginger, cornflour, syrup, juice and extract in a large bowl; toss to coat fruit in mixture. Divide mixture among six 1-cup (250ml) ovenproof dishes.

3 Process nuts until chopped roughly. Transfer to a medium bowl, stir in oats, oil and extra syrup and extract; spoon over fruit mixture.

4 Bake, uncovered, for 1 hour. Cover with foil; bake a further 15 minutes or until crumble topping is golden and pears are soft.

5 To serve, sprinkle pomegranate seeds over the top and accompany with yoghurt.

tips *Freeze dried pomegranate seeds are available from health food stores or substitute with unsweetened cranberries for extra antioxidants.*

I AM
VEGAN
HIGH IN FIBRE
SUGAR-FREE

PINEAPPLE & COCONUT

granita

PREP + COOK TIME **40 MINUTES (+ COOLING & FREEZING)** SERVES **4**

1 stick fresh lemon grass, white part
   only, bruised
½ cup (135g) coarsely grated
   palm sugar
⅔ cup (160ml) water
½ small pineapple (600g), peeled,
   chopped coarsely
2 teaspoons finely grated lime rind
2 tablespoons lime juice
¾ cup (200g) greek-style yoghurt
½ medium papaya (500g), peeled,
   sliced thickly
½ small rockmelon (650g), peeled,
   sliced thickly
¼ cup small fresh mint leaves

1 Place lemon grass, sugar and the water in a medium saucepan; cook, stirring, over low heat until sugar dissolves. Bring to the boil; remove from heat. Pour syrup into a large heatproof jug or bowl; cool.
2 Meanwhile, blend or process pineapple until smooth; you will need 1½ cups pulp. Whisk pineapple, rind, juice and yoghurt into cooled syrup. Pour pineapple mixture into a 20cm x 30cm (8-inch x 12-inch) (base measurement) metal slice pan. Freeze for 3 hours or until just beginning to freeze. Using a fork, scrape the mixture to break up ice crystals. Cover; freeze for 4 hours, scraping the mixture every hour, or until completely frozen.
3 Serve granita with papaya, rockmelon and mint.

tip Use vanilla-flavoured yoghurt instead of greek-style yoghurt, if you like.

I AM
VITAMIN RICH
HIGH IN FOLATE
LOW FAT

SQUASHED PLUM & RICOTTA

sandwiches

PREP + COOK TIME **15 MINUTES** SERVES **4**

2 tablespoons melted virgin
    coconut oil

2 teaspoons sugar-free icing mix
    (see tip)

1 teaspoon ground ginger

4 medium blood plums (340g),
    halved, stones removed

1 tablespoon pure maple syrup

8 x 2cm (¾-inch) slices
    sourdough bread

1 cup (240g) firm ricotta

1 Preheat a sandwich press. Brush press with half the coconut oil.

2 Combine icing mix and ginger in a small bowl.

3 Place plums, cut-side down, in the sandwich press. Cook, pressing down on the lid occasionally, for 6 minutes or until plums are tender and browned. Remove plums; wipe sandwich press clean.

4 Meanwhile, combine maple syrup and remaining coconut oil in a small bowl. Brush oil mixture over one side of each piece of bread.

5 Place four slices of bread, oiled-side down, on a board; spread with ricotta and top with plums. Top with remaining bread slices, oiled-side up. Cook in sandwich press, in two batches, for 3 minutes or until golden and heated through. Serve dusted with ginger mixture.

tip We used Natvia icing mix made from stevia. It is available in the baking aisle of most supermarkets.

I AM
SUGAR-FREE
HIGH IN VITAMIN C
EGG-FREE

PEACH & PISTACHIO
cake pots

PREP + COOK TIME **45 MINUTES** MAKES **12**

4 small peaches (460g), halved

1 cup (280g) greek-style yoghurt

2 medium apples (300g),
    grated coarsely

2 free-range eggs, beaten lightly

¼ cup (60ml) milk

2 tablespoons raw honey

2 cups (240g) ground almonds

2 teaspoons baking powder

⅓ cup (45g) pistachios,
    chopped coarsely

1½ tablespoons raw honey, extra

1 Preheat oven to 180°C/350°F. Cut 12 x 12cm (4-inch) squares from baking paper; line twelve ⅓ cup (80ml) ovenproof pots with paper squares (see tips).

2 Thinly slice three of the peaches. Coarsely chop remaining peach; blend or process to a coarse puree. Fold peach puree through yoghurt in a small bowl; cover and refrigerate until required.

3 Place apple, egg, milk, honey, ground almonds and baking powder in a large bowl; mix until just combined. Spoon mixture into pots; push peach slices 2cm (¾-inch) into the top of the batter.

4 Bake for 30 minutes or until a skewer inserted in the centre comes out clean.

5 Top cakes with pistachios; drizzle with extra honey. Serve warm with peach yoghurt.

tips We used peat seedling pots available from hardware stores and garden nurseries. You can also cook the cakes in a 12-hole (⅓ cup/80ml) muffin pan, lined with baking paper squares. This recipe is best made on day of serving.

I AM
GLUTEN-FREE
ANTIOXIDANT RICH
SUGAR-FREE

WITH MACADAMIA MILK ICE-CREAM

PREP + COOK TIME **30 MINUTES (+ REFRIGERATION & FREEZING)** SERVES **6**

You will need an ice-cream machine for this recipe.

3¼ cups (810ml) macadamia milk

1 cup (220g) maple sugar

2 teaspoons vanilla bean paste

100g (3 ounces) sugar-free dairy-free milk chocolate, chopped coarsely

1 teaspoon virgin coconut oil

2 tablespoons macadamias, roasted, chopped coarsely

CHOC FUDGE

2 cups (320g) blanched almonds

2 cups (160g) desiccated coconut

200g (6½ ounces) pitted medjool dates, chopped coarsely

½ cup (50g) cocoa powder

2 teaspoons salt flakes

¼ cup (60ml) pure maple syrup

50g (1½ ounces) cocoa butter, melted

1 Stir macadamia milk and maple sugar in a medium saucepan over medium heat for 2 minutes or until sugar dissolves. Stir in paste. Transfer to a heatproof bowl. Refrigerate until cold.

2 Pour chilled ice-cream mixture into an ice-cream machine. Churn, following manufacturer's instructions. Transfer to freezer.

3 Meanwhile, make choc fudge. Cut fudge into 2.5cm x 10cm (1-inch x 4-inch) pieces.

4 Place chocolate and coconut oil in a microwave-safe bowl. Microwave on HIGH (100%) in 30-second bursts until melted and smooth.

5 Serve scoops of ice-cream with fudge, drizzled with chocolate and sprinkled with macadamias.

choc fudge Grease and line a 20cm (8-inch) square cake pan with baking paper. Process almonds until finely ground. Add coconut and dates, process until mixture forms a soft paste. Add cocoa, salt, maple syrup and cocoa butter; process until smooth. Press mixture into pan. Refrigerate until firm.

tip Ice-cream and fudge can be made up to 1 week ahead.

I AM
GLUTEN-FREE
HIGH IN VITAMIN E
DAIRY-FREE

baked ricotta puddings

WITH ORANGE & DATE SALAD

PREP + COOK TIME **1 HOUR (+ COOLING & REFRIGERATION)** SERVES **4**

1 medium orange (240g)

1 medium blood orange (240g)

600g (1¼ pounds) ricotta

3 free-range eggs

⅓ cup (80ml) pure maple syrup

½ teaspoon ground cinnamon

4 fresh dates (80g), pitted, torn

2 tablespoons pine nuts, toasted

thyme sprigs, to serve

ORANGE SYRUP

½ cup (125ml) freshly squeezed
orange juice

2 tablespoons pure maple syrup

1 cinnamon stick

½ teaspoon fresh thyme leaves

1 Preheat oven to 180°C/350°F. Grease four ¾ cup (180ml), 10cm (4-inch) ovenproof dishes.

2 Finely grate rind from orange; you need 2 teaspoons. Cut the top and bottom from orange and blood orange; cut off the white pith, following the curve of the fruit. Holding the orange, cut down both sides of the white membrane to release each segment. Cut blood orange into thick slices. Set aside.

3 Process ricotta, eggs, syrup, cinnamon and rind until smooth. Pour mixture evenly into dishes.

4 Bake puddings for 20 minutes or until centre is just firm to touch. Cool to room temperature. Refrigerate for at least 1 hour or until cold.

5 Meanwhile, make orange syrup.

6 Serve puddings topped with orange segments, dates, syrup, pine nuts and thyme.

orange syrup Bring ingredients to the boil in a small saucepan. Reduce heat to low; simmer for 10 minutes or until syrupy. Refrigerate for 1 hour or until cold. Remove cinnamon stick.

I AM
PROTEIN RICH
HIGH IN CALCIUM
VITAMIN A RICH

UPSIDE DOWN GRAPE &
honey cake

PREP + COOK TIME **1 HOUR 30 MINUTES (+ STANDING)** SERVES **8**

8cm (3¼-inch) rosemary sprig

250g (8 ounces) small red seedless grapes, halved

½ cup (180g) honey

4 free-range eggs

½ cup (125ml) extra virgin olive oil

⅓ cup (95g) greek-style yoghurt

1 teaspoon finely grated lemon rind

1 cup (150g) plain (all-purpose) flour

⅔ cup (100g) plain (all-purpose) wholemeal flour

2 teaspoons baking powder

1 cup (280g) greek-style yoghurt, extra

RED WINE VINEGAR SYRUP

½ cup (125ml) red wine vinegar

¾ cup (270g) honey

1 Preheat oven to 140°C/280°F fan-forced. Grease and line base and side of a 22cm (8¾-inch) round cake pan, extending the paper 5cm (2 inches) above the edge.

2 Make red wine vinegar syrup; pour into pan to cover the base. Cool 5 minutes.

3 Place rosemary sprig in the centre of the syrup. Taking care as the syrup will still be hot, arrange grape halves snugly, cut-side up, in concentric circles starting from the outside of the pan, until syrup is covered.

4 Beat honey and eggs in a large bowl with an electric mixer on high speed for 8 minutes or until almost tripled in volume. With the motor operating, gradually add oil, then yoghurt and rind, beating briefly just to combine.

5 Sift flours and baking powder over egg mixture, return husks to bowl. Using a balloon whisk, gently stir dry mixture into egg mixture, taking care not to deflate the mixture. Pour mixture into pan; level surface.

6 Bake cake, on the lowest shelf, for 1 hour 10 minutes or until a skewer inserted into the centre comes out clean. Stand in pan for 15 minutes.

7 Cut back the paper collar, then using a tea towel or oven mitts, invert the hot cake onto a serving plate. Cool completely. Serve cake with extra yoghurt.

red wine vinegar syrup Bring ingredients to the boil in a medium saucepan over medium heat, stirring, until well combined. Boil rapidly for 5 minutes or until syrupy and reduced to ½ cup (125ml).

tip This cake is best made on day of serving.

I AM
SUGAR-FREE
ANTIOXIDANT RICH
LOW FAT

Cacao nibs can be separated into cocoa butter and powder. Cocoa powder retains many beneficial antioxidants and is an easy way of adding cocoa into your diet without the kilojoules of chocolate.

Dutch-processed cacao powder is treated with an alkali to neutralize its acidity; it is darker and more mellow in taste.

Raw dark chocolate is made using cold-pressed raw cacao beans, that is, without the use of heat. It is high in antioxidants, and has good levels of chromium, iron and magnesium, which support healthy heart function.

Cacao (cocoa) butter is rich in saturated fats; about a third is stearic acid, but this acts differently to other saturated fats in that it doesn't raise cholesterol and, in fact, lowers LDL (bad) cholesterol. So this makes it a pretty healthy fat overall.

cacao

Mmmmmm, chocolate. We love it, crave it when we're feeling down, hide it for a special treat, think twice about sharing it... before we actually do. It's good to know then, that cocoa consumption has been associated with a number of health benefits.

Raw cacao powder is made by removing the cocoa butter using a process known as cold-pressing. It retains more of its nutrients than heat-processed cacao powder; it also has a stronger, slightly bitter, taste.

Cacao beans are contained inside the large cacao pod. The beans are used to make cocoa butter, cocoa powder, cocoa solids and ultimately chocolate.

PURE GOODNESS

fruit stacks

PREP TIME **30 MINUTES (+ REFRIGERATION)** MAKES **6**

Keep the unused coconut liquid from the cans of coconut cream for another use. Assemble fruit stacks on the day of serving. You will need to refrigerate the cans of coconut cream overnight first before you can continue with the recipe.

1 medium rockmelon (1.7kg), halved
    crossways, peeled, seeded
1 medium honeydew (1.5kg), halved
    crossways, peeled, seeded
½ whole seedless watermelon
    (2.25kg), rind removed
1 medium figs (60g), cut into
    six wedges
1 finger lime (60g), halved
    lengthways, pulp reserved
¼ cup (30g) finely chopped pistachios

WHIPPED COCONUT CREAM
2 x 400ml cans coconut cream

1 Make whipped coconut cream.
2 Cut rockmelon, honeydew and watermelon crossways into 4cm (1½-inch) thick slices. Using a 4.5cm (1¾-inch) round cutter, cut rounds from fruit slices; you should get 6 rounds from each fruit.
3 Top each fruit round with whipped coconut cream. Stack three rounds together. Top fruit stacks with fig wedge, finger lime pulp and pistachios. Refrigerate until ready to serve.

whipped coconut cream
Refrigerate cans of coconut cream standing upright overnight. Carefully remove lid, scoop the solid top from coconut cream into a small bowl of an electric mixer. Reserve remaining liquid in can for another use. Beat coconut cream until medium peaks form.

I AM
GLUTEN-FREE
MINERAL RICH
VEGAN

PEAR & CHOCOLATE
rye bread pudding

PREP + COOK TIME **1 HOUR 20 MINUTES** SERVES **4**

300g (9½-ounce) loaf rye bread,
    torn into pieces
8 small paradise pears (450g),
    unpeeled, halved, quartered
    and some left whole
40g (1½ ounces) butter, softened
100g (3 ounces) dark chocolate
    (70% cocoa), chopped coarsely
2 cups (500ml) milk
300ml pouring cream
¼ cup (60ml) pure maple syrup
¾ teaspoon ground cinnamon
pinch of salt
3 free-range eggs
2 tablespoons pure maple syrup,
    extra

1 Preheat oven to 160°C/325°F.
Grease a shallow 2-litre (8-cup)
ovenproof dish.
2 Place torn bread and pear in
dish, dot with butter then scatter
with chocolate.
3 Bring milk, cream, maple syrup,
cinnamon and salt to the boil in a
medium saucepan. Whisk eggs in
a large heatproof bowl. Gradually
whisk hot milk mixture into egg.
Pour mixture over bread mixture.
4 Bake pudding for 50 minutes or
until just set. Stand for 5 minutes
before serving, drizzled with extra
maple syrup.

I AM
HIGH FIBRE
HIGH IN VITAMIN B
PROTEIN RICH

red fruit salad

WITH CHAI SPICED YOGHURT

PREP + COOK TIME **15 MINUTES (+ COOLING & REFRIGERATION)** SERVES **4**

Red coloured fruits like strawberries, grapes and cherries are high in antioxidants.

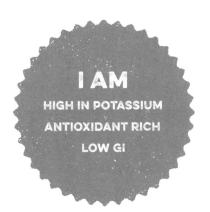

I AM
HIGH IN POTASSIUM
ANTIOXIDANT RICH
LOW GI

½ cup (125ml) water
2 tablespoons honey
1 cinnamon stick
3cm (1¼-inch) piece fresh ginger, cut into thin matchsticks
2 cardamom pods, bruised
2 whole cloves
1 whole star anise
500g (1-pound) piece watermelon, rind removed, cut into small wedges
250g (8 ounces) strawberries, halved
250g (8 ounces) red seedless grapes, halved
250g (8 ounces) cherries, halved, seeds removed
1½ cups (420g) greek-style yoghurt
¼ cup (30g) slivered pistachios
micro herbs, to serve (optional)

1 Stir the water, honey, cinnamon, ginger, cardamom, cloves and star anise in a small saucepan over medium heat until honey dissolves. Bring to the boil. Reduce heat; simmer, uncovered, for 2 minutes until liquid reduces by half. Remove from heat; cool completely.
2 Combine watermelon, strawberries, grapes and cherries in a bowl; drizzle with half the cooled syrup. Refrigerate for 10 minutes.
3 Stir remaining syrup through yoghurt.
4 Serve fruit salad topped with pistachios and micro herbs, along with the yoghurt mixture.

FLOURLESS CHOCOLATE CAKES
with avocado icing

PREP + COOK TIME **45 MINUTES (+ COOLING)** MAKES **6**

*Uniced cakes can be made
2 days ahead. Store in an
airtight container. Ice cakes
on day of serving.*

3 free-range eggs, separated

⅔ cup (150g) caster (superfine) sugar

1 teaspoon vanilla extract

75g (2½ ounces) dark chocolate
  (70% cocoa), grated finely

¾ cup (75g) ground hazelnuts

¼ cup (60g) virgin coconut oil,
  melted

125g (4 ounces) raspberries

AVOCADO ICING

1 large ripe avocado (320g)

2 tablespoons cocoa powder

2 tablespoons coconut oil, melted

2 tablespoons agave nectar

1 Preheat oven to 180°C/350°F.
Grease six ¾ cup (180ml) friand
pans; line bases and sides with
baking paper.

2 Beat egg yolks, ½ cup (110g) of
the sugar and the extract with an
electric mixer until thick and pale.
Fold in combined chocolate and
ground hazelnuts.

3 Beat egg whites in a small bowl
with electric mixer until soft peaks
form. Gradually add remaining
sugar; beat until sugar dissolves
between additions and mixture is
glossy and stiff. Gently fold egg
white mixture into egg yolk mixture
with coconut oil. Pour into pans.

4 Bake cakes for 20 minutes or
until a skewer inserted in the centre
comes out clean. Leave in pans for
10 minutes; turn, top-side up, onto
a wire rack to cool.

5 Make avocado icing.

6 Spread icing onto cooled cakes;
top with raspberries.

avocado icing Blend or process
ingredients until smooth and glossy.

I AM
GLUTEN-FREE
ANTIOXIDANT RICH
HIGH FIBRE

TO-DAYS PRICE 4'- per lb.

NO-BAKE BANANA

coconut pie

PREP TIME **30 MINUTES (+ REFRIGERATION)** SERVES **8**

Use coconut yoghurt instead of greek-style yoghurt, if you prefer, and omit the brown sugar and desiccated coconut. You will need about 2 passionfruit for this recipe.

I AM
HIGH FIBRE
RICH IN VITAMIN B
RAW

1 cup (160g) brazil nuts
180g (5½ ounces) fresh dates, pitted
½ cup (45g) traditional rolled oats
½ cup (40g) shredded coconut
3 teaspoons powdered gelatine
¼ cup (60ml) boiling water
3 cups (840g) greek-style yoghurt,
    at room temperature
¼ cup (55g) firmly packed light
    brown sugar
¼ cup (20g) fine desiccated coconut
2 teaspoons finely grated lime rind
2 medium bananas (400g), sliced
1 tablespoon lime juice
2 tablespoons passionfruit pulp
¼ cup (10g) flaked coconut, toasted

1 Lightly grease a 23cm (9¼-inch) round, 3cm (1¼-inch) deep, fluted flan tin with a removable base.
2 Process brazil nuts, dates, oats and shredded coconut until mixture forms a coarse paste. Press mixture evenly over base and side of tin.
3 Sprinkle gelatine over the just boiled water; whisk to dissolve, making sure there are no lumps. Stir into yoghurt with sugar, desiccated coconut and rind. Pour mixture into pie shell. Cover; refrigerate for 4 hours or until set.
4 Gently toss banana slices in lime juice. Serve tart topped with banana, passionfruit and flaked coconut.

Honey is one of the most natural sweeteners we can use. Local flora makes an impact on the flavour of the honey. Pure floral honeys have a low GI, but cheaper, blended honeys tend to be high. For a low GI honey look for Yellow Box, Stringy Bark, Red Gum, Iron Bark, Yapunya, Eucalypt or those labelled as pure floral honey.

Monk fruit is a subtropical melon that has been grown for hundreds of years in South-East Asia. The fruit contains a group of sweet tasting antioxidant compounds. A little like stevia, these compounds deliver sweetness without the sugar and kilojoules. Monk fruit sugar has 96% fewer kilojoules than sugar, and will not affect blood glucose or insulin levels.

Fresh honeycomb is the structure made of beeswax that houses the honey; it is an edible chewy comb, saturated with honey.

Agave syrup (or nectar) from the agave plant, has a low GI, but that is due to the high percentage of fructose present, which may be harmful in high quantities.

Barley malt syrup, made from sprouted barley, isn't as sweet as sugar or honey. It is produced similarly to brown rice syrup.

Brown rice syrup is made by cooking brown rice flour with enzymes to break down its starch into sugars from which the water is removed.

sugar-free

The popularity of cutting sugar from our diet comes with much confusion. Sure, cutting out processed and packaged foods, which are full of added sugar, makes sense, but we certainly shouldn't be cutting out fruits and vegetables, which are also full of beneficial antioxidants, vitamins, minerals and fibre.

Pure maple syrup is the concentrated sap of the maple tree, whereas maple-flavoured syrups are usually just processed glucose syrup with added flavourings. Real maple syrup is much tastier and contains significant amounts of nutrients and antioxidant compounds. It has a low GI, making it a good choice for blood glucose control.

Stevia comes from a plant, so is promoted as a natural sweetener, however, once processed, the end product becomes highly refined. It has a minimal effect on blood glucose levels and has no kilojoules, so it can be a useful way to reduce sugar intakes.

GOLDEN BEETROOT &
carrot cakes

PREP + COOK TIME **40 MINUTES** MAKES **8**

You will need 2 bunches (1kg) baby golden beetroot for this recipe: 1 bunch to get 1 cup grated, and 1 bunch for the candied beetroot.

3 cups (300g) ground hazelnuts

3 teaspoons baking powder

⅓ cup (55g) sultanas

⅓ cup (45g) coarsely chopped roasted hazelnuts

⅓ cup (120g) honey

¼ cup (60g) virgin coconut oil

1 teaspoon vanilla extract

1 teaspoon mixed spice

3 free-range eggs

1½ cups (175g) coarsely grated carrot

1 cup (50g) coarsely grated golden beetroot (beets)

vanilla yoghurt, to serve (optional)

CANDIED BEETROOT

1 bunch baby golden beetroot (beets) (500g), scrubbed and trimmed

1½ cup (375ml) pure maple syrup

1 Preheat oven to 180°C/350°F. Grease and line 8 holes of a 12-hole (¾ cup/180ml) straight sided, loose-based mini cheese cake pan.

2 Combine ground hazelnuts, baking powder, sultanas and hazelnuts in a medium bowl.

3 Whisk honey, coconut oil, extract, mixed spice and eggs in a medium bowl until smooth. Pour honey mixture over dry ingredients; mix well. Fold in grated carrot and beetroot. Spoon mixture into holes.

4 Bake cakes for 30 minutes or until a skewer inserted in the centre comes out clean. Leave cakes in pan for 5 minutes before transferring to a wire rack to cool.

5 Meanwhile, make candied beetroot.

6 Serve cakes topped with candied beetroot and yoghurt.

candied beetroot Using a mandoline or V-slicer, cut beetroot into very thin slices. Place slices in a medium saucepan with maple syrup; cook over medium heat for 10 minutes or until beetroot is candied.

tip While the cakes themselves are dairy-free, if you serve them with the vanilla yoghurt, they are not; for a dairy-free option use coconut milk yoghurt.

I AM
HIGH FIBRE
HIGH IN FOLATE
DAIRY-FREE

kumara & coconut tarts

WITH PECAN PRALINE

PREP + COOK TIME **45 MINUTES (+ COOLING & REFRIGERATION)** SERVES **6**

1½ cups (180g) ground almonds

⅓ cup (50g) coconut flour

2 tablespoons tapioca flour

2 tablespoons coconut sugar

1 teaspoon ground ginger

2 free-range eggs

⅓ cup (80g) virgin coconut oil, melted

500g (1 pound) kumara (orange
    sweet potato), cut into 3cm
    (1¼-inch) pieces

1 tablespoon water

¾ cup (180ml) coconut cream

2 free-range eggs, extra

¼ cup (60ml) pure maple syrup

1 teaspoon mixed spice

1 cup (280g) coconut yoghurt

PECAN PRALINE

¾ cup (90g) pecan halves

½ cup (80g) coconut sugar

½ cup (125ml) water

1 Preheat oven to 180°C/350°F.
Grease six 10cm (4-inch) round flan
tins with removable bases.

2 Process ground almonds, flours,
coconut sugar and ginger in a food
processor to combine. Add eggs and
coconut oil, processing until just
combined. Press mixture evenly
over base and sides of tins. Place
tins on an oven tray.

3 Bake for 10 minutes or until golden.

4 Meanwhile, place kumara and the
water in a small microwave-safe bowl;
cover with plastic wrap. Microwave
on HIGH (100%) for 8 minutes or
until tender. Drain; cool.

5 Blend or process kumara with
coconut cream, extra eggs, maple
syrup and mixed spice until smooth.
Pour mixture into tart shells.

6 Bake tarts for 15 minutes until
just set with a slight wobble in the
centre. Turn oven off; cool in oven.
Refrigerate for 2 hours.

7 Make pecan praline.

8 Just before serving, top tarts with
yoghurt and praline.

pecan praline Spread nuts on a
baking-paper-lined oven tray. Stir
coconut sugar and the water in a
small saucepan over medium-high
heat, without boiling, until sugar
dissolves. Bring to the boil; boil,
uncovered, without stirring, for
6 minutes until it reaches hard
crack stage (when a drizzle of syrup
dropped into iced water turns into
hard brittle shards). Pour toffee over
nuts on tray, titling to spread into
a thin even layer. Allow to cool and
set. Break praline into pieces.

*tips Tarts can be made up to 2 days
ahead; store, covered in the fridge.
Top with yoghurt and praline before
serving. Praline can be stored in an
airtight container for up to 2 weeks.*

I AM
GLUTEN-FREE
PROTEIN RICH
DAIRY-FREE

spelt & oat scones

WITH BERRY CHIA SEED JAM

PREP + COOK TIME **50 MINUTES** SERVES **8**

This jam takes only 10 minutes to make. It won't store as long as regular jam, however it can be frozen in portions to extend the shelf life.

1 cup (150g) wholemeal plain (all-purpose) flour

1 cup (150g) white spelt flour

2 teaspoons baking powder

1 teaspoon fine sea salt flakes

100g (3 ounces) cold butter, chopped coarsely

¾ cup (180ml) buttermilk

1 tablespoon raw honey

1 tablespoon buttermilk, extra

2 tablespoons rolled oats

50g (1½ ounces) butter, extra

BERRY CHIA SEED JAM

400g (12½ ounces) frozen mixed berries

¼ cup (35g) white chia seeds

1 tablespoon pure maple syrup

1 teaspoon finely grated lemon rind

1 teaspoon lemon juice

1 vanilla bean, split lengthways, seeds scraped

1 Make berry chia seed jam.

2 Preheat oven to 220°C/425°F fan-forced (see tips). Line an oven tray with baking paper.

3 Sift flours, baking powder and salt into a large bowl; rub in butter until mixture resembles coarse breadcrumbs. Add buttermilk and honey. Using a dinner knife, cut liquid through mixture until it starts to clump. Turn out onto a floured surface; knead gently for 45 seconds or until dough just comes together. (Don't over work the dough or it will be tough.)

4 Shape dough into a 16cm (6½-inch) round on tray with floured hands. Mark the round into eight wedges, using the back of a floured knife. Brush top with extra buttermilk; sprinkle with oats.

5 Bake scones for 20 minutes or until top is golden. Serve warm with extra butter and jam.

berry chia seed jam Cook frozen berries in a medium saucepan over medium heat, stirring occasionally, for 5 minutes or until berries release their juices. Reduce heat to low, add chia seeds and syrup; cook, stirring occasionally, for 6 minutes or until thickened slightly. Stir in rind, juice and vanilla seeds (keep vanilla pod for another use).

tips The even heat provided by the fan function of the oven will help give these scones an extra boost. For conventional ovens, increase the temperature by 10-20 degrees. Scones are best made on the day of serving. The jam can be made up to 3 days ahead; store in an airtight container in the fridge for up to 2 weeks or freeze for up to 1 month.

I AM
SUGAR-FREE
ANTIOXIDANT RICH
HIGH FIBRE

BLOOD ORANGE
fizzed jelly

PREP + COOK TIME **30 MINUTES (+ STANDING & FREEZING)** SERVES **6**

The trick to creating these delightful fizzy jellies is to chill the glasses first and set the jellies quickly in the freezer, preserving all the bubbles.

3 cups (750ml) blood orange juice

½ cup (100g) norbu (monk fruit sugar)

2½ leaves titanium-strength gelatine (12.5g)

1¼ cups (310ml) soda water, chilled

2 tablespoons micro basil or small basil leaves

BLOOD ORANGE SALAD

4 medium blood oranges (680g)

2 pink grapefruit (700g)

100g (3 ounces) strawberries, sliced thickly

1 teaspoon shredded fresh basil leaves

1 teaspoon norbu (monk fruit sugar)

I AM
SUGAR-FREE
HIGH IN VITAMIN C
GLUTEN-FREE

1 Chill six ½ cup (125ml) dessert glasses in the freezer.

2 Strain blood orange juice into a heavy-based medium saucepan. Add norbu; stir over medium heat until dissolved. Bring to the boil. Reduce heat; simmer, for 15 minutes or until reduced to 1⅔ cups, skimming off any foam.

3 Soak gelatine leaves in cold water for 3 minutes or until softened. Squeeze out excess water, add gelatine to reduced juice; stir until dissolved. Cool to room temperature.

4 Transfer syrup to a large jug. Add soda water, pour into chilled glasses; freeze for 1½ hours or until set. (If you are not serving jellies immediately, cover, place in the fridge.)

5 Just before serving, make blood orange salad.

6 Serve jellies topped with blood orange salad and basil.

blood orange salad Using a small knife, cut rind with the white pith away from 1 orange. Hold the orange over a bowl to catch juices, then cut between the membrane on either side of segments to release the segment into the bowl. Using your hands, squeeze remaining juice from membrane over segments. Repeat with remaining oranges and grapefruit. Add strawberries, basil and norbu to the bowl; stir to combine. Cover; refrigerate until required.

tips When blood oranges are out of season use sugar-free blood orange juice (available from most supermarkets), and regular oranges for the salad. You can use 1½ tablespoons powdered gelatine instead of the leaf gelatine. Sprinkle over reduced blood orange juice in step 2; whisk to dissolve. Omit step 3. Jellies can be made the day before and will keep in the fridge for up to 4 days.

MIXED BERRY & COCONUT
layer cake

PREP + COOK TIME **40 MINUTES (+ COOLING)** SERVES **6**

6 free-range eggs

2 teaspoons vanilla bean paste

¾ cup (165g) maple sugar

¼ cup (60g) virgin coconut oil, melted

1½ cups (180g) ground almonds

3 teaspoons gluten-free baking powder

500g (1 pound) coconut yoghurt

125g (4 ounces) fresh raspberries

125g (4 ounces) fresh blueberries

1 Preheat oven to 180°C/350°F. Grease and line two 20cm (8-inch) round cake pans with baking paper.

2 Beat eggs, paste and maple sugar in a small bowl with an electric mixer for 10 minutes or until light and creamy. Add coconut oil; beat for a further 3 minutes.

3 Transfer mixture to a large bowl; gently stir in ground almonds and baking powder. Spoon mixture evenly between pans.

4 Bake cakes, rotating pans halfway through cooking, for 25 minutes or until cakes spring back when lightly pressed with a finger. Turn cakes immediately, top-side down, onto wire racks to cool.

5 Place one cake layer on serving plate; top with half the yoghurt and half the berries. Top with second cake, then remaining yoghurt and remaining berries.

tip Cake is best made and assembled on day of serving.

I AM

GLUTEN-FREE

PROTEIN RICH

DAIRY-FREE

SLOW-ROASTED ROSÉ & VANILLA

quince galette

PREP + COOK TIME **6 HOURS (+ COOLING)** SERVES **6**

3 medium quince (1kg)

¼ cup (90g) honey

3 cups (750ml) water

1½ cups (375ml) rosé wine

1 cinnamon stick

1 vanilla bean, split lengthways
   into thirds

6 sheets fillo pastry

2 tablespoons extra virgin olive oil

1 teaspoon ground cinnamon

⅓ cup (75g) caster (superfine) sugar

⅓ cup (40g) ground almonds

¼ cup (40g) roasted almonds,
   chopped

1 cup (280g) vanilla bean
greek-style yoghurt

1 Preheat oven to 150°C/300°F.

2 Peel quince; reserve half the peel. Cut quince into quarters, do not core.

3 Stir honey, the water, wine, cinnamon and vanilla in a large cast iron casserole or baking dish over medium heat until honey dissolves. Add quince and reserved peel, bring to the boil; cover with a piece of baking paper then cover tightly with foil, or a lid (make sure quince is submerged in the liquid).

4 Bake quince for 5 hours, turning twice, until quince are tender and deep red in colour. Leave quince in syrup to cool.

5 Remove quince from syrup with a slotted spoon. Cut cores from quince; cut each quarter in half lengthways. Strain syrup; reserve vanilla bean, discard peel. Reserve 2 cups (500ml) of the syrup. Return quince to remaining syrup; stand until required. Place reserved syrup in a saucepan over medium heat; simmer for 5 minutes or until thickened. Cool.

6 Preheat oven to 210°C/420°F. Grease a large oven tray; place tray in oven while heating.

7 Layer pastry sheets in alternate directions, on a large piece of baking paper, brushing each layer with some of the oil.

8 Combine cinnamon and sugar in a small bowl; reserve 2 tablespoons cinnamon sugar. Combine ground almonds with remaining cinnamon sugar. Sprinkle almond mixture over pastry leaving a 10cm (4-inch) border. Top with drained quince, fold edges of pastry over quince. Transfer galette, on baking paper, to preheated tray. Brush pastry with remaining oil; sprinkle pastry with reserved cinnamon sugar.

9 Bake galette for 20 minutes or until pastry is golden. Drizzle with reduced syrup, top with chopped almonds and reserved vanilla beans; serve with yoghurt.

tip Quince can be prepared to the end of step 4, up to 3 days ahead; keep, covered, in the fridge.

I AM
EGG-FREE
HIGH IN VITAMIN C
HIGH FIBRE

Raw brownies

The brownie mixtures can also be pressed into greased mini muffin pans.
Carefully remove from pan with a palette knife.

DATE & RASPBERRY

PREP TIME **20 MINUTES (+ REFRIGERATION)**
MAKES **25**

Grease and line base and sides of a 20cm (8-in) square
cake pan with baking paper. Process 2¼ cups (270g)
pecans until finely chopped. With motor operating,
add 2¼ cups (520g) fresh pitted dates, ⅓ cup raw
cacao powder, 3 teaspoons water and 1½ teaspoons
virgin coconut oil; process until mixture comes
together. Press mixture evenly into pan; level with
a palette knife. Refrigerate for 1 hour or until firm.
Drizzle with 50g (1½oz) melted 70% dark chocolate;
top with 60g (2oz) raspberries. Cut into 25 squares.

CRUNCHY WALNUT

PREP TIME **20 MINUTES (+ REFRIGERATION)**
MAKES **25**

Grease and line base and sides of a 20cm (8-in) square
cake pan with baking paper. Process 2¼ cups (270g)
pecans until finely chopped. With motor operating,
add 2¼ cups (520g) fresh pitted dates, ⅓ cup (35g)
raw cacao powder, 3 teaspoons water, 1½ teaspoons
virgin coconut oil and 1 teaspoon ground cinnamon;
process until mixture comes together. Transfer to a
bowl; stir in ½ cup (55g) chopped walnuts and ¼ cup
(40g) cacao nibs. Press mixture evenly into pan; level
with a palette knife. Refrigerate for 1 hour or until firm.
Dust with 1 teaspoon cocoa powder. Cut into 25 squares.

PEANUT BUTTER

PREP TIME **20 MINUTES (+ REFRIGERATION)**
MAKES **25**

Grease and line base and sides of a 20cm (8-in) square
cake pan with baking paper. Combine 2 tablespoons
sesame seeds, 1 tablespoon linseeds and ⅓ cup (65g)
pepitas in a small bowl. Process 2¼ cups (270g) pecans
until finely chopped. With motor operating, add
2¼ cups (520g) fresh pitted dates, ⅓ cup (35g) raw
cacao powder, 3 teaspoons water and 1½ teaspoons
virgin coconut oil; process until mixture comes together.
Transfer to a bowl; stir in half the seed mixture. Press
half the mixture into pan; top with ½ cup (140g) natural
peanut butter, in teaspoonfuls. Press on remaining date
mixture. Refrigerate for 1 hour or until firm. Spread
top with an extra ½ cup (140g) natural peanut butter;
sprinkle with remaining seed mixture. Refrigerate for
30 minutes or until firm. Cut into 25 squares.

CITRUS & PISTACHIO

PREP TIME **20 MINUTES (+ REFRIGERATION)**
MAKES **25**

Grease and line base and sides of a 20cm (8-in) square
cake pan with baking paper. Process 2¼ cups (270g)
pecans until finely chopped. With motor operating,
add 2¼ cups (520g) fresh pitted dates, ⅓ cup (35g) raw
cacao powder, 3 teaspoons water, 1½ teaspoons virgin
coconut oil, 2 teaspoons finely grated orange rind and
2 teaspoons finely grated lemon rind; process until
mixture comes together. Transfer to a bowl; stir in
½ cup (70g) chopped pistachios. Press mixture evenly
into pan; press on ½ cup (70g) chopped pistachios.
Refrigerate for 1 hour or until firm. Cut into 25 squares.

POWER JUICES

JUICES

STRAWBERRY, POMEGRANATE &

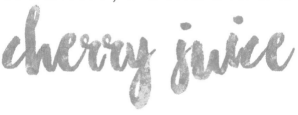

cherry juice

PREP TIME **10 MINUTES** SERVES **2**

1 cup (130g) chopped strawberries
1 cup (150g) frozen cherries, pitted
½ cup (125ml) pomegranate juice
1 pink lady apple (150g), cored,
  quartered

1 Blend ingredients in a high-speed blender until smooth.
2 Serve immediately with crushed ice and fresh cherries, if you like.

tips You can push all of the ingredients through a juicer for a thinner consistency if you prefer. This juice will separate on standing, however a quick stir will bring it back together.

I AM
HEART HEALTHY
ANTIOXIDANT RICH
DAIRY-FREE

ZINGY APPLE &
CELERY JUICE

PREP TIME **10 MINUTES** SERVES **2**

3 green apples (450g), quartered

2 stalks celery (300g), untrimmed

1 medium lemon (140g), peeled,
  quartered

4cm (1½-inch) piece fresh ginger
  (20g), unpeeled

8cm (3¼-inch) piece fresh turmeric
  (60g), unpeeled

1 Push ingredients through a juice
extractor into a jug. Stir to combine.
2 Serve immediately with celery
sticks, if you like.

tip *This juice will separate on
standing, however a quick stir
will bring it back together.*

I AM
ANTI-INFLAMMATORY
GREAT POST-EXERCISE
HIGH IN IRON

NASHI, PINEAPPLE &

lemon grass juice

PREP TIME **10 MINUTES** SERVES **2**

15cm (6-inch) stalk fresh lemon grass, chopped

2 large nashi (500g), unpeeled, quartered

½ medium pineapple (625g), peeled, chopped coarsely

2 small limes (100g), peeled

1 Starting with the lemon grass, push ingredients through a juice extractor into a jug. Stir to combine.

2 Serve immediately with crushed ice, lime wedges and lemon grass stalks, if you like.

tips *This juice will separate on standing, however a quick stir will bring it back together. Replace the nashi with regular pears if you like. This is a sweeter juice which will make it a family favourite.*

I AM
REVITALISING
HIGH IN VITAMINS B & C
ANTIOXIDANT RICH

STRAWBERRY &
watermelon juice

PREP TIME **10 MINUTES** SERVES **2**

250g (8 ounces) strawberries, hulled
150g (4½ ounces) chopped seedless watermelon

1 Blend ingredients until smooth.

tips Freeze the watermelon first for an icy cold drink. Strawberries have been known as "the queen of fruits" and for a good reason. They pack a serious antioxidant punch, are rich in immune-boosting vitamin C and also contain ellagic acid which has been found to help prevent collagen damage. Refreshing juicy watermelon is rich in vitamins A, B6 and C, is a good source of lycopene and amino acids and has anti-inflammatory properties.

I AM
RICH IN VITAMIN C
ANTI-INFLAMMATORY
HIGH IN LYCOPENE

ELECTROLYTE BOOSTER

PREP TIME 10 MINUTES

SERVES 2

1 cup (250ml) coconut water
200g (6½ ounces) frozen pineapple
½ small avocado (100g)
¼ baby fennel bulb (35g)
¼ cup loosely packed fresh
   mint leaves
1 cup firmly packed baby
   spinach leaves
1 tablespoon lime juice
ice cubes

1 Blend ingredients in a high-speed blender until smooth.
2 Serve immediately over ice, topped with lime slices, if you like.

tips Frozen pineapple is available from supermarkets or freeze your own portioned, peeled, cored and chopped pineapple in zip-top bags. Electrolytes (sodium, potassium, calcium, magnesium, phosphate) are responsible for stimulating the muscles and nervous system. They also regulate fluids within the body. This natural booster is a far better choice than sugary purchased sports drinks.

I AM

POTASSIUM RICH

HIGH IN VITAMINS B & C

HIGH FIBRE

GAZPACHO JUICE

PREP TIME 5 MINUTES
SERVES 2

2 medium ripe tomatoes (300g),
    chopped coarsely
½ small red capsicum (bell pepper)
    (75g), chopped coarsely
½ small lebanese cucumber (65g),
    chopped coarsely
1 green onion (scallion),
    chopped coarsely
2 teaspoons finely chopped
    fresh basil leaves
½ teaspoon red wine vinegar

1 Blend ingredients until smooth.

*tips Store any remaining juice
in the fridge overnight. Tomatoes
are a great source of lycopene
(the carotenoid pigment) which is a
powerful antioxidant and has been
found to help prevent some cancers
and heart disease. Tomatoes and
capsicums provide a good dose
of vitamin C. Capsicums pack
an antioxidant punch, increase
metabolism and aid digestion.*

I AM
HIGH IN VITAMIN C
ANTIOXIDANT RICH
A DIGESTION AID

BROCCOLI, ORANGE &

carrot juice

PREP TIME **10 MINUTES** SERVES **2**

125g (4 ounces) broccoli stalks,
    chopped coarsely

4 medium oranges (960g), peeled

2 large carrots (360g), unpeeled,
    halved lengthways

½ cup loosely packed fresh thai
    basil leaves

1 Push ingredients through a juice extractor into a jug. Stir to combine. Serve immediately.

I AM
HIGH IN VITAMIN C
ANTI-INFLAMMATORY
HIGH IN FOLATE

tips This juice will separate on standing, however a quick stir will bring it back together. This is a good way to use broccoli stalks. You will need a 425g (13½-ounce) head of broccoli. There is a lot of vitamin C in broccoli, oranges and carrots. The thai basil adds a nice flavour twist.

BEETROOT, CARROT &

ginger juice

PREP TIME **5 MINUTES** MAKES **2 CUPS**

1 large fresh beetroot (200g),
   trimmed, cut into wedges
2 medium carrots (240g), chopped
2 medium red-skinned apples (300g),
   chopped coarsely
2cm (¾-inch) piece fresh ginger
   (10g), peeled, grated finely

1 Push beetroot, carrot and apple
through a juice extractor into a
medium jug; stir in ginger.
2 Serve immediately topped with
crushed ice, if you like.

tips Beetroot is a great source of
folic acid and a good source of fibre,
manganese and potassium. It has
been found to increase white blood
cells and reduce blood pressure.
It is one of the richest sources of
the amino acid, glutamine which is
essential to intestinal tract health.

I AM
HIGH IN FOLIC ACID
GOOD FOR HEALTHY SKIN
GLUTAMINE RICH

I AM

HIGH FIBRE

VITAMIN & MINERAL RICH

A DIGESTION AID

GREEN TEA & KIWI SIPPER

PREP TIME 10 MINUTES (+ COOLING) SERVES 2

1 green tea bag

1 cup (250ml) boiling water

2 teaspoons raw honey

½ cup (90g) frozen green grapes

1 medium kiwifruit (85g), peeled, chopped coarsely

½ cup loosely packed fresh mint leaves

½ cup firmly packed baby spinach leaves

1 Brew green tea in the boiling water for 5 minutes. Discard tea bag. Stir in honey. Cool in the refrigerator.

2 Place cooled tea in a high-speed blender with remaining ingredients; blend until smooth.

3 Serve immediately over ice and topped with mint leaves, if you like.

tips This drink separates quickly, so it is best made just before serving. Kiwifruit contain loads of fibre, vitamins C & E, antioxidants and minerals (zinc, calcium, iron, magnesium, copper, potassium). Kiwifruit are great for keeping skin, hair and nails glowing, healthy and strong and contain the enzyme actinidin which aids in digestion.

I AM

HIGH FIBRE
ANTIOXIDANT RICH
DAIRY-FREE

GREEN
SUPER JUICE

PREP TIME 5 MINUTES
SERVES 2

1 lebanese cucumber (130g),
  chopped coarsely
2 celery sticks (300g), trimmed,
  chopped coarsely
2 medium trimmed kale leaves (40g)
30g (1 ounce) baby spinach leaves
1 small ripe pear (180g), quartered,
  cored
¼ lemon (35g), peeled
1 sprig fresh mint
⅔ cup (180ml) coconut water
⅔ cup ice cubes

1 Blend ingredients in a high-speed
blender for 1 minute or until smooth.
If necessary, stop the blender and
push the ingredients down before
blending again.

PEACH, PAPAYA &
raspberry crush

PREP TIME **10 MINUTES** SERVES **2**

2 medium peaches (300g),
  chopped coarsely
100g (3 ounces) coarsely chopped
  red papaya
100g (3 ounces) raspberries
½ cup (125ml) water

1 Blend or process peaches, papaya,
raspberries and the water until
smooth.
2 Serve over crushed ice and top
with raspberries, if you like.

tips Use nectarines instead of
peaches, if you like. Peaches are rich
in vitamin A, beta-carotene and
vitamin C; they are also a good source
of vitamins E, K, B1, B2, B3 and B6,
folate and pantothenic acid. Papaya
is also rich in vitamins A and C and
contains papain, an enzyme that
aids digestion. Raspberries are rich
in antioxidants, vitamins and ellagic
acid, a phenolic compound that fights
against the formation of cancer cells.

I AM
A DIGESTION AID
HIGH IN VITAMINS A & C
ANTIOXIDANT RICH

ROCKMELON, CUCUMBER &

ginger juice

PREP TIME **10 MINUTES** SERVES **2**

½ medium rockmelon (800g),
  peeled, chopped
½ telegraph cucumber (200g),
  peeled, chopped
25g (¾-ounce) piece fresh ginger
½ cup loosely packed fresh coriander
  (cilantro), leaves and stalks
1 medium lime (90g), peeled

1 Push ingredients through a juice extractor into a jug. Stir to combine. Serve immediately.

tips The juice will separate on standing, however a quick stir will bring it back together. Use honeydew melon instead of rockmelon, if you like. This drink is a zesty and refreshing start to the day. Cucumber hydrates and the ginger gives a burst of warmth.

I AM
BETA-CAROTENE RICH
GREAT FOR HYDRATION
LOW CARB

peachy GREEN

PREP TIME **10 MINUTES** SERVES **2**

2 medium peaches (300g), stones
   removed, quartered

2 medium kiwifruit (170g), peeled,
   halved

8 cos (romaine) lettuce leaves,
   washed

3 sprigs fresh mint

1 small lime (65g), peeled, quartered

2 lebanese cucumbers (260g),
   unpeeled, quartered lengthways

1 Push ingredients through a juice
extractor into a jug. (Push the
lettuce and mint through the juicer
in the middle of the order so the
remaining ingredients help to push
them through.)

2 Serve over crushed ice and
topped with mint and peach
wedges, if you like

*tips This juice can also be made
in a blender. Add 1 cup (250ml)
coconut water for a thinner
consistency. If you're new to green
juices, this is a great introduction.
The sweetness of the peaches are
a perfect accompaniment to the
vitamin C, E & K rich kiwifruit,
hydrating cucumber, refreshing cos
lettuce and alkalising lime juice.*

I AM
HIGH FIBRE
HIGH IN POTASSIUM
VITAMIN RICH

REJUVENATING

refresher

PREP TIME **10 MINUTES (+ REFRIGERATION)** SERVES **2**

2 hibiscus tea bags
1 cup (250ml) boiling water
4 cups (650g) chopped seedless
   watermelon
½ cup loosely packed fresh
   mint leaves
1 medium lime (65g), peeled

I AM
ANTIOXIDANT RICH
COOLING & HYDRATING
HIGH IN LYCOPENE

1 Brew tea bags in the boiling
water in a heatproof jug or bowl for
5 minutes. Refrigerate for 1 hour or
until cold. Discard tea bags.
2 Push watermelon, mint, lime
and cooled hibiscus tea through
a juice extractor into a jug. (It's
a good idea to add the mint half
way through juicing so that the
watermelon pushes it through.)
Stir juice to combine.
3 Serve immediately with sliced
watermelon and micro mint,
if you like.

tips *Watermelon is made up of
92% water, so is the perfect hydrating
juice first thing in the morning.
It also contains lycopene, a powerful
antioxidant that research shows
reduces the risk of stroke and
protects against ovarian cancer.
Hibiscus tea lowers blood pressure.*

I AM

HIGH IN GLUTAMINE

GREAT FOR GUT HEALTH

HIGH FIBRE

INVIGORATING FRUIT & VEGIE JUICE

PREP TIME 10 MINUTES

SERVES 2

2 large beetroot (beets) (400g),
   chopped coarsely

2 celery stalks (300g), trimmed

130g (4 ounces) silver beet
   (swiss chard) leaves

2 large green apples (400g),
   chopped

1 cup loosely packed fresh
   flat-leaf parsley leaves

1 medium lemon (140g), segmented

20g (¾ ounce) fresh ginger, peeled

1 Push ingredients through a
juice extractor into a jug. Stir to
combine. Serve immediately.

tips *Make this juice just before
serving to retain the nutrients in
the fruit and vegetables. With a
good dose of leafy greens, vitamin-
rich vegetables and fruits and an
invigorating hit of ginger, this juice
will give your digestion a kick-start
and your body the fuel it needs to
get up and go.*

APPLE, KALE, AVOCADO & GINGER JUICE

PREP TIME 10 MINUTES
SERVES 2

1 medium lime (90g)
1 medium apple (150g), chopped
1 lebanese cucumber (130g),
   chopped
½ medium avocado (125g),
   chopped
1⅓ cups (330ml) coconut water
30g (1 ounce) baby spinach leaves
1 teaspoon finely grated fresh ginger
50g (1½ ounces) baby kale leaves

1 Remove rind with pith from lime;
discard. Coarsely chop lime flesh.
2 Blend or process lime and
remaining ingredients until
smooth. Divide between two
glasses.
3 Serve immediately topped with
crushed ice, if you like.

tips Avocado is packed with fibre
and healthy fats (particularly oleic
acid that maintains moisture in
the epidermal layer, keeping skin
soft and hydrated). It also contains
potassium (more than bananas!),
which is known to reduce blood
pressure levels and increases blood
flow to the brain. Kale is rich in
carotenoids (which can reduce
the risk of age-related macular
degeneration and cataracts), and
is a good source of vitamins A, C
and K, and calcium.

I AM
POTASSIUM RICH
GOOD FOR HEALTHY SKIN
HIGH FIBRE

PICK
-ME-
UPS

lo-cal SIPPER

PREP TIME **5 MINUTES** SERVES **2**

1 small fennel bulb (200g)

1 medium pink grapefruit (425g),
    peeled, quartered

6 small mandarins (600g), peeled

1 Trim and slice the fennel bulb
(reserve some fronds for serving,
if you like). Starting with the
sliced fennel, push ingredients
through a juice extractor into a
jug. Stir to combine.

2 Serve immediately with reserved
fronds, if you like.

*tips This juice will separate on
standing, however a quick stir will
bring it back together. The fennel
and grapefruit make this a sharper-
tasting juice. Fennel aids digestion,
is rich in fibre and vitamin C.
Pink grapefruit is low in calories
and high in vitamin C and water.
Mandarins are also low in calories
and full of fibre.*

I AM

A DIGESTION AID

HIGH IN VITAMIN C

HIGH FIBRE

MATCHA *magic*

PREP TIME **5 MINUTES** SERVES **2**

1½ cups (375ml) coconut water
½ cup ice cubes
½ medium avocado (125g), peeled
½ teaspoon matcha green tea powder
3 fresh dates (60g), pitted

1 Place ingredients in a high-speed blender; blend until smooth. Adjust the consistency by adding extra coconut water, if necessary.
2 Serve immediately, dusted with a little extra matcha powder, if you like.

tips Matcha green tea powder is available from all good health food stores and Japanese food stores. Matcha is a powdered green tea, which contains 137 times more antioxidants than regular green tea.

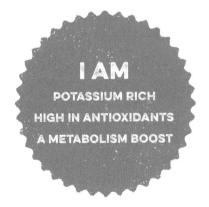

I AM
POTASSIUM RICH
HIGH IN ANTIOXIDANTS
A METABOLISM BOOST

I AM

ANTIOXIDANT RICH
A METABOLISM BOOST
HIGH FIBRE

HOT! HOT! HOT! CHOCOLATE

PREP + COOK TIME
20 MINUTES SERVES 2

1 vanilla bean, split lengthways
1 fresh long red chilli
3 cups (750ml) coconut milk blend
  (see tip)
2 tablespoons raw cacao powder
1 tablespoon rice malt syrup

1 Scrape vanilla seeds, using the tip of a knife; add seeds and pod to a small saucepan. Cut chilli into four pieces, add three pieces to pan; thinly slice remaining piece, reserve for serving. Add coconut milk blend to pan; bring to the boil. Remove from heat; stand for 5 minutes. Discard chilli.
2 Stir cacao powder and syrup into infused milk, return to heat; simmer, stirring, for 2 minutes or until cacao is dissolved and milk heated through.
3 Serve topped with reserved chilli and extra cacao powder, if you like.

tip We used Pureharvest Coco Quench, a blend of coconut and rice milks; it has a thinner consistency than canned coconut milk, but still has a great coconut milk taste.

ICED ALMOND CHAI TEA

PREP + COOK TIME
25 MINUTES
(+ REFRIGERATION)
MAKES **1.25 LITRES (5 CUPS)**

3 cups (750ml) water
2 teaspoons black tea leaves
2 cinnamon sticks
1 vanilla bean, split lengthways
1 tablespoon raw honey
5 thick slices fresh ginger
6 cloves
8 cardamom pods, bruised
½ teaspoon black peppercorns
1 litre (4 cups) almond milk

1 Place the water in a large
saucepan with tea leaves,
cinnamon, vanilla, honey,
ginger, cloves, cardamom and
peppercorns; bring to the boil.
Reduce heat; simmer, uncovered,
for 20 minutes or until reduced
to 1 cup. Pour into a small jug;
refrigerate until chilled.
2 To serve, fill four tall glasses
with ice cubes; pour ¼ cup of
chai mix into each glass (strain
first if you prefer), then top up
with almond milk.

tip Store the chai mix in the fridge
for up to 2 weeks.

I AM
SUGAR-FREE
HIGH IN ANTIOXIDANTS
POTASSIUM RICH

AFTERNOON
brain reboot

PREP TIME **10 MINUTES** SERVES **2**

1 cup (250ml) canned coconut milk

1 cup (150g) frozen blueberries

1 small beetroot (beet) (100g),
   washed, grated

2 tablespoons cacao powder

1 Place ingredients in a high-speed blender and blend until smooth. Adjust the consistency by adding extra coconut milk, if necessary.
2 Serve topped with a little extra coconut milk and cacao powder, if you like.

tips Make this smoothie in advance and keep it in the fridge in a sealed jar for an afternoon boost. Stir or shake to bring it back together. Coconut boosts brain function due to the medium chain triglycerides. The antioxidants in blueberries stimulate the flow of blood and oxygen to the brain; similarly, the nitrates in beetroot cleanses the blood and encourages blood flow to the brain. Cacao is rich in flavanols which protect brain cells from toxins and inflammation.

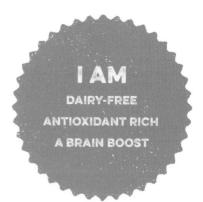

I AM
DAIRY-FREE
ANTIOXIDANT RICH
A BRAIN BOOST

HOT SALTED CAROB LATTE

PREP + COOK TIME
10 MINUTES SERVES 2

1 vanilla bean, split lengthways
3 cups (750ml) soy milk
1½ tablespoons carob powder
pinch salt flakes
2 teaspoons honey

1 Scrape seeds from one vanilla pod half using the tip of a knife; add seeds and pod half to a small saucepan. Add soy milk, carob powder, salt and honey. Place pan over low-medium heat; simmer, stirring constantly, for 5 minutes or until carob powder dissolves and mixture is heated. Discard pod.
2 Transfer to a blender; blend until frothy. Pour into heatproof glasses.
3 Serve dusted with a little carob powder, if you like.

tip Store unused vanilla pod half in a jar of caster (superfine) sugar to make your own vanilla sugar.

I AM
DAIRY-FREE
LOW IN CHOLESTEROL
MINERAL RICH

I AM
HIGH IN VITAMIN C
COOLING & HYDRATING
SUGAR-FREE

POST-RUN REFRESHER

PREP TIME 5 MINUTES
SERVES 2

½ telegraph cucumber (200g),
  unpeeled, chopped coarsely
¼ cos (romaine) lettuce (125g),
  chopped coarsely
1 medium pear (230g), unpeeled,
  chopped coarsely
¼ medium lemon (35g), peeled
½ cup (125ml) chilled unsweetened
  coconut water

1 Push the cucumber, lettuce,
pear and lemon through a juice
extractor, into a jug. Stir in
coconut water.
2 Serve immediately.

tips *This juice will separate on
standing, however a quick stir will
bring it back together. Swap the
pear for apple as a variation.*

 MOCKTAIL

PREP TIME **10 MINUTES** SERVES **2**

75g (2½ ounces) green kale
¾ cup firmly packed fresh mint leaves
350g (11 ounces) peeled pineapple, chopped coarsely
1 medium lime (90g), peeled
½ cup (125ml) chilled unsweetened coconut water

MINT SALT RIMS
1 tablespoon sea salt flakes
1 tablespoon fresh mint leaves
1 lime wedge

1 Make the mint salt rims.
2 Push kale, mint, pineapple and lime through a juice extractor into a jug. Stir in coconut water.
3 Pour into prepared glasses, over crushed ice, if you like.

mint salt rims Crush the salt and mint in a mortar and pestle; transfer mixture to a small plate. Run the lime around the rim of two glasses. Press the rims into the salt mixture.

tips This juice darkens a lot on standing but the flavour is fine. If you don't have a mortar and pestle you could process the salt in a small food processor or spice grinder. This mocktail is very refreshing. Coconut water has electrolytes to help quench thirst. And kale adds a host of vitamins, minerals and antioxidants.

I AM
VITAMIN C RICH
HIGH IN MINERALS
ANTIOXIDANT RICH

MID-MORNING *boost*

PREP TIME **5 MINUTES (+ REFRIGERATION)** SERVES **2**

2 cups (500ml) boiling water

2 teaspoons honey

2 rooibos tea bags

60g (2 ounces) blueberries

¼ cup loosely packed fresh
    mint leaves

½ medium lemon (70g),
    unpeeled, sliced

1 Place the boiling water and honey in a medium heatproof jug. Add tea bags; stand for 2 minutes. Discard tea bags. Refrigerate for 1 hour or until cold.

2 Crush blueberries and mint in a small bowl with the end of a wooden spoon or rolling pin. Add to the tea with lemon slices. Refrigerate for 1 hour.

3 Serve over crushed ice topped with micro mint, if you like.

tips *This will keep in the refrigerator for at least 24 hours. Stir just before serving. Rooibos tea is caffeine free and low in tannins, but high in minerals and antioxidants. Blueberries are high in antioxidants that help maintain brain function.*

I AM
SUGAR-FREE
ANTIOXIDANT RICH
A BRAIN BOOST

 MINT TEA

PREP TIME **5 MINUTES** SERVES **1**

½ cup loosely packed fresh mint leaves
1 teaspoon cacao nibs
1 teaspoon honey
1 cup (250ml) boiling water

1 Place mint, cacao and honey in a heatproof mug.
Add the boiling water; stand for at least 5 minutes.

*tips This tea could also be made with dried
peppermint leaves. The ultimate flavour combo,
choc mint, is brought to your afternoon cuppa with
the digestive and anti-inflammatory benefits of
fresh mint tea and the gentle stimulating qualities
of raw cacao nibs. Nibble on the cacao nibs once
you've finished for an extra pick-me-up.*

I AM
SUGAR-FREE
ANTI-INFLAMMATORY
AN ENERGY BOOSTER

Tonics

SMOOTHIE

PREP TIME **5 MINUTES** SERVES **2**

1 dragonfruit (460g), peeled, chopped coarsely

½ cup (45g) rolled oats

2 tablespoons blanched almonds

2 teaspoons honey

¼ teaspoon ground cinnamon

¾ cup (180ml) chilled soy milk

1 Blend ingredients in a high-speed blender until smooth.

2 Serve topped with extra oats and ground cinnamon, if you like.

I AM
HIGH IN VITAMIN E
LOW IN CHOLESTEROL
HIGH FIBRE

tips We used white fleshed dragonfruit, you can also use pink fleshed dragonfruit. Dragonfruit is also called pitaya. This drink will stand so you can make it ahead of time and refrigerate until required. Dragonfruit helps to decrease bad cholesterol levels and increase good ones. Oats are high in magnesium which helps to regulate blood pressure and aids the heart muscle. They are a "superfood" wholegrain, a source of fibre and contain beta-glucan, which helps lower cholesterol re-absorption. Almonds and soy milk also help lower bad cholesterol.

ANTI-INFLAMMATORY

boost

PREP TIME **5 MINUTES** SERVES **2**

2 medium carrots (240g), unpeeled, chopped coarsely

4 medium oranges (960g), peeled, chopped coarsely

15g (½ ounce) fresh turmeric, unpeeled

1 Push carrot, orange and turmeric through a juice extractor into a jug. Stir to combine.

2 Serve immediately topped with crushed ice, ground black pepper and baby carrot-tops, if you like.

tips This juice will separate on standing, however a quick stir will bring it back together. Turmeric is strongly coloured and can stain your hands and chopping boards, so be careful what you chop it on. Oranges, carrots, turmeric and pepper all contain anti-inflammatory antioxidants.

I AM
ANTIOXIDANT RICH
HIGH IN VITAMIN A & C
ANTI-INFLAMMATORY

DIGESTION  *tonic*

PREP TIME **5 MINUTES (+ 1 WEEK STANDING)** MAKES **2 CUPS**

1 baby fennel bulb (130g)

1 teaspoon fennel seeds

2 tablespoons honey

2 tablespoons raw sugar

2 cups (500ml) unfiltered cider
vinegar (see tips)

ice cubes

sparkling water, chilled

1 Reserve stems and fronds of
fennel for serving. Thinly slice
fennel bulb.

2 Combine sliced fennel, fennel
seeds, honey and sugar in a
sterilised 3-cup (750ml) capacity
jar (see tips). Pour vinegar over
fennel mixture. Seal jar; store in a
dark, cool place for 1 week. Strain
the vinegar into a clean jar.

3 Just before serving, place
2 tablespoons of the vinegar
tonic in a glass with ice cubes;
top up each glass with ¾ cup
(180ml) sparkling water. Serve
with lemon wedges and reserved
fennel, if you like.

*tips You will need to start this recipe
a week ahead. For information on
how to sterilise jars, see page 486.
Unfiltered cider vinegar contains
the 'mother' which is strand-like
enzymes of connected protein
molecules with living nutrients and
bacteria, great for gut health. It's
available from health food stores
and some major supermarkets.
This tonic will last for a year in a
cool, dark place.*

I AM

HIGH IN VITAMIN C

GOOD FOR GUT HEALTH

POTASSIUM RICH

Drink Boosters

Raw cacao powder is made by removing the cocoa butter using a process known as cold-pressing. It retains more of its nutrients than heat-processed cocoa powder; it also has a stronger bitter, chocolate taste. Blend a couple of teaspoons into dairy or nut-milk based smoothies.

Whey protein is a dairy-based supplement. Evidence has shown that if consumed immediately after a strength-training workout, it leads to better muscle repair than other forms of protein. Blend a scoop into vegetable or fruit based smoothies.

Maca powder is claimed to help with menstrual problems and chronic fatigue and to act as an aphrodisiac, there is some evidence of the latter, but no evidence for the others. It is a rich source of vitamins C and B6, iron and calcium. Blend a teaspoon of this fairly neutral-tasting powder into either a fruit or vegetable based smoothie.

Spirulina is a blue-green algae that is rich in protein and contains all the essential amino acids. It is also a good source of iron, making it a great supplement for vegans and vegetarians. Blend 1-2 teaspoons into a green smoothie. It should be avoided by people with hyperparathyroidism and those who have serious allergies to seafood or seaweed.

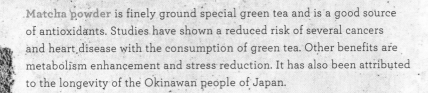

Matcha powder is finely ground special green tea and is a good source of antioxidants. Studies have shown a reduced risk of several cancers and heart disease with the consumption of green tea. Other benefits are metabolism enhancement and stress reduction. It has also been attributed to the longevity of the Okinawan people of Japan.

Acaï powder is made from acais, a wild berry grown in the Amazon famed as a rich source of antioxidants, especially anthocyanin, which gives the powder its rich red hue. This powerful antioxidant can help protect the body from free-radical damage, attributed with age-related diseases. Incorporate a few teaspoons of this pleasant slightly tart powder into a fruit or vegetable based smoothie for an added health boost.

Pea protein is a non-dairy protein supplement derived from yellow peas, making it ideal for vegans, or those that can't have dairy. As with whey protein isolate it is high in BCAAs (branched chain amino acids) which studies have shown can help with muscle repair and keep you energised and sated between meals. Blend a scoop into fruit or vegetable based smoothies.

Activated charcoal is an ancient treatment used to trap toxins. Medical grade charcoal (the only type you should consume) is made from a variety of sources, including coconut shells. It is useful for digestion issues, bloating and general detoxification. Take it a few hours after vitamin supplements and consult your doctor if you are on other medication, as it may interfere with absorption.

 SOOTHER

PREP TIME **5 MINUTES** SERVES **2**

½ medium avocado (125g),
   chopped coarsely
1 lebanese cucumber (130g),
   peeled, chopped coarsely
20g (¾ ounce) baby spinach leaves
2 tablespoons raw cashew nuts
4 fresh dates (80g), pitted
1 cup (250ml) water

1 Blend ingredients in a high-speed blender until smooth and creamy.
2 Serve over crushed ice topped with cacao nibs, if you like.

tips This drink will stand so you can make it ahead of time; refrigerate until required. Avocado is high in vitamin E and omega-9 fatty acids which are great for skin. Cucumbers contain antioxidants and silica; they are also high in water, so good for retaining moisture in your skin. Spinach is high in beta carotene which helps with skin cell development and skin tone.

I AM
ANTIOXIDANT RICH
GREAT FOR SKIN HEALTH
HIGH FIBRE

weight loss
TONIC

PREP TIME **10 MINUTES (+ REFRIGERATION & STANDING)**   MAKES **1 LITRE (4 CUPS)**

1 peppermint tea bag

1 cup (250ml) boiling water

800g (1½ pounds) chopped seedless
   watermelon

2 medium limes (180g), peeled

½ cup (125ml) chilled aloe vera juice

1½ tablespoons white chia seeds

1 Place tea bag and the boiling water in a large heatproof jug; stand for 2 minutes. Discard tea bag. Refrigerate 1 hour or until cold.

2 Push watermelon and limes through a juice extractor into a jug. Add to chilled tea with aloe vera and chia seeds; stir to combine. Refrigerate for at least 15 minutes or until chia seeds have swollen and softened.

3 Serve with extra watermelon and limes, if you like.

tips *This tonic will keep in the refrigerator for 24 hours. Stir just before serving. Peppermint tea is good for digestion and is an appetite suppressant. Aloe vera is good for bloating. Chia seeds are good for digestion and high in fibre, making you feel full. Watermelon has a high water content.*

I AM
HIGH FIBRE
GREAT FOR GUT HEALTH
RICH IN VITAMIN C

CRAMP *cure*

PREP TIME **10 MINUTES (+ FREEZING)** SERVES **2**

2 large bananas (460g),
   chopped coarsely
1½ cups (375ml) almond milk
1 tablespoon cacao powder
1 tablespoon chia seeds
1 tablespoon tahini
1 teaspoon maca powder
1 teaspoon ground cardamom

1 Place banana in an airtight container or resealable plastic bag. Freeze for 4 hours or until firm.
2 Blend frozen banana with remaining ingredients in a high-speed blender until smooth.
3 Serve immediately dusted with cacao powder, if you like.

tips *To create a striped affect in your serving glass, blend 2 teaspoons cocoa powder and 1 tablespoon honey to form a paste. Spread paste on the inside of each glass. If you know that you suffer from cramps, you may like to enjoy this smoothie in the week leading up to your period as a preventative. This smoothie will help relieve menstrual cramps. Banana, full of potassium, helps to relieve muscle contractions. Cacao and tahini are rich in magnesium which, when taken regularly, relieves muscle cramps. Maca is a great support for hormone health, chia seeds are rich in omega-3 and cardamom is an antispasmodic.*

I AM
DAIRY-FREE
HIGH IN POTASSIUM
MAGNESIUM RICH

BLOOD SUGAR
balancer

PREP TIME **5 MINUTES** SERVES **2**

6 medium golden kiwifruit (500g),
   peeled
250g (8 ounces) strawberries
½ telegraph cucumber (200g),
   unpeeled, chopped coarsely

1 Push ingredients through a juice
extractor into a jug. Stir to combine.
2 Serve juice immediately with
kiwifruit, strawberry and cucumber
ribbon skewers, if you like.

tips The juice will separate on
standing, however a quick stir will
bring it back together. For maximum
flavour, make sure all the fruit is nice
and ripe. Kiwifruit, strawberries and
cucumbers are all low GI which help
maintain your blood sugar levels.

I AM
FOLATE RICH
HIGH IN VITAMIN C
LOW GI

SLEEPY TIME TONIC

PREP + COOK TIME
25 MINUTES (+ STANDING & REFRIGERATION)
MAKES 1 LITRE (4 CUPS)

1.25 litres (5 cups) water
⅓ cup dried chamomile flowers (or 3 tea bags)
¼ cup fresh lemon thyme sprigs
4 slices lemon
1 tablespoon raw honey

1 Bring the water to the boil in a medium saucepan; remove from heat. Add chamomile, lemon thyme and lemon slices. Stir in honey until dissolved. Cover; stand for 20 minutes. Strain tea; discard solids.
2 Refrigerate at least 1 hour or until cooled. Serve tea mixture over ice with extra slices of lemon and extra sprigs fresh lemon thyme, if you like.

tip Chamomile tea is known for its soothing and calming effect, making this tonic the perfect bedtime drink.

I AM
ANTIOXIDANT RICH
A GREAT SLEEP AID
SUGAR-FREE

TURMERIC & HONEY TONIC

PREP + COOK TIME
15 MINUTES (+ STANDING)
SERVES 2

2 cups (500ml) unsweetened
   almond milk
1 tablespoon raw honey
2 teaspoons grated fresh turmeric
1 cinnamon stick
4 slices fresh ginger

1 Stir almond milk, honey,
turmeric, cinnamon stick and
ginger in a small saucepan over
low-medium heat; bring almost
to the boil. Remove from heat;
stand for 10 minutes.
2 Strain through a fine sieve into
heatproof glasses; discard solids.
Serve with extra cinnamon sticks
and dusted with ground cinnamon,
if you like.

tip *The anti-inflammatory
properties of turmeric and honey,
plus the antimicrobial properties
of honey and its use as a cough
suppressant, make this tonic a
tasty and natural way to deal
with seasonal allergies.*

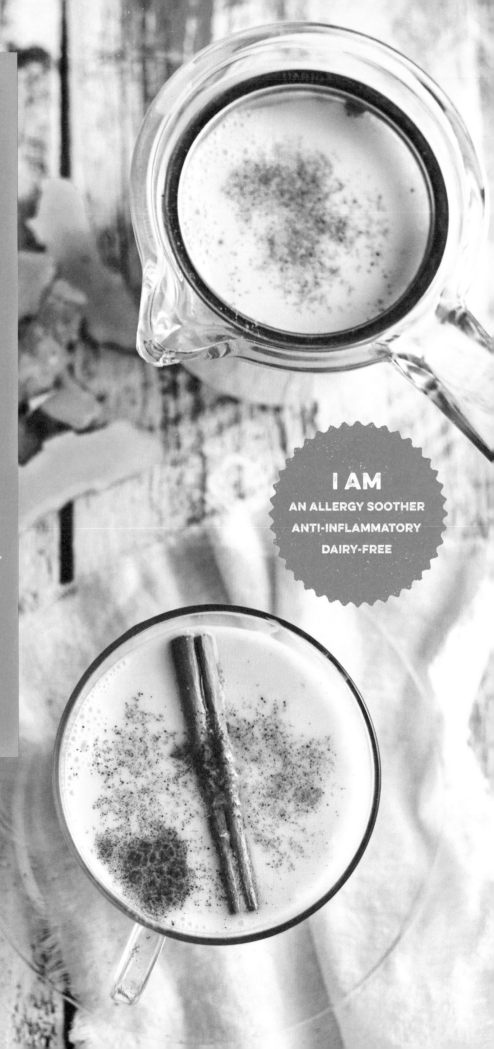

I AM
AN ALLERGY SOOTHER
ANTI-INFLAMMATORY
DAIRY-FREE

PRE-BENDER *booster*

PREP TIME **5 MINUTES** SERVES **2**

2 medium pears (460g), unpeeled,
   quartered
2 stalks celery (300g), untrimmed
1 small lemon (100g), peeled,
   quartered
½ cup loosely packed fresh
   basil leaves

1 Push pears alternately with celery,
lemon and basil through a juice
extractor into a jug. Stir to combine.
Serve immediately.

tips *It's best to drink this
immediately, as the pear will
discolour quickly. Research shows
that drinking pear juice prior to
drinking alcohol reduces the
effects of a hangover. Remember
to stay hydrated with water
throughout the night and drink
responsibly. No amount of pear
juice will remedy over-indulging.*

I AM
LOW GI
HIGH IN VITAMINS
MINERAL RICH

APRICOT SMOOTHIE

PREP TIME **10 MINUTES (+ STANDING)** SERVES **2**

You need to start this recipe the day before.

½ cup (75g) raw cashews
1 chamomile tea bag
1 cup (250ml) boiling water
½ cup (75g) dried apricots
1 cup (250ml) filtered water
2 tablespoons rolled oats
1 tablespoon raw honey

I AM
DAIRY-FREE
AN ANXIETY AID
HIGH FIBRE

1 Rinse cashews in a sieve under cold running water. Place cashews in a small bowl with enough cold water to cover. Cover the bowl with a clean tea towel; stand at room temperature overnight. Drain nuts through a sieve; rinse under running water.
2 Place tea bag and the boiling water in a heatproof jug or bowl; stand 5 minutes. Add apricots; cool to room temperature. Refrigerate tea mixture until cold. (This step can be done the night before.) Discard tea bag.
3 Blend rinsed cashews and chilled tea mixture with filtered water, oats and honey in a high-speed blender until smooth.
4 Serve topped with shaved fresh coconut, if you like.

tips Soaking cashews overnight softens them and helps to neutralise the phytic acid that makes nuts difficult to digest. Chamomile tea is known for its calming effect; apricots are rich in vitamins A and C; cashews and oats help to soothe. Oats are rich in copper, zinc, selenium, thiamine and niacin which all contribute to support and soothe skin health. Cashews are one of the highest known plant sources of tryptophan and vitamin B6; both are a precursor to the feel-good hormone, serotonin, and work to create a relaxed state that helps fight anxiety and a tense mood.

love POTION

PREP TIME **10 MINUTES** SERVES **2**

400g (12½ ounces) chopped
    seedless watermelon

250g (8 ounces) peeled pineapple,
    chopped coarsely

1 long fresh red chilli, stem removed,
    chopped coarsely

¼ cup (60ml) pure pomegranate juice

1 teaspoon honey

1 Push the watermelon, pineapple
and chilli through a juice extractor
into a jug. Add pomegranate juice
and honey. Stir to combine.

2 Serve immediately with extra
chilli, if you like.

tips *The juice will separate on
standing, however a quick stir
will bring it back together. Long
red chillies can vary in their level
of heat so if you don't like things
too spicy, have a taste before you
juice the chilli and add more or less
accordingly. If you prefer, remove
the seeds and membrane from the
chilli first as these contain most of
the heat. All of these ingredients are
thought to be natural aphrodisiacs.
They also happen to contain lots of
vitamins, minerals and antioxidants.*

I AM
HIGH IN VITAMINS C & K
A METABOLISM BOOST
ANTIOXIDANT RICH

strong BONES

PREP TIME **5 MINUTES** SERVES **2**

1 large orange (300g)

1 cup (250ml) almond milk

2 small fresh figs (100g), chopped

1 tablespoon vanilla protein powder
   (see tip)

1 tablespoon hulled tahini

1 tablespoon chia seeds

1 Grate 1 teaspoon of rind from the orange; squeeze juice.

2 Blend rind and juice with remaining ingredients in a high-speed blender until smooth.

3 Serve in jars or glasses with thinly sliced fresh figs, if you like.

tips If you are opting for a dairy-free smoothie, then choose a vegan protein powder such as pea or brown rice protein. If dairy is not an issue, you can use a whey protein powder. Non-dairy calcium-rich foods include tahini, figs and almonds. Protein and omega-3 in chia seeds are essential for bone health.

I AM
DAIRY-FREE
HIGH IN CALCIUM
PROTEIN RICH

To peel or not to peel

Citrus Juice a washed wedge-sized piece of mandarin or lemon rind, it contains 20 times the flavonoids of the flesh. Avoid large citrus.

Ginger Peeling is unnecessary, however a quick rinse is a good idea. The nutritional benefits of the skin are minimal.

Carrot Peel non-organic carrots. Leave the skin on scrubbed organic carrots for extra nutrients and include a handful of the green tops if you like.

Kiwifruit While the skins are edible they can add bitterness, so peeling is the norm. In a few individuals kiwifruit can be allergenic.

Apple Buy organic and keep the skin on as two-thirds of its fibre is in the skin. It is also rich in minerals and antioxidants.

Beetroot Keep the skin on for extra nutrients and fibre content. Trim the tops as this is where the dirt collects; scrub well.

Melon Peel rockmelon; it can be contaminated. Don't peel honeydew and watermelon, as nutrients are concentrated.

Banana Banana flesh can't be juiced, but the peel can. It is a rich source of potassium, fibre and lutein for eye health.

Cucumber Peel if non-organic. While the skins are edible they are often listed as a vegetable most likely to contain pesticides.

BANANA PAPAYA

SMOOTHIE

PREP TIME **5 MINUTES (+ FREEZING)** SERVES **2**

2 medium bananas (460g),
    chopped coarsely
2 cups (340g) chopped papaya
1½ cups (375ml) almond milk
2 teaspoons flaxseed oil
2 teaspoons grated fresh turmeric
1 teaspoon ground cinnamon

1 Place banana in an airtight container or resealable plastic bag. Freeze for 4 hours or until firm.
2 Blend frozen banana with papaya, almond milk, flaxseed oil, turmeric and cinnamon in a high-speed blender until smooth.
3 Serve immediately with crushed ice and lime rind, if you like.

tips Don't waste bananas that are a little too ripe to eat. Chop them coarsely and freeze in resealable plastic bags in 1-2 banana quantities, so they are ready to add to smoothies. You will need half a medium papaya. Papaya, turmeric and cinnamon are all good for reducing inflammation. Banana is rich in potassium. Flaxseed oil, rich in omega 3, is helpful for joint lubrication; it also helps the body absorb the curcumin which is the anti-inflammatory component of turmeric.

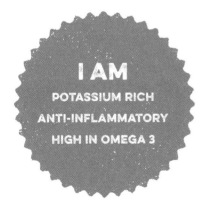

I AM
POTASSIUM RICH
ANTI-INFLAMMATORY
HIGH IN OMEGA 3

vegan's DREAM

PREP TIME **5 MINUTES (+ FREEZING)** SERVES **2**

1 large banana (230g),
   chopped coarsely

2 cups (500ml) almond milk

400g (12½ ounces) canned cooked
   black beans, drained, rinsed

2 fresh dates (40g), pitted

1 tablespoon vegan cacao powder

1 tablespoon tahini

1 teaspoon ground cinnamon

1 Place banana in an airtight container or resealable plastic bag. Freeze for 4 hours or until firm.

2 Blend frozen banana with remaining ingredients in a high-speed blender until smooth.

3 Serve topped with vegan chocolate and cacao powder, if you like.

tips *Beans are a great way to thicken smoothies and add extra protein. Try cannellini or butter beans in a banana and vanilla bean smoothie. Tahini is high in calcium and iron and cacao is magnesium-rich. Almond milk is high in calcium and protein and is a great dairy alternative.*

I AM
HIGH FIBRE
HIGH IN PROTEIN
CALCIUM RICH

CHERRY, LIME &
chia fresca

PREP TIME **10 MINUTES (+ REFRIGERATION)**   MAKES **1.25 LITRES (5 CUPS)**

1 cup (150g) pitted fresh cherries
3 cups (750ml) water
¼ cup (60ml) light agave syrup
2 tablespoons lime juice
1 tablespoon white chia seeds

1 Blend cherries, the water and agave syrup in a blender until smooth. Strain into a large jug. Add lime juice and chia seeds; stir to combine. Refrigerate for 15 minutes or until chia seeds have swollen and softened.
2 Serve with sliced lime and crushed ice, if you like.

tips *You can use thawed frozen cherries for this recipe. This drink will keep in the refrigerator for 24 hours. Stir just before serving. Chia seeds are good for digestion and keep you feeling full. Cherries are rich in antioxidants.*

I AM
ANTIOXIDANT RICH
GREAT FOR DIGESTION
HIGH FIBRE

ORANGE & VANILLA BEAN

coconut water

PREP TIME **5 MINUTES (+ REFRIGERATION)** MAKES **1 LITRE (4 CUPS)**

1 small navel orange (190g)
1 litre (4 cups) pure unsweetened coconut water
1 vanilla bean, split lengthways

1 Using a vegetable peeler, peel rind from orange
into long wide strips, avoiding any white pith.
Squeeze juice.
2 Place orange rind and juice in a large jug with
coconut water and vanilla bean; stir to combine.
Refrigerate for 1 hour or until cold.

*tips This will keep in the refrigerator for 24 hours.
Coconut water has electrolytes which rehydrate
you. Oranges are high in vitamin C.*

I AM
HIGH IN VITAMIN C
GREAT FOR HYDRATION
SUGAR-FREE

green
WATER

PREP TIME **10 MINUTES** SERVES **2**

1 whole young coconut (1.1kg)

1 teaspoon spirulina powder

I AM
ANTI-INFLAMMATORY
MINERAL & VITAMIN RICH
HIGH IN ANTIOXIDANTS

1 Using a sharp knife, carefully cut the top off the coconut. Pour the water from centre of coconut through a sieve into a jug; you need 1½ cups (375ml) coconut water.

2 Place coconut on a board; cut in half with a cleaver or heavy knife. The coconut flesh should be white; if flesh is purple or brown-tinged, don't use it. Use a spoon to scoop out the white flesh.

3 Blend coconut water and flesh in a high-speed blender for 1 minute or until smooth. Add spirulina; blend briefly until well combined.

tips *The young coconut should be heavy and when shaken, should be completely full with liquid. Spirulina is a powerful super food containing high levels of protein, vitamins B1, B2 and B3, as well as copper and iron, and decent amounts of magnesium, potassium and manganese. It is high in antioxidants, contains anti-inflammatory properties and according to research, has anti-cancer properties.*

I AM

ANTIOXIDANT RICH

COOLING & HYDRATING

HEART HEALTHY

ICED GREEN TEA & CUCUMBER SIPPER

PREP TIME 5 MINUTES (+ REFRIGERATION)

MAKES 1 LITRE (4 CUPS)

2 green tea bags

3½ cups (875ml) boiling water

1 tablespoon raw honey

crushed ice

½ cup (125ml) cucumber juice (see tips)

1 tablespoon lime juice

½ cup fresh mint leaves

1 lebanese cucumber (130g), sliced thinly

½ pink lady apple (75g), sliced thinly

1 Place tea bags and the boiling water in a heatproof jug; stand for 5 minutes. Discard tea bags. Stir in honey until dissolved. Refrigerate until chilled.

2 Half fill a large jug with ice, then add cucumber juice, lime juice, mint, sliced cucumber, apple and chilled tea; stir to combine.

tips You will need to juice 2 medium (260g) lebanese cucumbers for the amount of juice required here. If you don't have a juicer, use a blender, then strain mixture through a fine sieve.

PASSIONFRUIT & PINEAPPLE SPRITZER

PREP TIME 15 MINUTES (+ REFRIGERATION)
MAKES 1 LITRE (4 CUPS)

1 small ripe pineapple (900g)
½ cup (125ml) passionfruit pulp
1½ cups (375ml) chilled sparkling
    mineral water
¼ cup torn fresh mint leaves

1 Peel, core and coarsely chop
pineapple. Push pineapple pieces
through a juice extractor into a
jug; you need about 2 cups (500ml)
juice. Refrigerate until chilled.
2 Place chilled pineapple juice in a
large jug with passionfruit, mineral
water and mint; stir to combine.
Pour into serving glasses.
3 Serve topped with crushed ice,
passionfruit pulp and micro mint,
if you like.

*tip You will need about
6 passionfruit for this recipe.*

I AM
POTASSIUM RICH
FOR A HEALTHY GUT
HIGH IN VITAMIN C

ICED LEMON & MINT

green tea

PREP TIME **5 MINUTES (+ REFRIGERATION)** SERVES **2**

2 green tea bags
1 medium lemon (140g), rind cut into long thin strips
2 cups (500ml) hot water
2 teaspoons lemon juice
1 tablespoon fresh mint leaves
ice cubes

1 Place tea bags, rind and the hot water in a small heatproof jug; stir to combine. Refrigerate for 1 hour or until cold.
2 Discard tea bags; stir in juice and mint leaves, then ice cubes. Serve with lemon slices, if you like.

tip Lemon revitalises the body, while mint and green tea refresh and aid in digestion.

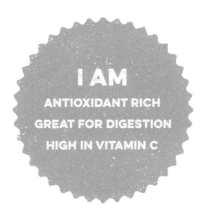

I AM
ANTIOXIDANT RICH
GREAT FOR DIGESTION
HIGH IN VITAMIN C

CUCUMBER, LIME & COCONUT WATER

PREP TIME 10 MINUTES

SERVES 2

1 lebanese cucumber (130g), chopped coarsely
3 cups (750ml) coconut water
2 tablespoons lime juice

1 Push cucumber through a juice extractor into a jug. Stir in coconut water and lime juice.
2 Serve topped with crushed ice and mint sprigs, if you like.

tips You can use fresh coconut juice from a young coconut, if you like. Cucumber hydrates, coconut water contains electrolytes to quench your thirst, and lime is an alkaliser.

I AM

HIGH IN VITAMIN K
A THIRST QUENCHER
POTASSIUM RICH

STRAWBERRY & BASIL SUNSHINE ICED TEA

PREP + COOK TIME
10 MINUTES (+ REFRIGERATION)
MAKES 1.25 LITRES (5 CUPS)

1 litre (4 cups) water
3 white tea bags
½ cup loosely packed fresh
    basil leaves
250g (8 ounces) ripe strawberries
2 teaspoons stevia granules
2 tablespoons lemon juice
ice cubes
2 sprigs fresh basil, extra
10 strawberries, extra, halved

1 Bring the water to the boil in a
medium saucepan; remove from
heat. Add tea bags and basil; stand
for 5 minutes. Discard tea bags and
basil. Refrigerate tea until chilled.
2 Blend strawberries, stevia and
¼ cup of the chilled tea until
smooth. Strain through a fine sieve
to remove seeds. Add strawberry
puree and lemon juice to remaining
chilled tea; stir to combine.
3 Half fill a large jug with ice,
then add extra basil and extra
strawberries. Pour in tea mixture;
stir to combine.

tips White tea is one of the least
processed of all teas. Strawberries
are rich in immune-boosting
vitamin C and also contain ellagic
acid which has been found to help
prevent collagen damage.

I AM
HIGH IN VITAMIN C
ANTIOXIDANT RICH
SUGAR-FREE

ginger ale

PREP TIME **10 MINUTES** MAKES **1 LITRE (4 CUPS)**

10cm (4-inch) piece fresh ginger
  (50g), unpeeled
1 medium lemon (140g), peeled
2 tablespoons pure maple syrup
1 litre (4 cups) sparkling
  mineral water

1 Push ginger and lemon through a
juice extractor into a jug; you should
have about ¼ cup (60ml) juice.
2 Combine juice mixture and maple
syrup in a large jug; stir in mineral
water. Serve over ice cubes, if you like.

*tips The ginger and lemon juice
can be made up to 2 days ahead;
store in a sealed glass jar in the
refrigerator. This drink makes a
great alternative to sugar-laden
ginger ale and has the added
benefits of reducing inflammation
and aiding digestion. This would
be a good tonic for nausea or
morning sickness.*

I AM
HIGH IN VITAMIN C
GREAT FOR DIGESTION
SUGAR-FREE

SMOOTHIES

PREP TIME **10 MINUTES (+ STANDING)** MAKES **2 CUPS (500ML)**

1 cup (160g) blanched almonds
2 cups (500ml) water

1 Place almonds in a large bowl with enough cold water to cover. Stand, covered, for 4 hours or overnight. Drain; rinse under cold water.
2 Process almonds with the water in a high-speed blender until smooth. Pour mixture through a strainer lined with a fine cloth into a large bowl. Keep any blended nuts left behind for another use (see tips).

spiced nut milk Make nut milk using 1 cup pecans. Stir in cinnamon sticks, star anise and saffron threads.

vanilla nut milk Make nut milk using ½ cup almonds and ½ cup cashews. Scrape the seeds from a split vanilla bean into the milk; stir to combine.

tips Using blanched or skinless nuts will create a whiter coloured milk. Use a high-powered blender such as a Vitamix to create a smoother textured milk. Instead of throwing out the blended nuts left behind after straining, keep them to sprinkle on your breakfast cereal or add to curries and pastes. Place the strained, blended nuts on an oven tray in a 150°C/300°F oven until mixture is dry. You can make nut milks with most nuts: hazelnuts, almonds, cashews, pecans are particuarly good. If you want to sweeten the milk, add pure maple syrup, honey or pureed dates. Nut milks are a delicious and nutritious dairy-free, high-protein option.

I AM
DAIRY-FREE
LOW IN CHOLESTEROL
PROTEIN RICH

I AM
HIGH FIBRE
VITAMIN & MINERAL RICH
DAIRY-FREE

CREAMY RASPBERRY SMOOTHIE

PREP TIME 5 MINUTES (+ STANDING) SERVES 2

⅔ cup (100g) raw cashews
1 cup (250ml) coconut water
1 cup (150g) frozen raspberries
1 tablespoon pure maple syrup
½ lime, peeled
1 cup ice cubes
2 tablespoons coconut cream

1 Place cashews in a medium bowl with enough cold water to cover. Stand at room temperature for 3 hours. Drain; rinse well.
2 Blend drained cashews with remaining ingredients in a high-speed blender for 1 minute or until smooth.
3 Divide coconut cream between serving jars, swirl around the sides; pour in smoothie.

SUMMER SUNRISE

PREP TIME 10 MINUTES
SERVES 2

½ cup (125ml) coconut water
⅓ cup (80ml) fresh orange juice
1 medium apple (150g),
    quartered, cored
½ small ripe pineapple (450g),
    peeled, cored, chopped coarsely
1cm (½-inch) piece fresh ginger,
    peeled, sliced thinly
1 cup ice cubes

1 In this order, place coconut
water and orange juice, then apple,
pineapple and ginger in a blender.
Add ice cubes; blend on high-speed
for 1 minute or until smooth.
2 Serve topped with chopped
pineapple, mint and pineapple
fronds, if you like

*tip This low-carb icy smoothie
is packed full of vitamin C, fibre,
potassium and enzymes that aid
in gut health and digestion.*

I AM

HIGH IN VITAMIN C
GREAT FOR GUT HEALTH
LOW CARB

SOY, LINSEED &
raspberry smoothie

PREP TIME **5 MINUTES** SERVES **2**

1 large banana (230g),
  chopped coarsely
1 cup (150g) frozen raspberries
2 cups (500ml) soy milk
1 tablespoon tahini
1 tablespoon LSA (see tips)
1 tablespoon honey

1 Blend ingredients in a high-powered blender until smooth.
2 Serve smoothie topped with fresh raspberries and toasted sesame seeds, if you like.

tips LSA is a ground mixture of linseeds (L), sunflower seeds (S) and almonds (A). It is available from supermarkets and health food stores. LSA is rich in protein, healthy omega-3 fats and minerals (calcium, zinc and magnesium). Tahini is a good non-dairy form of calcium, plus is high in iron and magnesium (which has been linked to relieving muscle cramps). This recipe is dairy-free. You can use your favourite non-dairy milk here.

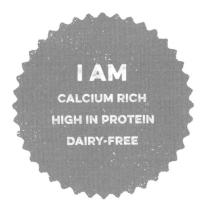

I AM
CALCIUM RICH
HIGH IN PROTEIN
DAIRY-FREE

HIGH-FIBRE BERRY SMOOTHIE

PREP TIME 5 MINUTES
SERVES 2

2 cups (500ml) milk
½ cup (50g) crushed Weet-Bix
   (see tips)
⅔ cup (190g) berry yoghurt
1 cup (150g) frozen mixed berries
   (see tips)

1 Blend or process ingredients
until smooth.
2 Served topped with fresh berries
and edible flowers, if you like.

tips *You need about 2 Weet-Bix*
for the crushed quantity required.
Weet-Bix is a wheat-based breakfast
cereal biscuit containing oven-
roasted whole wheat grains, sugar,
salt and barley malt extract.
You can use ¼ cup of fresh mixed
berries and 2 ice cubes instead
of the frozen berries.

I AM
ANTIOXIDANT RICH
HIGH IN CALCIUM
HIGH FIBRE

HONEYDEW SMOOTHIE

PREP TIME 5 MINUTES
SERVES 2

2 small apples (260g), peeled,
  cored, chopped coarsely
12 medium baby cos (romaine)
  lettuce leaves (100g)
50g (1½ ounces) baby spinach
  leaves
200g (6½ ounces) coarsely
  chopped honeydew melon
1½ cups (375ml) water

1 Blend or process ingredients
until smooth.
2 Serve immediately topped with
crushed ice and baby spinach
leaves, if you like.

tips *Store all the ingredients in the*
fridge for an extra cold smoothie.
This smoothie will separate on
standing, however a quick stir will
bring it back together. Honeydew
melon has a high water content
and is a good source of potassium,
making it good for maintaining
healthy blood pressure levels.
Its high vitamin C and copper
content aid collagen production
and tissue repair. Lettuce has a
cooling effect, spinach provides
calcium and both, along with the
apple and melon, provide a healthy
dose of dietary fibre.

I AM
HIGH FIBRE
GREAT POST-EXERCISE
POTASSIUM RICH

TROPICAL FRUIT
smoothie

PREP TIME **10 MINUTES** SERVES **2**

½ cup (125ml) freshly squeezed
orange juice

½ small pineapple (450g), chopped
coarsely

⅓ cup (80ml) strained passionfruit
juice

250g (8 ounces) low-fat yoghurt

1 tablespoon wheat germ

1 Blend or process ingredients until smooth.

2 Serve smoothie topped with crushed ice and passionfruit, if you like.

tips *You will need about 5 passionfruit. To increase the fibre content of this smoothie, stir some of the strained passionfruit seeds into the smoothie after blending. For a non-dairy smoothie, use soy or coconut yoghurt instead. Wheat germ adds a boost of folate and vitamin E to this fresh fruit smoothie that's already packed with vitamins, potassium, calcium and loads of fibre and enzymes for gut health and digestion.*

I AM
CALCIUM RICH
GREAT FOR GUT HEALTH
HIGH IN FOLATE

CHOCOLATE THICK SHAKE

PREP TIME 10 MINUTES
SERVES 2

1 cup (250ml) unsweetened
   almond milk
1 medium frozen banana (200g),
   chopped coarsely
½ small avocado (100g), chopped
½ cup firmly packed baby
   spinach leaves
1 tablespoon cacao powder
2 tablespoons vanilla bean whey
   protein powder (optional)
   or yoghurt
2 teaspoons raw honey

1 Blend ingredients in a high-
speed blender until smooth
2 Serve immediately over ice
cubes, dusted with cacao powder
and topped with banana chips,
if you like.

tip *This high-protein, sugar-free
smoothie is just like a chocolate
thick shake... only better for you.*

I AM
POTASSIUM RICH
HIGH IN PROTEIN
SUGAR-FREE

ALMOND & AVOCADO PROTEIN SMOOTHIE

PREP TIME 5 MINUTES
SERVES 2

1 cup (250ml) unsweetened
  almond milk
1 tablespoon vanilla-flavoured
  protein powder
2 tablespoons almond spread
½ medium ripe avocado (125g)
1 tablespoon raw honey
½ medium banana (100g)
1 cup ice cubes

1 Blend ingredients in a high-
speed blender for 1 minute or
until smooth.

*tip This creamy, high-protein
smoothie is the perfect post-
workout drink to help kickstart
your body's recovery processes.*

HORCHATA

porridge shake

PREP + COOK TIME **15 MINUTES (+ REFRIGERATION)** SERVES **2**

You need to start this recipe the day before.

½ vanilla bean
2 cups (500ml) unsweetened
   almond milk
½ cup (45g) rolled oats
2 teaspoons raw honey
2 teaspoons rolled oats, extra
2 tablespoons flaked almonds
¼ teaspoon sea salt
¼ teaspoon ground cinnamon

1 Using the tip of a small knife, scrape out vanilla seeds. Place vanilla seeds and pod in a medium jug with almond milk, oats and honey; stir to combine. Refrigerate, covered, overnight.
2 Preheat oven to 180°C/ 350°F. Place extra oats on a small oven tray; roast for 5 minutes. Add almonds; roast for another 5 minutes or until lightly golden.
3 Discard vanilla bean from milk mixture. Blend or process milk mixture until smooth; stir in salt.
4 Pour shake into serving glasses, top with roasted almond mixture; dust with cinnamon. Serve immediately.

tips For a quick version, leave out the oats (and the overnight refrigeration); blend chilled milk, vanilla seeds, honey and salt together. Serve immediately. This recipe is perfect for a breakfast on the go, simply pour into a bottle, jar or jug with a lid and away you go.

I AM
DAIRY-FREE
GREAT FOR PROTEIN
HIGH FIBRE

BANANA, CHIA & KIWI SMOOTHIE

PREP TIME 10 MINUTES
SERVES 2

1 medium banana (200g), chopped
2 medium kiwifruit (170g), chopped
30g (1 ounce) baby spinach leaves
1 cup (250ml) almond milk
1 tablespoon honey
2 teaspoons chia seeds

1 Blend ingredients until smooth.
2 Serve immediately topped with crushed ice, extra chia seeds and sliced kiwifruit, if you like.

tips You can use black or white chia seeds in this recipe, available from supermarkets and health food stores. Kiwifruit contains loads of fibre, vitamins C & E, antioxidants and minerals – zinc, iron, calcium, magnesium, copper and potassium. Kiwifruit are great for keeping skin, hair and nails glowing, healthy and strong and contains the enzyme actinidin which aids in gut health and digestion. Chia seeds are good for digestion and high in fibre, making you feel full.

I AM
HIGH FIBRE
GOOD FOR HEALTHY SKIN
DAIRY-FREE

PB & J SMOOTHIE

PREP TIME 5 MINUTES
SERVES 2

1½ cups (225g) frozen strawberries
1½ tablespoons smooth light
    peanut butter
2 tablespoons wheat germ
1 tablespoon brown rice malt syrup
1½ cups (375ml) low-fat milk

1 Blend ingredients until smooth.
2 Spread a little extra peanut butter
on the inside of each serving glass,
if you like, before pouring in the
smoothie.

*tips You could use honey or agave
syrup instead of brown rice malt
syrup, if you prefer. This low-carb
smoothie really does taste like
an indulgent peanut butter and
jelly sandwich in a glass, without
the sugar-laden jam, with a
boost of extra fibre and healthier
unsaturated fats.*

I AM
HIGH FIBRE
HIGH IN VITAMIN C
LOW CARB

STRAWBERRY SOY PROTEIN

smoothie

PREP TIME **10 MINUTES** SERVES **2**

125g (4 ounces) strawberries
1½ cups (375ml) reduced-fat soy milk
150g (4½ ounces) firm silken tofu
1 tablespoon honey

1 Blend 50g (1½ ounces) of the strawberries until smooth; reserve.
2 Blend remaining strawberries, milk, tofu and honey until smooth.
3 Pour into serving glasses; drizzle with reserved strawberry puree.

tips Silken tofu refers to the manufacturing method of straining the soya bean liquid though silk, while firm tofu is made by compressing bean curd to remove most of the water. Tofu is an excellent source of amino acids, iron, calcium and protein. This smoothie is a delicious creamy, dairy-free option.

I AM
DIARY-FREE
HIGH IN CALCIUM & IRON
PROTEIN RICH

Crunchy toppers

Vanilla Munch

Combine ⅓ cup coconut flakes, ⅓ cup sliced brazil nuts and the scraped seeds from 1 split vanilla bean in a small jar; seal the lid.

Rose Tang

Combine ¼ cup freeze-dried pomegranate seeds, 1 tablespoon dried rose petals and ¼ cup halved dry-roasted natural almonds in a small jar; seal the lid.

Black Magic

Combine 1 tablespoon sunflower seeds, 1 tablespoon pepitas (pumpkin seeds), 1 tablespoon linseeds and 2 tablespoons black chia seeds in a small jar; seal the lid.

Yellow Power

Combine ¼ cup coarsely chopped raw cashews, thinly sliced rind of 1 mandarin (or orange), 1 teaspoon ground turmeric and ¼ teaspoon ground cardamom in a small jar; seal the lid.

Golden Glow

Combine 1 cup roasted halved macadamias, 2 tablespoons millet seeds and 2 tablespoons LSA in a small jar; seal the lid.

Hot Chocolate

Combine ¼ cup halved roasted hazelnuts, 2 tablespoons cocoa nibs, 2 tablespoons activated buckwheat (buckinis) and a pinch of ground chilli in a small jar; seal the lid.

Berry Seeds

Combine ½ cup toasted shredded coconut, ½ cup goji berries (or cranberries or dried cherries) and 2 tablespoons poppy seeds in a small jar; seal the lid.

Green Crunch

Combine 1 tablespoon white chia seeds, 1 tablespoon pepitas (pumpkin seeds) and 1 tablespoon bee pollen in a small jar; seal the lid.

CHERRY & WALNUT

smoothie

PREP TIME **15 MINUTES (+ STANDING)** SERVES **2**

You need to start this recipe the day before.

¼ cup (25g) walnuts
2 tablespoons almonds
1 cup (250ml) water
375g (12 ounces) frozen pitted
   cherries
1 teaspoon pure maple syrup

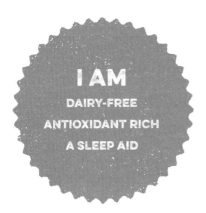

I AM
DAIRY-FREE
ANTIOXIDANT RICH
A SLEEP AID

1 Rub walnuts in a clean
tea towel to remove most of the
skins. Combine walnuts, almonds
and the water in a medium bowl.
Cover; stand overnight.
2 Blend nut mixture in a high-speed
blender until as smooth as possible.
Strain the mixture through a muslin
or tea-towel lined sieve over
a medium jug, twist and press the
cloth to extract as much nut milk as
possible. Discard solids.
3 Blend nut milk, cherries and syrup
until smooth.
4 Serve immediately, topped with
crushed ice, chopped walnuts, chia
seeds and fresh cherries, if you like.

tips *For a thicker smoothie,
blend the chia seeds with the other
ingredients. Cherries are rich in
powerful antioxidants. Some research
also suggests they help prevent the
risk of stroke, reduce post-exercise
muscle pain and contain melatonin
that supports healthy sleep.*

I AM
CALCIUM RICH
VITAMIN & MINERAL RICH
HIGH FIBRE

MANGO, BANANA & BERRY SMOOTHIE

PREP TIME 10 MINUTES
SERVES 4

⅔ cup (100g) frozen raspberries
2 cups (500ml) milk
2 small bananas (260g), chopped
3 small mangoes (900g), chopped
2 tablespoons lime juice

1 Blend raspberries and ½ cup of the milk until smooth; reserve ¼ cup in a small bowl. Add banana, mango and juice to remaining raspberry mixture; blend until smooth.
2 Divide into serving glasses, top with reserved raspberry mixture. If you like, serve topped with crushed ice, frozen raspberries and mango cheeks.

tips For a super-chilled summery smoothie, freeze the chopped banana and mango overnight before using. Mangoes are a good source of vitamins C, A, B6 and K and, like bananas, potassium. This smoothie is packed full of fibre and antioxidants. For a dairy-free option, use soy, rice, coconut or nut milk.

FROZEN YO-BERRY

PREP TIME 10 MINUTES (+ FREEZING) SERVES 2

1½ cups (420g) greek-style yoghurt
1 tablespoon honey
200g (7 ounces) peeled, coarsely
   chopped pineapple
250g (8 ounces) strawberries, halved
250g (8 ounces) fresh mixed berries

1 Blend yoghurt, honey, pineapple
and strawberries until smooth.
Pour mixture into three 14-hole
ice-cube trays (1 tablespoon
capacity). Freeze for 4 hours or
until frozen.
2 Serve frozen yo-berry cubes
with fresh berries and, if you like,
topped with micro mint.

*tips The yo-berry cubes will soften
into a slushly-style drink. Vary the
fruit according to your taste and
what's in season; just make sure
you use the same quantities.
Yoghurt and pineapple promote
gut health and digestion. Yoghurt
provides calcium. Strawberries
provide powerful antioxidants and
have a high concentration of ellagic
acid, a phenolic compound that has
been found to prevent the growth
of some cancer cells and prevent
collagen damage.*

I AM

HIGH IN CALCIUM

GREAT FOR GUT HEALTH

ANTIOXIDANT RICH

spiced apple pie

OAT SMOOTHIE

PREP TIME **5 MINUTES** SERVES **2**

1 cup (90g) rolled oats

2 tablespoons maca powder

1 cup (250ml) almond milk

1 cup (250ml) pure apple juice

2 small red apples (260g), cored,
   chopped coarsely

¼ cup (70g) greek-style yoghurt

4 fresh medjool dates (20g), pitted,
   chopped coarsely

1 teaspoon ground cinnamon

¼ teaspoon ground nutmeg

1 vanilla bean, split lengthways,
   seeds scraped

6 ice cubes

1 Place ingredients in a high-speed blender; blend until smooth.
2 Pour smoothie into tall glasses. Serve sprinkled with ground cinnamon, if you like.

I AM
HIGH FIBRE
VITAMIN & MINERAL RICH
SUGAR-FREE

tips Medjool dates are available from the fresh food section of major supermarkets. When pears are in season, use a juicy variety such as packham instead of the red apples, and pear juice instead of apple juice. Maca powder is available from major supermarkets and health food stores. It is a rich source of vitamin C, iron, copper and calcium, and a very good source of riboflavin, niacin, vitamin B6, potassium and manganese. It also contains about 14% protein and provides a good dose of fibre.

BANANA BRAN SMOOTHIE

PREP TIME 5 MINUTES
SERVES 2

1 cup (250ml) milk
1 medium banana (200g),
    chopped coarsely
¼ cup (70g) greek-style yoghurt
2 teaspoons honey
2 teaspoons unprocessed bran
¼ teaspoon ground cinnamon

1 Blend or process ingredients
until smooth.
2 Serve sprinkled with ground
cinnamon, if you like.

tips Use frozen bananas or add ice
cubes to the blender for a thicker
smoothie. For a dairy-free option,
use soy, rice, coconut or nut milk
and soy or coconut yoghurt. The
popular combination of banana,
honey and cinnamon, with an
added fibre boost from bran, is
an easy way to get your family to
increase their fibre intake.

I AM
CALCIUM RICH
HIGH IN POTASSIUM
HIGH FIBRE

I AM
CALCIUM RICH
AN IMMUNITY BOOST
A DIGESTION AID

MELON & MANGO LASSI

PREP TIME 15 MINUTES
SERVES 2

150g (4½ ounces) strawberries,
  halved
1 tablespoon caster (superfine)
  sugar
1 cup (280g) greek-style yoghurt
½ cup (125ml) water
200g (6½ ounces) seeded, peeled,
  coarsely chopped rockmelon
2 small mangoes (600g), peeled,
  chopped coarsely
3 ice cubes

1 Process strawberries and sugar
until smooth; reserve ¼ cup in
a small bowl. Add remaining
ingredients to remaining berry
mixture; process until smooth.
2 Divide reserved strawberry
mixture between serving glasses;
swirl inside each glass. Pour in
lassi mixture.
3 Serve lassi topped with extra
strawberries, if you like.

*tips Rockmelon is a good source
of fibre, vitamins A and C and
potassium. This combination
of rockmelon with pineapple,
mango and strawberries will
provide a rich dose of vitamin C
and boost immunity as well as
aiding digestion.*

MANGO & COCONUT

smoothie

PREP TIME **10 MINUTES** SERVES **4**

1 whole young coconut (1.1kg)

2 large mangoes (1.2kg),
chopped coarsely

1½ cups (420g) greek-style yoghurt

1 tablespoon coconut sugar

2 passionfruit, to serve (optional)

1 Using a sharp knife, carefully cut the top off the coconut. Pour water from centre of coconut through a sieve into a blender. Cut open the shell; scrape out the flesh with a spoon into blender.

2 Add mango, yoghurt and sugar to blender; blend until smooth.

3 Serve with passionfruit pulp and mango wedges, if you like.

tips The young coconut should be heavy and when shaken, should be completely full with water. Freeze the coconut water and chopped mango ahead of time; this will chill your smoothie. Use coconut yoghurt for a non-dairy version and added coconut flavour. The water from a young coconut is a far better isotonic drink than sugar-laden sports drinks, providing high levels of electrolytes in their natural form.

I AM

SUGAR-FREE

HIGH IN BETA-CAROTENE

MUSCLE STIMULANT

I AM

DAIRY-FREE
ANTIOXIDANT RICH
HIGH IN PROTEIN

BERRY BERRY LUSCIOUS

PREP TIME 15 MINUTES
SERVES 2

2 tablespoons goji berries
2 cups (500ml) chilled coconut
 milk blend (see tips)
2 cups (300g) frozen mixed berries
1 cup firmly packed baby spinach

1 In a small bowl, soak goji
berries in half the coconut milk
for 10 minutes.
2 Transfer mixture to a high-
speed blender; add mixed berries,
spinach and remaining coconut
milk. Blend until smooth.
3 Serve over crushed ice, topped
with extra goji berries and fresh
mixed berries, if you like.

tips *We used Pureharvest Coco
Quench a blend of coconut and rice
milks; it has a thinner consistency
than canned coconut milk, but still
has a great coconut milk taste.
The berries in this recipe pack
some serious antioxidant punch,
plus provide vitamin C, beta-
carotene and fibre.*

MELON & BERRY FRAPPÉ

PREP TIME 10 MINUTES
SERVES 2

400g (12½ ounces) seedless
   watermelon, peeled, chopped
   coarsely
100g (3 ounces) frozen strawberries
1 teaspoon finely grated lime rind
1½ tablespoons lime juice

1 Blend ingredients until smooth.
2 Serve immediately in glasses
lined with thinly sliced strawberries,
topped with crushed ice and a lime
wedge. if you like.

*tips Use any melon and berry
combination; just make sure you
use the same quantities. Hydrating
watermelon is 92% water and rich
in vitamins A, B6 and C, is a good
source of lycopene and amino acids
(citrulline and arginine) and has
anti-inflammatory properties.*

I AM
ANTI-INFLAMMATORY
GREAT FOR HYDRATION
VITAMIN RICH

MANGO & ALMOND
smoothie

PREP TIME **5 MINUTES** SERVES **2**

1 large mango (600g),
  chopped coarsely
¼ cup (30g) ground almonds
1 cup (250ml) milk
½ cup (140g) yoghurt
1 teaspoon vanilla extract
1 tablespoon lime juice
2 teaspoons honey

1 Blend ingredients in a high-powered
blender until smooth.
2 Serve over crushed ice topped with
a little honey, extra finely chopped
mango and shredded lime rind,
if you like.

tips *Use frozen mango or drained
canned mango in natural juice,
if fresh is not available. Blend ice
with the ingredients for a thicker
smoothie. For a dairy-free version,
use soy, rice, coconut or nut milk
and soy or coconut yoghurt.
Mangoes are a good source of
vitamins C, A, B6 and K and
potassium. Almonds contain
vitamin E, high-quality protein,
iron and copper, as well as healthy
unsaturated fats.*

I AM
PROTEIN RICH
HIGH IN BETA-CAROTENE
CALCIUM RICH

SUPERSEED SMOOTHIE

PREP TIME 5 MINUTES
(+ FREEZING) SERVES 2

1 small banana (130g), peeled,
    chopped coarsely
½ cup (140g) greek-style yoghurt
1 cup (150g) frozen mixed berries
1 tablespoon dried goji berries
1 tablespoon honey
1 cup (250ml) milk
1 teaspoon ground linseeds
    (flaxseeds)
1 teaspoon chia seeds

1 Place banana in an airtight
container or resealable plastic bag.
Freeze for 4 hours or until firm.
2 Blend banana with remaining
ingredients in a high-powered
blender until smooth.
3 Serve immediately topped with
extra ground linseeds, chia seeds
and goji berries, if you like.

tips *Chia seeds are the richest
plant source of omega-3 fatty
acids, important for brain, heart
and nervous system function as
well as keeping skin soft. They
are packed with fibre, protein
and calcium and contain iron,
magnesium, zinc and B vitamins.*

I AM
HIGH FIBRE
ANTIOXIDANT RICH
A BRAIN BOOST

CHAI SMOOTHIE

PREP TIME 10 MINUTES

SERVES 1

1 black tea bag
⅓ cup (80ml) boiling water
½ teaspoon ground cinnamon
½ teaspoon ground cardamom
½ teaspoon ground clove
½ teaspoon ground ginger
4 hard ginger biscuits
1 cup (280g) greek-style yoghurt
1 tablespoon honey

1 Place tea bag in the boiling water in a small heatproof jug; stand for 3 minutes. Discard tea bag. Cool.
2 Blend tea with remaining ingredients until smooth.
3 Serve topped with extra crumbled ginger biscuits, if you like.

tip *We used gingernut biscuits.*

I AM
HIGH FIBRE
GOOD FOR GUT HEALTH
HGIH IN CALCIUM

BANANA & MAPLE
raspberry smoothie

PREP TIME **10 MINUTES** SERVES **2**

1 large ripe banana (230g), chopped coarsely
1 cup (135g) frozen raspberries
¾ cup (210g) greek-style yoghurt
¾ cup (180ml) milk
2 teaspoons pure maple syrup

1 Blend or process ingredients until smooth.
2 Serve over crushed ice, topped with extra
raspberries and extra maple syrup, if you like.

tips *Replace the raspberries with blueberries*
or strawberries, if you prefer, and add honey
and ground cinnamon. Blend crushed ice with
the ingredients for an even thicker smoothie.
For a non-dairy version, use soy or coconut
yoghurt and soy milk or light coconut milk.

I AM
SUGAR-FREE
POTASSIUM RICH
HIGH IN CALCIUM

chunky toppers

Chocolate Monkey

Combine ½ cup each of banana chips, roasted unsalted peanuts and coconut flakes in a small jar. Chop 50g (1½oz) dark chocolate (70% cocoa) into small squares. Add to jar; seal the lid.

Shortcake Crumble

Preheat oven to 200°C/400°F. Combine ½ cup ground almonds and 2 tablespoons rolled oats in a bowl; rub in 25g (¾oz) cold butter. Spread out on a baking-paper-lined oven tray; bake for 10 minutes or until golden. Cool.

Apricot Blossom

Combine ⅓ cup each of dried apricot halves, pistachios and roasted walnut halves, 1 tablespoon each of toasted sesame seeds and halved dried inca berries, and 1 teaspoon orange blossom water in a jar; seal the lid.

Pink Sprinkle

Combine 2 tablespoons each of dried cranberries and goji berries, ¼ cup quinoa flakes, 1 tablespoon acai powder and 2 teaspoons pink peppercorns in a jar; seal the lid.

Honey Crumble

Heat 1 tablespoon virgin coconut oil in a frying pan. Stir in ¼ cup quinoa, 1 tablespoon each of honey and sesame seeds, and ½ teaspoon ground cinnamon until golden. Spread on a baking-paper-lined tray; cool. Break into pieces.

Date & Almond Rawnola

Pulse ½ cup natural almonds, 8 pitted dates, 2 tablespoons cocoa nibs and 1 tablespoon natural almond butter or spread in a food processor until coarsely chopped; transfer to a jar. Stir in 1 cup shredded coconut; seal the lid.

Cacao Crunch

Heat ¼ cup honey and 2 teaspoons virgin coconut oil in a medium pan until foamy. Stir in 1 tablespoon each of cacao and activated buckwheat (buckinis), 2 cups multi puffs and ¼ cup chopped almonds.

Crimson Blast

Combine ½ cup each of dried blueberries, macadamia halves and crimson raisins with ¼ cup golden flaxmeal in a small jar; seal the lid.

POMEGRANATE *smoothie*

PREP TIME **10 MINUTES (+ FREEZING)** SERVES **2**

2 medium pomegranates (640g)

1 cup (280g) greek-style yoghurt

1 tablespoon honey

1 large banana (230g),
   chopped coarsely

I AM

ANTIOXIDANT RICH

ANTI-INFLAMMATORY

HIGH IN VITAMIN C

1 Cut pomegranates in half crossways. Hold each half, cut-side down, in the palm of your hand over a medium bowl, then hit the outside firmly with a wooden spoon. The seeds should fall out easily; discard any white pith that falls out with them. Divide 2 tablespoons of the seeds among the holes of an ice-cube tray; top with water. Freeze for 4 hours or until frozen.

2 Grind remaining pomegranate seeds in a mortar and pestle to release the juice. Strain through a sieve into a blender; discard solids.

3 Add yoghurt, honey and banana to blender; blend until smooth.

4 Pour smoothie into glasses. Serve immediately topped with pomegranate ice-cubes and, if you like, slivered pistachios.

tips You can use ⅔ cup (160ml) pure pomegranate juice in the smoothie if pomegranates are out of season. For a thicker smoothie, freeze banana for 4 hours or until firm before blending. Pomegranates are an excellent source of vitamin C and polyphenol ellagitannin – a powerful antioxidant and anti-inflammatory.

SMOOTHIE
BOWLS

WARM FIG &
tahini bowl

PREP & COOK TIME **25 MINUTES** SERVES **2**

½ cup (100g) white quinoa

1 cup (250ml) water

½ cup (100g) soft and juicy
  whole dried figs

1½ cups (375ml) almond milk

1 tablespoon tahini

2 teaspoons honey

½ teaspoon ground cinnamon

¼ teaspoon ground cardamom

1 small banana (130g),
  chopped coarsely

3 fresh figs (225g), torn in half

2 tablespoons pistachios

HONEY QUINOA CRUMBLE

1 tablespoon virgin coconut oil

¼ cup (50g) white quinoa

1 tablespoon honey

1 tablespoon sesame seeds

½ teaspoon ground cinnamon

1 Make honey quinoa crumble.

2 Place quinoa and the water in a
small saucepan; bring to the boil.
Reduce heat to low; cook, covered,
for 15 minutes or until tender.
Remove pan from heat.

3 Place dried figs, almond milk,
tahini, honey and spices in a medium
saucepan; stir to combine. Bring to a
simmer; remove from heat.

4 Blend cooked quinoa and warm
fig mixture with the banana until
smooth. Pour into serving bowls.
Serve topped with fresh fig,
pistachios and crumble.

honey quinoa crumble Heat
coconut oil in a medium frying
pan over low heat; cook quinoa,
honey, sesame seeds and cinnamon,
stirring, for 5 minutes or until
lightly golden. Spread mixture
on a baking-paper-lined tray; cool.
Break into small pieces.

*tips Quinoa is high in protein
so will keep you feeling fuller for
longer. Tahini paste is a good non-
dairy form of calcium. This recipe
is suitable for vegans.*

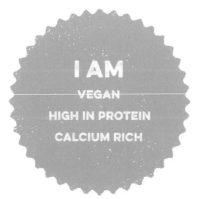

I AM
VEGAN
HIGH IN PROTEIN
CALCIUM RICH

COCONUT &

mango bowl

PREP TIME **10 MINUTES** SERVES **2**

2 medium chilled ripe mangoes
   (860g), peeled
1 cup (250ml) chilled coconut milk
2 tablespoons flaxmeal
4 passionfruit, halved
⅓ cup (55g) coarsely chopped
   brazil nuts
2 tablespoons shaved fresh coconut
2 teaspoons linseeds (flaxseeds)

1 Chop the flesh of one mango;
thinly slice second mango.
2 Blend chopped mango, coconut
milk, flaxmeal and the pulp from
2 passionfruit until smooth.
3 Pour smoothie into serving bowls;
top with sliced mango, brazil nuts,
remaining passionfruit, the coconut,
linseeds and, if you like, edible flowers.
Serve immediately.

*tips Don't use more flaxmeal than
required in the recipe as it can have
a laxative effect. This smoothie will
thicken on standing so is best served
immediately. Mangoes contain high
levels of fibre and vitamins C and A.
Flaxmeal is high in fibre and omega-3
fatty acids. This recipe is suitable
for vegans.*

I AM
POTASSUM RICH
HIGH IN BETA-CAROTENE
VEGAN

ACAI BERRY

PREP TIME **10 MINUTES (+ FREEZING)** SERVES **2**

2 medium bananas (400g),
   chopped coarsely
½ cup (75g) frozen blueberries
100g (3 ounces) frozen unsweetened
   pure acai
1 cup (280g) greek-style yoghurt
2 teaspoons bee pollen
⅓ cup (50g) fresh raspberries
2 tablespoons fresh blueberries
2 tablespoons goji berries
2 teaspoons bee pollen, extra

1 Place banana in an airtight container or resealable plastic bag. Freeze for 4 hours or until firm.
2 Blend frozen banana with frozen blueberries, acai, yoghurt and bee pollen until smooth.
3 Pour into serving bowls. Top with fresh raspberries and blueberries, goji berries, extra bee pollen and, if you like, edible flowers. Serve immediately.

tips Freeze the bananas for several hours or overnight. Acai can be found in the freezer section of some health food stores. Acai, blueberries, goji, chia and bee pollen are all superfoods. They should help boost your energy levels and immune system. Yoghurt provides protein and banana provides fibre to keep you fuller for longer.

I AM
HIGH FIBRE
ANTIOXIDANT RICH
AN ENERGY BOOST

CHOC ALMOND
banana bowl

PREP TIME **15 MINUTES (+ FREEZING)** SERVES **2**

2 small bananas (260g),
   chopped coarsely
1 cup (250ml) almond milk
1 cup (90g) rolled oats
2 tablespoons natural almond butter
   or spread (see tips)
6 fresh dates (120g), pitted
1 tablespoon cacao powder
½ teaspoon vanilla extract
½ teaspoon ground cinnamon
2 tablespoons halved almonds
2 small bananas (200g), extra,
   sliced lengthways

DATE & ALMOND RAWNOLA
½ cup (80g) almonds
8 fresh dates (160g), pitted
2 tablespoons cacao nibs
1 tablespoon natural almond butter
   or spread
1 cup (75g) shredded coconut

1 Place chopped banana in an airtight container or resealable plastic bag. Freeze for 4 hours or until firm.
2 Make date and almond rawnola.
3 Blend frozen banana with almond milk, oats, almond butter, 4 dates, cacao, extract and cinnamon until smooth.
4 Pour into serving bowls; divide ½ cup rawnola between serves. Top with halved almonds, remaining dates and extra bananas. If you like, drizzle with honey and dust with a little extra cacao powder. Serve immediately.

date & almond rawnola Place nuts, dates, cacao nibs and almond butter in a food processor; pulse until coarsely chopped. Transfer to a bowl; stir in coconut. (Makes 2½ cups)

tips We used a natural almond spread made from 100% almonds; there are other products which only contain 23% almonds. Store leftover rawnola in an airtight container. Sprinkle on yoghurt and other desserts. Rolled oats are low GI so will keep you fuller for longer. They also help to lower cholesterol. Cacao is high in antioxidants. Bananas are high in potassium.

I AM
PROTEIN RICH
LOW IN CHOLESTEROL
VEGAN

strawberry
SHORTCAKE

PREP + COOK TIME **20 MINUTES (+ COOLING)** SERVES **2**

1 cup (250ml) canned coconut milk

2 cups (250g) frozen strawberries

½ medium avocado (125g)

¼ cup (20g) rolled oats

1 vanilla bean, split lengthways,
seeds scraped

1 teaspoon ground cinnamon

1 tablespoon honey

160g (5 ounces) fresh strawberries,
halved

SHORTCAKE CRUMBLE

½ cup (60g) ground almonds

2 tablespoons rolled oats

25g (¾ ounce) cold butter, chopped

1 Make shortcake crumble.

2 Reserve 1 tablespoon of the coconut milk. Blend remaining coconut milk with frozen strawberries, avocado, oats, vanilla seeds, cinnamon and honey, in a high-powered blender until smooth.

3 Pour into serving bowls. Top with shortcake crumble, fresh strawberries and, if you like, micro herbs. Drizzle with reserved coconut milk just before serving.

shortcake crumble Preheat oven to 200°C/400°F. Line an oven tray with baking paper. Combine ground almonds and oats in a medium bowl; rub in butter. Spread mixture onto tray; bake for 10 minutes or until golden. Cool.

tips *You can store the shortcake crumble in an airtight container for up to 3 days. All the flavours of your favourite afternoon tea treat are here in a delicious and nutritious smoothie bowl. The beauty of this strawberry shortcake is that it's a satiating meal replacement that packs an antioxidant, complex slow-release carbs, and protein punch. The shortcake crumble is the pièce de résistance; you'd be forgiven if you thought you were eating the real thing.*

I AM
HIGH FIBRE
HIGH IN VITAMIN C
PROTEIN RICH

PECAN & MAPLE BANANA
soft serve bowl

PREP TIME **10 MINUTES (+ FREEZING)** SERVES **2**

4 large bananas (920g), sliced
1½ tablespoons carob powder
⅓ cup (80ml) pure maple syrup
⅓ cup (40g) pecans

1 Place banana in an airtight container or resealable plastic bag. Freeze for at 4 hours or until firm (see tips).
2 Process frozen banana until smooth and the texture of soft serve ice-cream. Add 2 teaspoons of the carob powder and 2 tablespoons of the maple syrup; process until just combined. Add ¼ cup of the pecans; pulse briefly until just combined.
3 Combine remaining carob powder with remaining maple syrup. Smear half the carob syrup mixture on the inside of serving jars.
4 Spoon banana mixture into serving jars; top with remaining pecans and drizzle with remaining carob syrup mixture.

tips You must use frozen bananas for this recipe to work. If the ice-cream becomes too soft while you're preparing it, return it to the freezer for a few minutes to firm up. This vegan four-ingredient ice cream bowl will make you rethink the way you eat ice cream. The ice cream itself is made up of one ingredient only – bananas. Until you actually make this you won't believe it's possible.

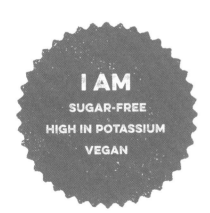

I AM
SUGAR-FREE
HIGH IN POTASSIUM
VEGAN

CARMEN MIRANDA
smoothie bowl

PREP TIME **10 MINUTES (+ FREEZING)** SERVES **2**

2 cups (400g) coarsely chopped
   mango

1 large banana (230g),
   chopped coarsely

1 whole young coconut (1.1kg)

1 small lime (70g)

1 medium peach (150g),
   seed removed, quartered

1 passionfruit

1 tablespoon chia seeds

250g (8 ounces) strawberries, halved

2 small bananas (260g), extra, sliced

1 passionfruit, extra

1 teaspoon chia seeds, extra

1 Place mango and banana in an airtight container or resealable plastic bag. Freeze for 4 hours or until firm.

2 Using a sharp knife, carefully cut the top off the coconut. Pour water from centre of coconut through a sieve into a jug. You need 2 cups (500ml) coconut water. Place coconut on a board; cut in half with a cleaver or heavy knife. The coconut flesh should be white; if flesh is purple or brown-tinged, don't use it. Use a spoon to scoop out the white flesh.

3 Cut lime in half; cut one half in half again. Reserve wedges for serving. Thickly peel remaining half.

4 Blend coconut water and flesh, frozen mango and banana, peeled lime, half the peach, the passionfruit pulp and chia seeds in a high-powered blender until smooth.

5 Pour into serving bowls. Serve topped with halved strawberries, sliced extra banana, remaining peach wedges, extra passionfruit pulp, extra chia seeds and reserved lime wedges.

tips *The young coconut should be heavy and when shaken, should be completely full with liquid. You need about 2 medium mangoes. This smoothie bowl is over the top, just like the flamboyant Brazilian performer it was named after, but that's what's so fun about it. Full of fresh summer fruits and sweet hydrating coconut you'll be transported to an idyllic tropical island oasis. Best shared among friends and eaten with a spoon.*

I AM
MINERAL RICH
GREAT FOR HYDRATION
VEGAN

 TURKISH DELIGHT

PREP TIME **10 MINUTES (+ STANDING)** SERVES **2**

1 cup (150g) raw cashews

1½ cups (375ml) filtered water

2 cups (250g) frozen raspberries

4 fresh dates (80g), pitted

½ teaspoon rosewater essence

¼ teaspoon vanilla bean paste

1 tablespoon pistachios

2 tablespoons dried rose buds

2 teaspoons cacao nibs

I AM
SUGAR-FREE
HIGH IN PROTEIN
CALCIUM RICH

1 Rinse cashews in a sieve under running water. Place in a bowl with enough water to cover. Cover bowl with a clean tea towel; stand at room temperature overnight. Drain cashews; rinse in a sieve under running water.

2 Blend cashews with the filtered water, raspberries, dates, rosewater and vanilla paste in a high-powered blender until smooth.

3 Pour smoothie into bowls. Top with pistachios, rose buds and cacao nibs. Drizzle with a little extra almond milk, if you like.

tips Soaking cashews overnight softens them and helps to neutralise the phytic acid that makes nuts difficult to digest. This delicious smoothie bowl has all of the flavours of a Turkish delight, but without the sugar and other guff. Raw cashews give it a velvety smooth consistency, while the subtle splash of rosewater combined with the tartness of raspberries is a perfect pairing.

Glossary

ACAI POWDER a small, round fruit with a large, hard, inedible pit and a dark purple, pulpy skin, that tastes like a blend of berries and chocolate. It supposedly has a high concentration of antioxidants, although further scientific studies are needed.

ACTIVATED BUCKINIS made with buckwheat, which, despite its name, is not actually a wheat, but is a fruit belonging to the same family as rhubarb. It's gluten free, high in protein and essential amino acids, and is a rich source of minerals and B vitamins.

AGAVE SYRUP from the agave plant; has a low GI, but that is due to the high percentage of fructose present, which may be harmful in large quantities.

ALLSPICE also known as pimento or jamaican pepper; so-named because it tastes like a combination of nutmeg, cumin, clove and cinnamon. Available whole or ground.

ALMONDS

blanched brown skins removed from the kernel.

flaked paper-thin slices.

ground also called almond meal; almonds are powdered to a coarse flour-like texture.

slivered small pieces cut lengthways.

ANCHOVIES small oily fish. Anchovy fillets are preserved and packed in oil or salt in small cans or jars, and are strong in flavour. Fresh anchovies are much milder in flavour.

BAKING PAPER also called parchment paper or baking parchment – is a silicone-coated paper that is used for lining baking pans and oven trays so cooked food doesn't stick, making removal easy.

BAKING POWDER a raising agent consisting mainly of two parts cream of tartar to one part bicarbonate of soda (baking soda).

BARLEY a nutritious grain used in soups and stews. Hulled barley, the least processed, is high in fibre. Pearl barley has had the husk removed then been steamed and polished so that only the 'pearl' of the original grain remains, much the same as white rice.

BAY LEAVES aromatic leaves from the bay tree available fresh or dried; adds a strong, slightly peppery flavour.

BEANS

black also called turtle beans or black kidney beans; an earthy-flavoured dried bean completely different from the better-known Chinese black beans (fermented soybeans). Used mostly in Mexican and South American cooking.

broad (fava) available dried, fresh, canned and frozen. Fresh should be peeled twice (discarding both the outer long green pod and the beige-green tough inner shell); the frozen beans have had their pods removed but the beige shell still needs removal.

butter cans labelled butter beans are, in fact, cannellini beans. Confusingly, it's also another name for lima beans, sold both dried and canned; a large beige bean with a mealy texture and mild taste.

cannellini a small white bean similar in appearance and flavour to other white beans (great northern, navy or haricot), all of which can be substituted for the other. Available dried or canned.

green also known as french or string beans (although the tough string they once had has generally been bred out of them), this long thin fresh bean is consumed in its entirety once cooked.

sprouts tender new growths of assorted beans and seeds germinated for consumption as sprouts.

white a generic term we use for canned or dried cannellini, haricot, navy or great northern beans belonging to the same family, phaseolus vulgaris.

BEE POLLEN is collected and sold as a health-food product with claims of being 'nature's perfect food'. However, there have been documented cases of severe anaphylactic reactions to bee pollen. Pregnant and breast-feeding mothers should avoid bee pollen.

BEETROOT (BEETS) firm, round root vegetable.

BICARBONATE OF SODA (BAKING SODA) a raising agent.

BLOOD ORANGE a virtually seedless citrus fruit with blood-red-streaked rind and flesh; sweet, non-acidic, salmon-coloured pulp and juice having slight strawberry or raspberry overtones. The rind is not as bitter as a regular orange.

BROCCOLINI a cross between broccoli and chinese kale; it has long asparagus-like stems with a long loose floret, both are edible. Resembles broccoli but is milder and sweeter in taste.

BRUISING a cooking term to describe the slight crushing given to aromatic ingredients, particularly garlic and herbs, with the flat side of a heavy knife or cleaver to release flavour and aroma.

BUCKWHEAT a herb in the same plant family as rhubarb; not a cereal so it is gluten-free. Available as flour; ground (cracked) into coarse, medium or fine granules (kasha) and used similarly to polenta; or groats, the whole kernel sold roasted as a cereal product.

BUTTER use salted or unsalted (sweet) butter; 125g (4 ounces) is equal to one stick of butter.

BUTTERMILK originally the term given to the slightly sour liquid left after butter was churned from cream, today it is made from no-fat or low-fat milk to which specific bacterial cultures have been added. Despite its name, it is actually low in fat.

CACAO

beans are contained inside the large cacao pod. The beans are used to make cocoa butter, cocoa powder, cocoa solids and chocolate.

cacao (cocoa) butter is rich in saturated fats; about a third is stearic acid, but this acts differently to other saturated fats in that it doesn't raise cholesterol and, in fact, lowers LDL (bad) cholesterol. So this makes it a pretty healthy fat overall.

dutch-processed cacao powder is treated with an alkali to neutralize its acidity; it is darker and more mellow in taste.

nibs can be separated into cocoa butter and powder. Cocoa powder retains many beneficial antioxidants and is an easy way of adding cocoa into your diet without the kilojoules of chocolate.

raw cacao powder is made by removing the cocoa butter using a process known as cold-pressing. It retains more of its nutrients than heat-processed cacao powder; it also has a stronger, slightly bitter, taste.

raw dark chocolate is made using cold-pressed raw cacao beans, that is, without the use of heat. It is high in antioxidants, and has good levels of chromium, iron and magnesium, which support healthy heart function.

CAPERS grey-green buds of a warm climate shrub (usually Mediterranean), sold either dried and salted or pickled in a vinegar brine. Capers must be rinsed well before using.

CAPSICUM (BELL PEPPER) also called pepper. Comes in many colours: red, green, yellow, orange and purplish-black. Be sure to discard seeds and membranes before use.

CARDAMOM a spice native to India and used extensively in its cuisine; can be purchased in pod, seed or ground form. Has a distinctive aromatic, sweetly rich flavour.

CASHEWS plump, kidney-shaped, golden-brown nuts having a distinctive sweet, buttery flavour and containing about 48% fat. Because of this high fat content, they should be kept, sealed tightly, under refrigeration to avoid becoming rancid. We use roasted unsalted cashews in this book, unless otherwise stated; they're available from health-food stores and most supermarkets.

CAVOLO NERO (TUSCAN CABBAGE) has long, narrow, wrinkled leaves and a rich and astringent, mild cabbage flavour. It doesn't lose its volume like silver beet or spinach when cooked, but it does need longer cooking.

CHEESE

cream commonly called philadelphia or philly; a soft cow-milk cheese, its fat content ranges from 14 to 33%.

fetta Greek in origin; a crumbly textured goat- or sheep-milk cheese having a sharp, salty taste. Ripened and stored in salted whey.

fetta, persian a soft, creamy fetta marinated in a blend of olive oil, garlic, herbs and spices; available from most major supermarkets.

goat's made from goat's milk, has an earthy, strong taste; available in both soft and firm textures, in various shapes and sizes, and sometimes rolled in ash or herbs.

gorgonzola a creamy Italian blue cheese with a mild, sweet taste; good as an accompaniment to fruit or used to flavour sauces (especially pasta).

haloumi a firm, cream-coloured sheep-milk cheese matured in brine; haloumi can be grilled or fried, briefly, without breaking down. Should be eaten while still warm as it becomes tough and rubbery on cooling.

mascarpone an Italian fresh cultured-cream product made in much the same way as yoghurt. Whiteish to creamy yellow in colour, with a buttery-rich, luscious texture. Soft, creamy and spreadable, it is used in Italian desserts and as an accompaniment to fresh fruit.

mozzarella a delicate, semi-soft, white cheese traditionally made from buffalo milk. Sold fresh, it spoils rapidly so will only keep, refrigerated in brine, for 1 or 2 days at the most.

parmesan also called parmigiano; is a hard, grainy cow-milk cheese originating in Italy. Reggiano is the best variety.

pecorino the Italian generic name for cheeses made from sheep milk; hard, white to pale-yellow in colour. If you can't find it, use parmesan instead.

ricotta a soft, sweet, moist, white cow-milk cheese with a low fat content and a slightly grainy texture.

CHIA SEEDS contain protein and all the essential amino acids and a wealth of vitamins, minerals and antioxidants, as well as being fibre-rich.

CHICKPEAS (GARBANZO BEANS) an irregularly round, sandy-coloured legume. Has a firm texture even after cooking, a floury mouth-feel and robust nutty flavour; available canned or dried (soak for several hours in cold water before use).

CHILLI available in many different types and sizes. Use rubber gloves when seeding and chopping fresh chillies as they can burn your skin. Removing seeds and membranes lessens the heat level.

cayenne pepper a long, thin-fleshed, extremely hot red chilli usually sold dried and ground.

chipotle pronounced cheh-pote-lay. The name used for jalapeño chillies once they've been dried and smoked. Having a deep, intensely smokey flavour, rather than a searing heat, chipotles are dark brown, almost black in colour and wrinkled in appearance.

flakes also sold as crushed chilli; dehydrated deep-red extremely fine slices and whole seeds.

green any unripened chilli; also some particular varieties that are ripe when green, such as jalapeño, habanero, poblano or serrano.

jalapeño pronounced hah-lah-pain-yo. Fairly hot, medium-sized, plump, dark green chilli; available pickled, sold canned or bottled, and fresh, from greengrocers.

long available both fresh and dried; a generic term used for any moderately hot, thin, long (6-8cm/2¼-3¼ inch) chilli.

red thai also known as 'scuds'; small, very hot and bright red; can be substituted with fresh serrano or habanero chillies.

CHIVES related to the onion and leek; has a subtle onion flavour. Used more for flavour than as an ingredient; chopped finely, they're good in sauces, dressings, omelettes or as a garnish.

CHOCOLATE, DARK (SEMI-SWEET) also called luxury chocolate; made of a high percentage of cocoa liquor and cocoa butter, and little added sugar. Dark chocolate is ideal for use in desserts and cakes.

CINNAMON available both in the piece (called sticks or quills) and ground into powder; one of the world's most common spices, used universally as a sweet, fragrant flavouring for both sweet and savoury foods. The dried inner bark of the shoots of the Sri Lankan native cinnamon tree; much of what is sold as the real thing is in fact cassia, Chinese cinnamon, from the bark of the cassia tree. Less expensive to process than true cinnamon, it is often blended with Sri Lankan cinnamon to produce the type of "cinnamon" most commonly found in supermarkets.

CLOVES the dried flower buds of a tropical tree; used whole or ground. They have a strong scent and taste so use sparingly.

COCOA POWDER also called unsweetened cocoa; cocoa beans (cacao seeds) that have been fermented, roasted, shelled, ground into powder then cleared of most of the fat content.

COCONUT

cream comes from the first pressing of the coconut flesh, without the addition of water; the second pressing (less rich) is sold as coconut milk. Look for coconut cream labelled as 100% coconut, without added emulsifiers.

flaked dried flaked coconut flesh.

flour is a low carbohydrate, high fibre, gluten-free flour made from fresh dried coconut flesh. It has a sweetish taste and is suitable for those on a paleo diet.

milk not the liquid found inside the fruit (coconut water), but the diluted liquid from the second pressing of the white flesh of a mature coconut (the first pressing produces coconut cream).

oil is extracted from the coconut flesh so you don't get any of the fibre, protein or carbohydrates present in the whole coconut. The best quality is virgin coconut oil, which is the oil pressed from the dried coconut flesh, and doesn't include the use of solvents or other refining processes.

shredded thin strips of dried coconut.

sugar is not made from coconuts, but from the sap of the blossoms of the coconut palm tree. The refined sap looks a little like raw or light brown sugar, and has a similar caramel flavour. It also has the same amount of kilojoules as regular table (white) sugar.

water is the liquid from the centre of a young green coconut. It has fewer kilojoules than fruit juice, with no fat or protein. There are sugars present, but these are slowly absorbed giving coconut water a low GI.

young are coconuts that are not fully mature. As a coconut ages, the amount of juice inside decreases, until it eventually disappears and is replaced by air.

CORIANDER (CILANTRO) also known as pak chee or chinese parsley; a bright-green leafy herb with a pungent flavour. Both stems and roots of coriander are also used in cooking; wash well before using. Also available ground or as seeds; these should not be substituted for fresh as the tastes are completely different.

CORN, PUFFED whole grain corn is steamed until it puffs up.

CORNFLOUR (CORNSTARCH) thickening agent available in two forms: 100% corn (maize), which is gluten free, and a wheaten cornflour (made from wheat) which is not.

COUSCOUS a fine, grain-like cereal product made from semolina; from the countries of North Africa. A semolina flour and water dough is sieved then dehydrated to produce minuscule even-sized pellets of couscous; it is rehydrated by steaming or with the addition of a warm liquid and swells to three or four times its original size; eaten like rice with a tagine, as a side dish or salad ingredient.

CRANBERRIES, DRIED they have the same slightly sour, succulent flavour as fresh cranberries. Available in most supermarkets.

CREAM

pouring also called pure, fresh or single cream. It has no additives and contains a minimum fat content of 35%.

sour a thick commercially-cultured soured cream with a 35% fat content.

thickened (heavy) a whipping cream that contains a thickener. It has a minimum fat content of 35%.

CUCUMBER

lebanese short, slender and thin-skinned. Probably the most popular variety because of its tender, edible skin, tiny, yielding seeds, and sweet, fresh and flavoursome taste.

telegraph also known as the european or burpless cucumber; long and slender with shallow ridges running down the length of its thin dark-green skin.

CUMIN also known as zeera or comino; resembling caraway in size, cumin is the dried seed of a plant related to the parsley family. Its spicy, almost curry-like flavour is essential to the traditional foods of Mexico, India, North Africa and the Middle East. Available dried as seeds or ground. Black cumin seeds are smaller than standard cumin, and dark brown rather than true black; they are mistakenly confused with kalonji.

CURRANTS tiny, almost black raisins so-named after a grape variety that originated in Corinth, Greece.

CURRY PASTES some recipes in this book call for commercially prepared pastes of varying strengths and flavours. Use whichever one you feel best suits your spice-level tolerance.

massaman rich, spicy flavour reminiscent of Middle Eastern cooking; favoured by southern Thai cooks for use in hot and sour stew-like curries and satay sauces.

tikka in Indian cooking, the word "masala" loosely translates as paste and the word "tikka" means a bite-sized piece of meat, poultry or fish. Tikka paste is any maker's choice of spices and oils, mixed into a mild paste, frequently coloured red. Used for marinating or for brushing over meat, seafood or poultry, before or during cooking instead of as an ingredient.

DAIKON also called white radish; this long, white horseradish has a wonderful, sweet flavour. After peeling, eat it raw in salads or shredded as a garnish; also great when sliced or cubed and cooked in stir-fries and casseroles. The flesh is white but the skin can be either white or black; buy those that are firm and unwrinkled from Asian food shops.

DILL also known as dill weed; used fresh or dried, in seed form or ground. Its anise/celery sweetness flavours the food of the Scandinavian countries, and Germany and Greece. Its feathery, frond-like fresh leaves are grassier and more subtle than the dried version or the seeds (which slightly resemble caraway in flavour). Use dill leaves with smoked salmon and sour cream, poached fish or roast chicken; use the seeds with simply cooked vegetables, or home-baked dark breads.

DUKKAH an Egyptian specialty spice mixture made up of roasted nuts, seeds and an array of aromatic spices.

EDAMAME (SHELLED SOY BEANS) available frozen from Asian food stores and some supermarkets.

EGGPLANT also called aubergine. Ranging in size from tiny to very large and in colour from pale green to deep purple.

EGGS some recipes in this book may call for raw or barely cooked eggs; exercise caution if there is a salmonella problem in your area. The risk is greater for those who are pregnant, elderly or very young, and those with impaired immune systems.

ESSENCE/EXTRACT an essence is either a distilled concentration of a food quality or an artificial creation of it. Coconut and almond essences are synthetically produced substances used in small amounts to impart their respective flavours to foods. An extract is made by actually extracting the flavour from a food product. In the case of vanilla, pods are soaked, usually in alcohol, to capture the authentic flavour. Essences and extracts keep indefinitely if stored in a cool dark place.

FENNEL a white to very pale green-white, firm, crisp, roundish vegetable about 8-12cm (3¼-4¾ inches) in diameter. The bulb has a slightly sweet, anise flavour but the leaves have a much stronger taste. Also the name of dried seeds having a licorice flavour.

FISH FILLETS, FIRM WHITE blue eye, bream, flathead, snapper, ling, swordfish, whiting, jewfish or sea perch are all good choices. Check for small pieces of bone and use tweezers to remove them.

FISH SAUCE called nuoc nam (Vietnamese) or nam pla (Thai); made from pulverised salted fermented fish, most often anchovies. Has a pungent smell and strong taste, so use sparingly.

FLOUR

chickpea (besan) creamy yellow flour made from chickpeas and is very nutritious.

plain (all-purpose) a general all-purpose wheat flour.

rice very fine, almost powdery, gluten-free flour; made from ground white rice. Used in baking, as a thickener, and in some Asian noodles and desserts. Another variety, made from glutinous sweet rice, is used for chinese dumplings and rice paper.

self-raising plain flour sifted with baking powder in the proportion of 1 cup flour to 2 teaspoons baking powder.

tapioca made from the root of the cassava plant; a soft, fine, light white flour.

wholemeal also known as wholewheat flour; milled with the wheat germ so is higher in fibre and more nutritional than plain flour.

FREEKEH is cracked roasted green wheat and can be found in some larger supermarkets, health food and specialty food stores.

GAI LAN also known as chinese broccoli, gai larn, kanah, gai lum and chinese kale; used more for its stems than its coarse leaves.

GARAM MASALA a blend of spices that includes cardamom, cinnamon, coriander, cloves, fennel and cumin. Black pepper and chilli can be added for heat.

GELATINE we use dried (powdered) gelatine; it's also available in sheet form called leaf gelatine. Three teaspoons of dried gelatine (8g or one sachet) is about the same as four gelatine leaves.

GHEE a type of clarified butter used in Indian cooking; milk solids are cooked until golden brown, which imparts a nutty flavour and sweet aroma; it can be heated to a high temperature without burning.

GINGER

fresh also called green or root ginger; thick gnarled root of a tropical plant.

ground also called powdered ginger; used as a flavouring in baking but cannot be substituted for fresh ginger.

pickled pink or red in colour, paper-thin shavings of ginger pickled in a mixture of vinegar, sugar and natural colouring. Available from Asian food shops.

GLUTEN is a combination of two proteins found in wheat (including spelt), rye, barley and oats. When liquid is added to the flour, these two proteins bind to become gluten. Gluten gives elasticity to dough, helping it rise and keep its shape; it also gives the final product a chewy texture.

GOJI BERRIES (dried) small, very juicy, sweet red berries that grow on a type of shrub in Tibet. Believed to be high in nutrients and antioxidants.

GREASING/OILING PANS use butter (for sweet baking), oil or cooking-oil spray (for savoury baking) to grease baking pans; overgreasing pans can cause food to overbrown. Use paper towel or a pastry brush to spread the oil or butter over the pan.

HARISSA a Moroccan paste made from dried chillies, cumin, garlic, oil and caraway seeds. Available from Middle Eastern food shops and supermarkets.

HAZELNUTS also known as filberts; plump, grape-sized, rich, sweet nut having a brown skin that is removed by rubbing heated nuts together vigorously in a tea-towel.

ground is made by grounding the hazelnuts to a coarse flour texture for use in baking or as a thickening agent.

HOISIN SAUCE a thick, sweet and spicy Chinese paste made from salted fermented soya beans, onions and garlic.

HONEY the variety sold in a squeezable container is not suitable for the recipes in this book.

HORSERADISH a vegetable with edible green leaves but mainly grown for its long, pungent white root. Occasionally found fresh in specialty greengrocers and some Asian food shops, but commonly purchased in bottles at the supermarket in two forms: prepared horseradish and horseradish cream. These cannot be substituted one for the other in cooking but both can be used as table condiments. Horseradish cream is a commercially prepared creamy paste consisting of grated horseradish, vinegar, oil and sugar, while prepared horseradish is the preserved grated root.

KAFFIR LIME LEAVES also known as bai magrood and looks like two glossy dark green leaves joined end to end, forming a rounded hourglass shape. Used fresh or dried in many South-East Asian dishes, they are used like bay leaves or curry leaves, especially in Thai cooking. Sold fresh, dried or frozen, the dried leaves are less potent so double the number if using them as a substitute for fresh; a strip of fresh lime peel may be substituted for each kaffir lime leaf.

KUMARA (ORANGE SWEET POTATO) the Māori name of an orange-fleshed sweet potato often confused with yam.

LEEKS a member of the onion family, the leek resembles a green onion but is much larger and more subtle in flavour. Tender baby or pencil leeks can be eaten whole with minimal cooking but adult leeks are usually trimmed of most of the green tops then sliced.

LEMON GRASS a tall, clumping, lemon-smelling and -tasting, sharp-edged grass; the white part of the stem is used, finely chopped, in cooking.

LENTILS (red, brown, yellow) dried pulses often identified by and named after their colour; also known as dhal.

LETTUCE

butter (boston) small, round, loosely formed heads with a sweet flavour; soft, buttery-textured leaves range from pale green on the outer leaves to pale yellow-green inner leaves.

cos (romaine) the traditional caesar salad lettuce. Long, with leaves ranging from dark green on the outside to almost white near the core; the leaves have a stiff centre rib giving a slight cupping effect to the leaf on either side.

LSA A ground mixture of linseeds (L), sunflower seeds (S) and almonds (A); available from supermarkets and health food stores.

MANGO tropical fruit originally from India and South-East Asia. With skin colour ranging from green to yellow and deep red; fragrant, deep yellow flesh surrounds a large flat seed. Slicing off the cheeks, cross-hatching them with a knife then turning them inside out shows the sweet, juicy flesh at its best. Mangoes can also be used in curries and salsas, or pureed for ice-cream, smoothies or mousse. Mango cheeks in light syrup are available canned. Sour and crunchy, green mangoes are just the immature fruit that is used as a vegetable in salads, salsas and curries.

MAPLE SYRUP, PURE distilled from the sap of sugar maple trees found only in Canada and the USA. Maple-flavoured syrup or pancake syrup is not an adequate substitute for the real thing.

MILK we use full-cream homogenised milk unless otherwise specified.

soy rich creamy 'milk' extracted from soya beans that have been crushed in hot water and strained. It has a nutty flavour.

MIRIN a Japanese champagne-coloured cooking wine; made of glutinous rice and alcohol and used expressly for cooking. Should not be confused with sake.

MIZUNA a mustard green from Japan where it is traditionally used in soups and other cooked main dishes. It's often found in mesclun, but its mild, aromatic jagged green leaves can also stand alone. Refrigerate in a plastic bag, unwashed, for up to 5 days.

MORTAR AND PESTLE a cooking tool whose design has remained the same over the centuries: the mortar is a bowl-shaped container and the pestle a rounded, bat-shaped tool. Together, they grind and pulverise spices, herbs and other foods. The pestle is pressed against the mortar and rotated, grinding the ingredient between the two surfaces. Essential for curry pastes and crushing spices.

MUSHROOMS

flat large, flat mushrooms with a rich earthy flavour. They are sometimes misnamed field mushrooms, which are wild mushrooms.

oyster also known as abalone; grey-white mushrooms shaped like a fan. Prized for their smooth texture and subtle, oyster-like flavour.

porcini also known as cèpes; the richest-flavoured mushrooms. Expensive, but because they're so strongly flavoured, only a small amount is required.

portobello are mature, fully opened swiss browns; they are larger and bigger in flavour.

swiss brown also known as cremini or roman mushrooms; are light brown mushrooms with a full-bodied flavour.

MUSTARD

dijon pale brown, creamy, distinctively flavoured, fairly mild French mustard.

wholegrain also known as seeded. A French-style coarse-grain mustard made from crushed mustard seeds and dijon-style french mustard.

NORBU (MONK FRUIT SUGAR) monk fruit is a subtropical melon that contains a group of sweet tasting antioxidant compounds. Used as an alternative to cane sugar, as it has 96% fewer kilojoules and will not affect blood glucose or insulin levels.

NORI a type of dried seaweed used as a flavouring, garnish or for sushi. Sold in thin sheets, plain or toasted (yaki-nori).

NUTMEG a strong and pungent spice ground from the dried nut of an evergreen tree native to Indonesia. Usually found ground but the flavour is more intense from a whole nut, available from spice shops, so it's best to grate your own.

OIL

coconut see *Coconut*

olive made from ripened olives. Extra virgin and virgin are the first and second press, respectively, of the olives; "light" refers to taste not fat levels.

peanut pressed from ground peanuts; most commonly used oil in Asian cooking because of its high smoke point (capacity to handle high heat without burning).

sesame used as a flavouring rather than a cooking medium.

vegetable oils sourced from plant rather than animal fats.

ONIONS

brown and white are interchangeable; white onions have a more pungent flesh.

green (scallions) also called, incorrectly, shallot; an immature onion picked before the bulb has formed, has a long, bright-green stalk.

red also known as spanish, red spanish or bermuda onion; a sweet-flavoured, large, purple-red onion.

shallots also called french or golden shallots or eschalots; small and brown-skinned.

OYSTER SAUCE Asian in origin, this thick, richly flavoured brown sauce is made from oysters and their brine, cooked with salt and soy sauce, and thickened with starches.

PAPRIKA a ground, dried, sweet red capsicum (bell pepper); there are many grades and types available, including sweet, hot, mild and smoked.

PECANS native to the US and now grown locally; pecans are golden brown, buttery and rich. Good in savoury as well as sweet dishes; walnuts are a good substitute.

PEPITAS (PUMPKIN SEEDS) are the pale green kernels of dried pumpkin seeds; they can be bought plain or salted.

PERSIMMONS an autumnal fruit available in two varieties: an astringent one, eaten soft, and a non-astringent, or sweet, variety also known as fuji fruit.

PINE NUTS not a nut but a small, cream-coloured kernel from pine cones. Toast before use to bring out their flavour.

PISTACHIOS green, delicately flavoured nuts inside hard off-white shells. Available salted or unsalted in their shells; you can also get them shelled.

POLENTA also known as cornmeal; a flour-like cereal made of ground corn (maize). Also the name of the dish made from it.

POMEGRANATE dark-red, leathery-skinned fruit about the size of an orange filled with hundreds of seeds, each wrapped in an edible lucent-crimson pulp with a unique tangy sweet-sour flavour.

POPPY SEEDS small, dried, bluish-grey seeds of the poppy plant, with a crunchy texture and a nutty flavour. Can be purchased whole or ground.

PRESERVED LEMON RIND a North African specialty; lemons are quartered and preserved in salt and lemon juice or water. To use, remove and discard pulp, squeeze juice from rind, rinse rind well; slice thinly. Once opened, store under refrigeration.

QUINOA pronounced keen-wa; is the seed of a leafy plant similar to spinach. It has a delicate, slightly nutty taste and chewy texture.

flakes the grains have been rolled and flattened.

puffed has been steamed until it puffs up.

RADICCHIO a red-leafed Italian chicory with a refreshing bitter taste that's eaten raw and grilled. Comes in varieties named after their places of origin, such as round-headed Verona or long-headed Treviso.

RADISH a peppery root vegetable related to the mustard plant. The small round red variety is the mildest, it is crisp and juicy, and usually eaten raw in salads.

RHUBARB a plant with long, green-red stalks; becomes sweet and edible when cooked.

RICE

basmati a white, fragrant long-grained rice; the grains fluff up beautifully when cooked. It should be washed several times before cooking.

black high in nutritional value; the grain has a similar amount of fibre to brown rice and, like brown rice, has a mild, nutty taste.

brown retains the high-fibre, nutritious bran coating that's removed from white rice when hulled. It takes longer to cook than white rice and has a chewier texture. Once cooked, the long grains stay separate, while the short grains are soft and stickier.

jasmine or Thai jasmine, is a long-grained white rice recognised around the world as having a perfumed aromatic quality; moist in texture, it clings together after cooking. Sometimes substituted for basmati rice.

RICE MALT SYRUP also known as brown rice syrup or rice syrup; is made by cooking brown rice flour with enzymes to break down its starch into sugars from which the water is removed.

ROASTING/TOASTING desiccated coconut, pine nuts and sesame seeds roast more evenly if stirred over low heat in a heavy-based frying pan; their natural oils will help turn them golden brown. Remove from pan immediately. Nuts and dried coconut can be roasted in the oven to release their aromatic essential oils. Spread them evenly onto an oven tray then roast at 180°C/350°F for about 5 minutes.

ROCKET (ARUGULA) also known as rugula and rucola; a peppery-tasting green leaf which can be used similarly to baby spinach leaves, eaten raw in salad or used in cooking. Baby rocket leaves, also known as wild rocket, are both smaller and less peppery.

ROLLED OATS flattened oat grain rolled into flakes and traditionally used for porridge. Instant oats are also available, but use traditional oats for baking.

ROSEWATER extract made from crushed rose petals; used for its aromatic quality.

SAFFRON available ground or in strands; imparts a yellow-orange colour to food once infused. The quality can vary greatly; the best is the most expensive spice in the world.

SAMBAL OELEK also ulek or olek; an Indonesian salty paste made from ground chillies and vinegar.

SILVER BEET also called swiss chard; mistakenly called spinach.

SEGMENTING CITRUS cut the top and bottom from the orange/lemon/lime. Cut off the rind with the white pith, following the curve of the fruit. Hold the fruit over a bowl to catch the juices, then cut down both sides of each segment close to the membrane to release the segment.

SESAME SEEDS black and white are the most common of this small oval seed, however there are also red and brown varieties. The seeds are used as an ingredient and as a condiment. Roast the seeds in a heavy-based frying pan over low heat.

SNOW PEAS also called mangetout; a variety of garden pea, eaten pod and all (although you may need to string them). Used in stir-fries or eaten raw in salads. Snow pea sprouts are available from supermarkets or greengrocers and are usually eaten raw in salads or sandwiches.

SOY SAUCE made from fermented soya beans. Several variations are available in most supermarkets and Asian food stores. We use japanese soy sauce unless stated otherwise.

SQUID also called calamari; a type of mollusc. Buy squid hoods to make preparation and cooking faster.

SPINACH also called english spinach and, incorrectly, silver beet.

STAR ANISE dried star-shaped pod with an astringent aniseed flavour; used to flavour stocks and marinades. Available whole and ground, it is an essential ingredient in five-spice powder.

STERLISING JARS it's important the jars be as clean as possible; make sure your hands, the preparation area, tea towels and cloths etc, are clean, too. The aim is to finish sterilising the jars and lids at the same time the preserve is ready to be bottled; the hot preserve should be bottled into hot, dry clean jars. Jars that aren't sterilised properly can cause deterioration of the preserves during storage. Always start with cleaned washed jars and lids, then follow one of these methods:

(1) Put jars and lids through the hottest cycle of a dishwasher without using any detergent.

(2) Lie jars down in a boiler with the lids, cover them with cold water then cover the boiler with a lid. Bring the water to the boil over a high heat and boil the jars for 20 minutes.

(3) Stand jars upright, without touching each other, on a wooden board on the lowest shelf in the oven. Turn the oven to the lowest possible temperature; leave jars to heat for 30 minutes.

Remove the jars from the oven or dishwasher with a towel, or from the boiling water with tongs and rubber-gloved hands; the water will evaporate from hot wet jars quite quickly. Stand jars upright and not touching on a wooden board, or a bench covered with a towel to protect and insulate the bench. Fill the jars as directed in the recipe; secure the lids tightly, holding jars firmly with a towel or an oven mitt. Leave at room temperature to cool before storing.

SUGAR

brown very soft, finely granulated sugar retaining molasses for its characteristic colour and flavour.

caster (superfine) finely granulated table sugar.

coconut see *Coconut*

palm also called nam tan pip, jaggery, jawa or gula melaka; made from the sap of the sugar palm tree. Light brown to black in colour and usually sold in rock-hard cakes; use brown sugar if unavailable.

SUGAR SNAP PEAS
also called honey snap peas; fresh small pea which can be eaten whole, pod and all.

SULTANAS
dried grapes, also known as golden raisins.

SUMAC
a purple-red, astringent spice ground from berries growing on shrubs flourishing wild around the Mediterranean; adds a tart, lemony flavour to food. Available from major supermarkets.

SUNFLOWER SEEDS
grey-green, slightly soft, oily kernels.

TAHINI
a rich, sesame-seed paste, used in most Middle-Eastern cuisines, especially Lebanese, in dips and sauces.

TAMARI
a thick, dark soy sauce made mainly from soya beans, but without the wheat used in most standard soy sauces.

TAMARIND
the tamarind tree produces clusters of hairy brown pods, each of which is filled with seeds and a viscous pulp, that are dried and pressed into the blocks of tamarind found in Asian food shops. Gives a sweet-sour, slightly astringent taste to marinades, pastes, sauces and dressings.

TAMARIND CONCENTRATE (OR PASTE)
the distillation of tamarind pulp into a condensed, compacted paste. Thick and purple-black, it requires no soaking. Found in Asian food stores.

TOFU
also called bean curd; an off-white, custard-like product made from the "milk" of crushed soybeans. Comes fresh as soft or firm, and processed as fried or pressed dried sheets. Fresh tofu can be refrigerated in water (changed daily) for up to 4 days.

firm made by compressing bean curd to remove most of the water. Good used in stir-fries as it can be tossed without disintegrating. Can also be flavoured, preserved in rice wine or brine.

silken not a type of tofu but reference to the manufacturing process of straining soybean liquid through silk; this denotes best quality.

TOMATO

canned whole peeled tomatoes in natural juices; available crushed, chopped or diced. Use undrained.

cherry also called tiny tim or tom thumb tomatoes; small and round.

paste triple-concentrated tomato puree used to flavour soups, stews, sauces and casseroles.

roma (egg) these are smallish, oval-shaped tomatoes used in Italian cooking or salads.

TURMERIC
also called kamin; is a rhizome related to galangal and ginger. Must be grated or pounded to release its acrid aroma and pungent flavour. Known for the golden colour it imparts, fresh turmeric can be substituted with the more commonly found dried powder. When fresh turmeric is called for in a recipe, the dried powder can be substituted (proportions are 1 teaspoon of ground turmeric for every 20g of fresh turmeric). Be aware that fresh turmeric stains your hands & plastic utensils (chopping boards, spatulas, the bowl of a food processor).

VANILLA

bean dried, long, thin pod from a tropical golden orchid; the minuscule black seeds inside the bean impart a luscious flavour in baking and desserts.

extract obtained from vanilla beans infused in water; a non-alcoholic version of essence.

paste made from vanilla beans and contains real seeds. Is highly concentrated: 1 teaspoon replaces a whole vanilla bean. Found in most supermarkets in the baking section.

VINEGAR

balsamic made from the juice of Trebbiano grapes; it is a deep rich brown colour with a sweet and sour flavour.

cider made from fermented apples.

rice wine made from rice wine lees (sediment left after fermentation), salt and alcohol.

wine based on red wine.

WALNUTS
as well as being a good source of fibre and healthy oils, nuts contain a range of vitamins, minerals and other beneficial plant components called phytochemicals. Each type of nut has a special make-up and walnuts contain the beneficial omega-3 fatty acids.

WATERCRESS
one of the cress family, a large group of peppery greens. Highly perishable, so must be used as soon as possible after purchase. It has an exceptionally high vitamin K content, which is great for eye health, and is an excellent source of calcium.

WOMBOK (NAPA CABBAGE)
also known as peking or chinese cabbage. Elongated in shape with pale green, crinkly leaves.

XANTHAN GUM
is a thickening agent produced by fermentation of, usually, corn sugar. When buying xanthan gum, ensure the packet states 'made from fermented corn sugar'. Found in the health-food section in larger supermarkets.

YEAST
(dried and fresh), a raising agent used in dough making. Granular (7g sachets) and fresh compressed (20g blocks) yeast can almost always be substituted for the other.

YOGHURT, GREEK-STYLE
plain yoghurt strained in a cloth (muslin) to remove the whey and to give it a creamy consistency.

ZUCCHINI
also called courgette; small, pale- or dark-green or yellow vegetable of the squash family.

conversion chart

MEASURES

One Australian metric measuring cup holds approximately 250ml; one Australian metric tablespoon holds 20ml; one Australian metric teaspoon holds 5ml.

The difference between one country's measuring cups and another's is within a two- or three-teaspoon variance, and will not affect your cooking results. North America, New Zealand and the United Kingdom use a 15ml tablespoon.

All cup and spoon measurements are level. The most accurate way of measuring dry ingredients is to weigh them. When measuring liquids, use a clear glass or plastic jug with the metric markings.

The imperial measurements used in these recipes are approximate only. Measurements for cake pans are approximate only. Using same-shaped cake pans of a similar size should not affect the outcome of your baking. We measure the inside top of the cake pan to determine sizes.

We use large eggs with an average weight of 60g.

DRY MEASURES

METRIC	IMPERIAL
15G	½OZ
30G	1OZ
60G	2OZ
90G	3OZ
125G	4OZ (¼LB)
155G	5OZ
185G	6OZ
220G	7OZ
250G	8OZ (½LB)
280G	9OZ
315G	10OZ
345G	11OZ
375G	12OZ (¾LB)
410G	13OZ
440G	14OZ
470G	15OZ
500G	16OZ (1LB)
750G	24OZ (1½LB)
1KG	32OZ (2LB)

LIQUID MEASURES

METRIC	IMPERIAL
30ML	1 FLUID OZ
60ML	2 FLUID OZ
100ML	3 FLUID OZ
125ML	4 FLUID OZ
150ML	5 FLUID OZ
190ML	6 FLUID OZ
250ML	8 FLUID OZ
300ML	10 FLUID OZ
500ML	16 FLUID OZ
600ML	20 FLUID OZ
1000ML (1 LITRE)	1¾ PINTS

LENGTH MEASURES

METRIC	IMPERIAL
3MM	⅛IN
6MM	¼IN
1CM	½IN
2CM	¾IN
2.5CM	1IN
5CM	2IN
6CM	2½IN
8CM	3IN
10CM	4IN
13CM	5IN
15CM	6IN
18CM	7IN
20CM	8IN
22CM	9IN
25CM	10IN
28CM	11IN
30CM	12IN (1FT)

OVEN TEMPERATURES

The oven temperatures in this book are for conventional ovens; if you have a fan-forced oven, decrease the temperature by 10-20 degrees.

	°C (CELSIUS)	°F (FAHRENHEIT)
VERY SLOW	120	250
SLOW	150	300
MODERATELY SLOW	160	325
MODERATE	180	350
MODERATELY HOT	200	400
HOT	220	425
VERY HOT	240	475

This book is published in 2016 by Octopus Publishing Group Limited based on materials licensed to it by Bauer Media Books, Australia.
Bauer Media Books is a division of Bauer Media Pty Limited, 54 Park St, Sydney; GPO Box 4088, Sydney, NSW 2001, Australia
phone (+61) 2 9282 8618; fax (+61) 2 9126 3702 www.awwcookbooks.com.au

BAUER MEDIA BOOKS
PUBLISHER JO RUNCIMAN
EDITORIAL & FOOD DIRECTOR PAMELA CLARK
DIRECTOR OF SALES, MARKETING & RIGHTS BRIAN CEARNES
CREATIVE DIRECTOR & DESIGNER HANNAH BLACKMORE
EDITOR AMANDA LEES
FOOD EDITOR REBECCA MELI
OPERATIONS MANAGER DAVID SCOTTO

PUBLISHED AND DISTRIBUTED IN THE UNITED KINGDOM BY
OCTOPUS PUBLISHING GROUP LTD
CARMELITE HOUSE
50 VICTORIA EMBANKMENT
LONDON, EC4Y 0DZ
UNITED KINGDOM
INFO@OCTOPUS-PUBLISHING.CO.UK;
WWW.OCTOPUSBOOKS.CO.UK

PRINTED IN CHINA BY LEO PAPER PRODUCTS LTD.

INTERNATIONAL FOREIGN LANGUAGE RIGHTS
BRIAN CEARNES, BAUER MEDIA BOOKS BCEARNES@BAUER-MEDIA.COM.AU

A CATALOGUE RECORD FOR THIS BOOK IS AVAILABLE FROM THE BRITISH LIBRARY.
ISBN: 9781742457178 (HARDBACK)
© BAUER MEDIA PTY LIMITED 2016
ABN 18 053 273 546